NAILING THE BILLIONAIRE

ERIN SWANN

SWANN PUBLICATIONS

Cover images licensed from Shutterstock.com, depositphotos.com

Cover design by Swann Publications

Edited by Jessica Royer Ocken

Proofreaders: Donna Hokanson, Tamara Mataya, Rosa Sharon

ISBN-13 978-1691336593

The following story is intended for mature readers. It contains mature themes, strong language, and sexual situations. All characters are 18+ years of age, and all sexual acts are consensual.

Find out more about the author and upcoming books online at:

WWW.ERINSWANN.COM

❀ Created with Vellum

ALSO BY ERIN SWANN

The Billionaire's Trust - Available on Amazon, also in AUDIOBOOK

(Bill and Lauren's story) He needed to save the company. He needed her. He couldn't have both. The wedding proposal in front of hundreds was like a fairy tale come true—Until she uncovered his darkest secret.

The Youngest Billionaire - Available on Amazon

(Steven and Emma's story) The youngest of the Covington clan, he avoided the family business to become a rarity, an honest lawyer. He didn't suspect that pursuing her could destroy his career. She didn't know what trusting him could cost her.

The Secret Billionaire – Available on Amazon, also in AUDIOBOOK

(Patrick and Elizabeth's story) Women naturally circled the flame of wealth and power, and his is brighter than most. Does she love him? Does she not? There's no way to know. When he stopped to help her, Liz mistook him for a carpenter. Maybe this time he'd know. Everything was perfect. Until the day she left.

The Billionaire's Hope - Available on Amazon, also in AUDIOBOOK

(Nick and Katie's story) They came from different worlds. She hadn't seen him since the day he broke her brother's nose. Her family retaliated by destroying his life. She never suspected where accepting a ride from him today would take her. They said they could do casual. They lied.

Previously titled: Protecting the Billionaire

Picked by the Billionaire – Available on Amazon

(Liam and Amy's story) A night she wouldn't forget. An offer she couldn't refuse. He alone could save her, and she held the key to his survival. If only they could pass the test together.

Saved by the Billionaire – Available on Amazon

(Ryan and Natalie's story) The FBI and the cartel were both after her for the same thing: information she didn't have. First, the FBI took everything, and then the cartel came for her. She trusted Ryan with her safety, but could she trust him with her heart?

Caught by the Billionaire – Available on Amazon

(Vincent and Ashley's story) Her undercover assignment was simple enough: nail the crooked billionaire. The surprise came when she opened the folder, and the target was her one-time high school sweetheart. What will happen when an unknown foe makes a move to checkmate?

The Driven Billionaire – Available on Amazon

(Zachary and Brittney's story) Rule number one: hands off your best friend's sister. With nowhere to turn when she returns from upstate, she accepts his offer of a room. Mutual attraction quickly blurs the rules. When she comes under attack, pulling her closer is the only way to keep her safe. But, the truth of why she left town in the first place will threaten to destroy them both.

Nailing the Billionaire – Available on Amazon

(Dennis and Jennifer's story) She knew he destroyed her family. Now she is close to finding the records that will bring him down. When a corporate shakeup forces her to work with him, anger and desire collide. Vengeance was supposed to be simple, swift, and sweet. It was none of those things.

Undercover Billionaire – Available on Amazon

(Adam and Kelly's story) Their wealthy families have been at war forever. When Kelly receives a chilling note, the FBI assigns Adam to protect her. Family histories and desire soon collide, causing old truths to be questioned. Keeping ahead of the threat won't be their only challenge.

Interested in FREE books?

Members of Erin's ARC-Team get early access to **FREE** copies of Erin's new releases for review purposes. Yes, you read that right – free books prior to the official release date. If you are interested in learning more about this opportunity CLICK HERE FOR MORE INFORMATION.

Want to hear about new releases and sales?

If you would like to hear about Erin's **new releases** and sales, join the newsletter HERE. We only email about sales or new releases, and we never share your information.

CHAPTER 1

JENNIFER

I'LL MAKE HIM PAY FOR WHAT HE DID.

My modified headlamp cast a dim glow on the recalcitrant lock.

The file needed to be back in place before it was missed. I had my copy, and when the news broke, this folder would attract attention.

I stretched my aching shoulders. The tensioner slipped out of the lock as I pulled the pick tool toward me.

Fuck.

After wiping my brow with my sleeve, I repositioned the tool at the bottom of the key slot to start picking the cylinder again—for the fourth time, or was it the fifth?

Normal file-cabinet locks wouldn't have been this hard, but the company hadn't gone with standard, hardware-store locks. These were a bitch, and the latex gloves I wore didn't help. The YouTubers made it look so much easier than it was.

The faint sound of a door opening down the corridor caught my attention.

I ducked low and quickly covered my light source with one hand before clicking it off with the other.

1

The door closed, and footsteps followed. They came closer, and then stopped for a few seconds before clomping my way.

Shimmying back to crouch behind a file cabinet with my bag, I worked to control my breathing, with limited success. The sound of my heart beating threatened to swamp the sounds from the corridor.

Every time this happened, I was more scared than the last. Getting caught in this file room would be something I could explain away during the work-day, perhaps. But after-hours, with the lights off? No way. It would be out-of-the-company time for yours truly, and most likely off to jail as well. Worst of all, I would fail at my mission.

There were days when jail didn't sound so bad—it would be a lot less stressful—but that was just me kidding myself. I couldn't live with what that would do to Ramona and Billy. Who would look after them if I couldn't? Certainly not Uncle Victor. Although, the thought of Ramona and him in the same room was amusing. She'd be after him day and night about his drinking, and I'd bet on Ramona carrying the day. She didn't lose many arguments.

I halted a laugh halfway up my throat. Silence was paramount until I knew the footsteps were far enough away. It didn't matter how funny my daydreams got, I had to concentrate on tonight's task.

Eventually I judged it had been long enough and struggled to my feet again.

I wasn't tall, but these locks were positioned for people shorter than me. Rolling a chair in here was out of the question, and hunching over for an hour was going to make this a multi-Tylenol evening. *Advil*, I reminded myself. I planned on a glass of wine, and research said not to take Tylenol with alcohol.

I started again on the file cabinet.

Somebody needed to invent an easier way to do this. Movie characters were always past the lock in less than five seconds, but Hollywood didn't need to be accurate. *Suspension of disbelief*, they called it.

One of those actors should come in here and tackle this lock. That would show them what the real world was like. Just because the script says *and the lock opened* doesn't make it so.

Suddenly, the tension tool loosened as the cylinder returned. Another quarter turn and the plug popped toward me with a loud clunk. At least it was open, but this stupid cabinet was all kinds of trouble.

I froze and listened intently for half a minute.

I couldn't detect any sounds, so I slowly pulled out the squeaky bottom drawer. Pulling my notes from my pocket, I double-checked where I'd originally found the file, just to be sure. Then I pulled the folder out of my messenger bag and slid it back in the drawer, exactly where it had been two days ago.

I eased the drawer closed, pushed in the lock plug, and turned the cylinder with my tension tool to the locked position.

Success.

Removing the headlamp, I clicked it off before closing it in my bag. With the tools back in place, I quickly pocketed the leather case of my pick set. It was too tall to fit well, but I'd deal with that later.

I shouldered the bag and made my way to the door.

The hallway was quiet, so I slipped through the door and closed it behind me.

Moving quietly, I started left. I couldn't relax until I'd made it out without being spotted.

At the corner, I listened before peeking around to look down the long corridor.

I pulled my head back quickly.

The bigger of the two night guards was halfway down the hall and coming this way.

I shuffled back the way I'd come as silently as I could.

The first office door I tried was locked, and the same with the second. There wasn't any time to try to pick one, and the file room door had locked behind me.

The sound of the guard rattling a doorknob just past the corner left me no alternative. I pushed my way into the bathroom, grabbed the handle to keep the spring-loaded door closer from doing its thing, and gently shut the door behind me.

I turned.

Shit.

I'd ended up in the men's room. Tiptoeing to the far stall, I slid inside.

A cough outside the door got my heart racing. He was just outside. If he came in here, I was done.

The sound of the door opening sealed my decision. With my hands braced against the stall walls, I put one foot on the toilet seat and climbed up, hoping it wouldn't squeak when I put my other foot on the opposite side of the seat and crouched.

It didn't, but as I lifted my other foot, my pick set case came loose from my pocket and fell to the floor, the light sound masked by the loud closing of the door to the corridor.

I closed my eyes and unsuccessfully willed my heartbeat to slow. Slow, silent breaths were agonizing as my lungs burned for more air.

The footsteps made their way inside and were followed by a grunt and the sound of a zipper coming down.

I opened my eyes, and the sight of my pick set on the floor only compounded my terror.

More grunts preceded humming and the sound of the guard peeing in the urinal.

A bead of sweat threatened to fall into my eye, but I didn't dare move to wipe it away.

The sound of the stream stopped and started a few times before the humming was replaced by another grunt as the zipper sound announced he was done.

The sound of flushing followed, then the door thudding shut.

Thankfully he hadn't bothered to wash his hands. If he had, he might have noticed the pick set on the floor in the mirror.

Finally able to breathe again, I wiped my brow with my sleeve, stepped off the toilet seat, and tried to compose myself. After retrieving the pick set and pocketing the latex gloves, I pulled two tissues from the box by the sink to dry my sweaty hands.

Two minutes went by on my watch before I listened at the bathroom door and found the hallway quiet enough to slip out again.

My path to the stairwell exit required a left down the long hallway, a right at the end, and another jog right. The path was clear as I made the final turn, and I could finally relax as I shuffled softly down the concrete stairs to the garage level.

The back of the garage had a separate set of stairs to the street, and no surveillance cameras.

Once back in the safety of my car, I pulled out my iPad, composed an email, and sent it.

To: HYDRA157

From: Nemesis666
The pony is back in the barn.

I twisted Mom's ring on my finger. "I'll get the proof for you."

The words dissipated in the empty car, but I was sure she could hear them.

CHAPTER 2

JENNIFER
(Four Days Later)

As I added pins to secure my French twist Monday morning, I wondered if the bomb would drop today. It had been four long days since I'd put the file back in place. A girl could hope.

I turned my head left and right, and a quick mirror check showed my twist to be perfect. A professional woman always presents a professional image—a habit Mom had taught me.

I ventured out to make breakfast for myself and my sister, Ramona. This meant pouring the Raisin Bran.

My nephew, Billy, had already poured himself a bowl of Cocoa Puffs. "Are you taking me to school today?" he asked.

"No, not today. Your mommy's taking you."

"Why?"

Ramona opened her door. "Because it's Monday, and it's my turn."

Billy spooned another mouthful of cereal, seeming content with the answer for a change.

Ramona joined us and dug into her cereal. "Anything planned for tonight?" she asked me.

I swallowed. "Nope."

She was clearly fishing for some sign of a third date with Simon, but he hadn't called again, at least not yet.

She gave up the quest, and ten minutes later, the two of them were out the door.

After the dishes, I gave in and sat down at my laptop.

It powered up, and I logged in to the bank's website.

I unfolded the bill I'd pulled from the drawer, and a double-check showed what I feared. My mouth dried. We'd skipped eating out, but with three mouths to feed, I didn't have enough to cover this today.

My pay wouldn't be direct-deposited until Friday. That meant this would be another late payment to deal with. The envelope went back in my purse, at the bottom this time.

Mom would have figured a way to make this all work, but I wasn't her.

Before I could close the computer, the new-email chime sounded, so I clicked on the icon. It was good news at last.

> To: Nemesis666
> From: HYDRA157
> The balloon is launched.
> Hope you can see it.

I grinned. I needed to hustle if I was going to see his reaction.

I deleted the message, closed the computer, and hefted my purse.

Mom would've been proud of the actions I was taking for our family. Ramona and Billy had a roof over their heads, and most importantly, I was avenging my stepfather, the only real dad I'd had.

My little car started with the typical fuss, another thing I needed to spend money on. Money I didn't have. It could use a good cleaning as well. I closed the window when I ended up behind a bus belching the black death of diesel fumes. The state told us we had to get our cars smog-checked every two years, but the city busses did whatever they wanted.

The traffic was heavy, but I made it to the Starbucks in time.

Inside, I ordered a tall mocha and took my preferred table. The coffee was expensive, but it couldn't be avoided. When hunting the rich, you had to go where they went.

7

Nursing my latte slowly, I turned on my tablet to read the news. Now all I had to do was wait for my target.

The table provided me a clear view of the place, but I had to get here extra early to snag it ahead of the two old ladies who seemed to think it had their names on it. It was important to get the chair facing the right direction.

I scrolled through the news on the tablet in front of me as if I were reading it. Each time the door opened, I glanced over.

So far he was a no-show.

My phone chirped that a text had arrived. I rummaged in my purse, hoping Ramona wasn't telling me she'd locked herself out again.

It wasn't that, but it was equally bad.

EB: Still thinking of U

My worse-than-useless ex-boyfriend couldn't get it through his thick skull that it was over. His now-occasional texts were like having a wasp land on you: swat it and invite a counterattack.

I'd tried responding negatively—that had made it worse. The last time I'd texted back that he should *bug off*, which had resulted in a string of sixty-seven more texts before he gave up. I'd counted.

I put the phone away and ignored him, just like last week.

At least he didn't come by at work. He'd tried that once, and the monster fit I'd thrown had so far prevented any re-occurrence.

Fireman Nick was in line now, with his daily list of a dozen beverages in hand, and my target usually beat him here. Checking my watch, I fretted that he might already have seen the article and decided to skip his mocha before work today. That would be disappointing, to say the least. I was perfectly positioned to see his response if he followed his normal routine.

I switched back to the *Times* website.

The story was third from the top, and probably would remain there all day. It would serve him right. I'd checked the print version already and knew the story was several column inches on the front page below the fold, and it continued on page three. It was guaranteed to get a reaction—and cost him a ton in the stock market.

It couldn't happen to a more deserving monster.

DENNIS

I WAS RUNNING LATER THAN USUAL AS I SHOVED MY PAPER UNDER MY ARM AND pushed through the door of my building out into the bright, early-morning sunshine.

Bad idea.

He stood directly in my path and shoved an envelope at me. "Dennis Benson, you've been served."

In retrospect, looking through the glass before I opened the door would have been a good idea. But I knew that wouldn't have accomplished anything other than putting off the inevitable.

If I'd ducked out the back, he would have tagged me at work, or back here in the evening. As distasteful as it was, there was no avoiding these legal arrows she sent my way.

My God, the woman could be vengeful. *Hell hath no fury,* they say, and that was understating it in this case. What a bitch.

I pocketed the envelope and set off on my morning walk to get my coffee. Rituals were good; rituals kept me grounded. I'd read that the first half hour of the day set one's mood for the rest of it, and a brisk walk followed by a delicious brew was my way of starting on the right foot.

The California sun on my face brightened my mood with every stride. Exercise and being outside, even if not in nature, was good for the mood and the soul. The smog wasn't as bad as yesterday, and the Santa Monica mountains were visible. Their winter shade of bright green had already given way to summer's duller colors. I tried to ignore the wretched envelope and take my mind back to walking the woods and the seashore, camping, and cooking over a campfire.

Back-to-basics activities brought us closer to nature and our roots as pioneers. The Benson family had been early settlers in California, and I was proud to be a fourth-generation Californian, not a recent transplant like so many of those I encountered.

Taking a deep breath, I pulled open the door and entered Starbucks.

The line wasn't long, but the fireman at the counter was reading from a list, and the last time I was behind him it had been quite a wait.

Looking around the tables, I saw a lot of regulars—including the cutie, my fantasy girl—plus three empty tables near the back. Mr. Infinite List ordering now wouldn't take a table, and with only two others ahead of me in line, at least I could catch a spot to relax this morning.

The envelope in my jacket pocket was a lead weight, but I refused to let *her* have that level of control over me. A good run is what I needed, something to get the endorphins flowing.

∼

JENNIFER

AN INCREASE IN STREET NOISE ANNOUNCED THE OPENING OF THE DOOR TO THE coffee shop.

I glanced over, and there he was. Mr. Immaculate—tall, imposing, with steely gray eyes and a defined, sharp jaw any woman would find attractive, especially compared to the short, bald guy just behind him in line. Mr. Immaculate's sandy blond hair was annoyingly in place, his suit perfectly tailored to span his broad shoulders and taper to his trim waist. The perfection of the man annoyed me to no end.

At least being in line behind Fireman Nick would annoy him.

He scanned the room.

I looked away and turned to catch the blonde to my left eying him.

Blondie was just short of drooling. Her eyes raked his form as she twirled the ends of her hair, and the corners of her mouth turned up. She was probably imagining his touch. She licked her lips. She moved her right hand over her left, concealing her ring.

Yuck. She disgusted me.

He disgusted me, because I knew what he'd done.

Blondie probably thought he was Adonis in a suit.

I knew better.

The suit hid the red skin of the devil himself, and the perfect hair hid his horns. One day soon, I would strip away the spit and polish and nail him to the wall, for all to see him as he really was: ghastly, cruel, and with an ugly soul.

Mr. Immaculate had his newspaper under his arm and his chin up, seeming confident that today he would win whatever struggles he encountered.

Think again.

I averted my eyes when he glanced my way. Looking back, I caught a smile on his lips as he approached the barista at the register.

He'd probably been checking out Blondie.

Straining to hear, I caught "grande mocha extra shot." It was his standard order.

Sticking to the routine was good. Like every hunter, I knew the predictable prey was the easiest to get.

He tipped the barista with a dollar bill as he always did, a subterfuge of generosity meant to conceal his true character.

I hid behind my raised tablet and watched him while he waited for his order.

He didn't check the paper.

Blondie stood.

Baldy, who'd been in line behind my prey, came over and kissed her before going to wait for his coffee.

Oops.

When Mr. Immaculate's order was ready, he took it to a table in the corner and opened his newspaper. He read with cup in hand, taking short sips.

It took thirty seconds or so for his jaw to drop when he found the article.

The door opened again, and I glanced reflexively in that direction.

Martha and Mona had arrived. The M&M girls, they called themselves. They made their way to me.

Martha arrived first. "Good morning, Jennie. Thought we'd come early today to see if you had any luck yet with—"

"Shh," Mona said, interrupting her and cocking her head in Mr. Immaculate's direction.

Martha looked over and put her hand to her mouth as she sat.

Mona took a seat as well. "Thank you for saving our table for us."

"My pleasure," I said. Each time they joined me, I couldn't bring myself to refuse.

Martha leaned over the table to whisper, "Did you approach him yet?"

"Not yet," I whispered back.

Mona adjusted her chair to see him better. "I don't see what the big deal is. I'll go talk to him, if you won't."

I reached out to touch Mona's hand. "Please don't. It's something I need to do myself."

"I agree," Martha interjected. "We're too old to be playing matchmaker."

"Speak for yourself," Mona shot back. "I'm not old; I'm mature."

"You're a year older than me," Martha corrected her.

These two could go at it for an hour, each jabbing at the other in a light-hearted way.

Martha stood. "Do you want your regular?" she asked Mona.

"Yes, please, but less cinnamon this time," Mona replied.

After Martha left for the counter, Mona leaned my way. "You should let me wave him over, and you could introduce yourself."

I had to keep nixing her suggestions, because I couldn't tell them my true intentions. "Thank you, but no. I need to do this my way."

She let out a loud breath. "At this rate, you'll be my age before you meet a man."

"There's nothing wrong with your age," I assured her.

That earned a smile. "You're a dear."

I glanced toward Mr. Immaculate. He'd put his cup down. His eyes got wider as he turned to the remainder of the article on page three.

I smiled as his jaw clenched.

The story corroded the confident exterior of the man, and wild anger grew in his eyes. His hands balled into fists as he probably planned his revenge against the writer—something along the lines of a meeting in a dark alley where he could pulverize him. Or would he choose the anonymity of a bullet from long range? Right now he was the rhino you didn't want to be in front of.

Mona giggled. "I saw that."

"What?"

"You like what you see when you look at him."

She couldn't possibly comprehend what made me smile this morning.

Mr. Immaculate stood to leave. He folded up his paper, tossed his cup, and headed for the door. His countenance showed the combination of anger and frustration I'd hoped for. The door closed behind him.

Martha returned with their coffees, and I excused myself shortly after that.

This would not be the last unmasking of his misdeeds, I promised myself as I walked to work. One by one I would reveal the skeletons in his closet, and the world would finally see the real Dennis Benson. His fancy suit wouldn't fool anyone then.

He deserved it all and more for what he'd done to me; what he'd done to my family.

CHAPTER 3

DENNIS

THE FLOORS DINGED BY AND THE RED NUMERALS INCREASED UNTIL THE uncomfortably hot compartment finally opened on the top floor.

I turned left toward my office, and my phone dinged with a text message. I stopped to check it.

DAD: We need to talk.

Dad was the only one I knew who bothered to make sure his punctuation was correct on a text message. Talking to him was not at the top of my list right now.

My assistant, Cindy, was away from her desk, and before I even reached my office, I could hear Jay Fisher, our CFO, and Larry Zerfoss, my strategic marketing guy, going at it about this morning's article. It would be the only thing talked about all day.

They were standing in my office, and they halted their argument mid-sentence when I entered.

I closed the door behind me and hung up my coat to cool off. "Morning."

"Did you see the *Times* this morning?" Larry asked.

I took my seat and put down the paper. "Just did."

"They make it sound like it's our fault," he complained.

I opened the paper. "I know."

Jay nodded.

"It's not fair, not fair at all," Larry continued. "This is going to tank us."

"What's the damage so far?" I asked.

Larry checked his phone. "Fourteen percent down and still dropping."

The stock market didn't like surprises or bad news, and this was both.

I turned to Jay. "Have you read it?"

He nodded. "Several times and—"

Larry interrupted. "We didn't even own the company when this was going on."

I put a hand up to stop him. "I know."

"Is there anything we can do legally?" I asked Jay.

His face telegraphed the answer. "No. I can't see anything factually wrong, and that means there's nothing to dispute." He turned to Larry. "Unless I'm missing something."

Larry took a breath. "It's just the way they present it—it makes us look like the guilty party here."

"It's America," Jay told him. "Spin is allowed. The First Amendment gives them freedom to print shit like this, twice a day if they want to."

Jay's answer was the same conclusion we'd come to after the previous article. We had no recourse with the paper.

I pointed to the byline. "Larry, where are we on finding out who Sigurd is?" Each of the articles had been penned by a *Sigurd*—no last name, or no first, whichever it was.

Dad had been the one to point out that Sigurd was a mythical Norse dragon slayer. Apparently, someone considered us their dragon.

"Nobody's talking, and we don't have any way to force them. The last article was submitted online through Romania, which is obviously a ruse."

Just like the last article, this one included details that had to have come from inside the company. We had a mole, and a destructive one at that.

"Better get your talking points sharpened up, then," I told him.

He held up a set of pink message slips. "I've got five analysts' calls and counting to return on this."

I stood. "Then get going. It's your job to turn this around."

He shook his head. "This isn't going to be easy."

"That's why we have you," I told him. "Just think of them as Eskimos you have to sell a refrigerator to."

The two left, with Larry still grumbling.

If we did have to sell refrigerators in Alaska, he was just the silver-tongued devil for the job.

I followed them out.

Cindy had returned to her desk. "Good morning."

I nodded. "Not from where I stand."

"Your father called."

"I know. I'll call him in a bit." He probably wanted to remind me of the mistake I'd made.

"And Melissa called as well," Cindy warned me.

"You might as well tell me I have a root canal scheduled today."

"I'm just the messenger," she shot back.

I withdrew into my office. The root canal message would have been better news than a call from my ex-wife. If I could ever have a do-over in life, that's one rash decision I wanted to unwind.

Her Bitchiness, Melissa, could chill for a while.

I dialed Dad after all.

"Dennis, thank you for calling back so quickly. I wanted to see how you're faring with this *Times* nonsense."

"Feeling a little persecuted," I admitted.

"Well, that's one of the problems with deciding to take your company public. You have others judging you all the time, and it's rarely fair."

There it was, the lecture about how I shouldn't have insisted on splitting off a portion into Vipersoft Corp. for me to run and financing it in the public markets.

"Dad, we've been over this."

"You always have the option of taking it private again and not having to deal with days like today."

Rehashing my decision to leave wouldn't do either of us any good. "That's not a discussion for today."

"And that's not why I called," he said. "I'm calling to see if there's anything I can do to help."

"Not unless you know a way to get the *Times* to stop picking on us."

He paused. "Dennis, is that who you think you have a problem with?"

"No. I know it's most likely the anonymous writer."

"That's the one you need to find. But in the meantime, this reminds me of your grandfather."

I sighed. I didn't need another down-home, don't-count-your-chickens-before-they-hatch kind of saying today.

"Your grandfather used to say you couldn't add anything to the lemonade to make it more sour, but you could always add sugar to make it sweeter."

"Thanks, Dad."

A lot of good that did.

"Sugar can sweeten the most bitter lemonade, if you have enough."

My brain kicked into gear, and I understood his message for a change. I had no idea why the great Lloyd Benson couldn't be more direct; it would have made life so much easier.

"Thanks, Dad. That's a good suggestion."

When I was sixteen, I'd been sure my generation was a lot smarter than our elders. Ever since then, I'd been getting reminders that we didn't know as much as we thought, and today was another one.

"Have a good rest of the day," he said. "And don't forget to ask for help if you need it."

We hung up.

Ask for help? That was his way of telling me I'd made a mistake by going off on my own, and he'd remind me of it forever if I went back to him for help. I'd handled tough situations before, and I'd handle this one. Sooner or later he'd get it through his thick skull that I wasn't a kid anymore.

I went to my jacket and pulled the awful envelope I'd been served out of the inside breast pocket. I was about to slice it open and get the bad news out of the way, when I stopped.

I put the letter face down on the desk. I'd had enough bad news for today. Picking up my phone, I was about to dial Dad back, when I decided against it. I didn't need validation. I knew what to do. The phone went face down on the envelope.

The phone and envelope made an odd pair. Melissa had given me the phone, a recent peace offering, and I'd avoided the urge to chuck it along with everything else that reminded me of her   that would have been giving in and letting her dictate my actions.

Keeping the phone had been my way of proving she couldn't control me or my mood. But the letter under the phone proved she wouldn't stop trying.

Those were the Jekyll and Hyde sides of Melissa—today she'd chosen the evil Hyde. And she'd already consumed more of my time than she deserved.

I walked to the door and opened it.

Thankfully, Cindy was at her desk.

"I need Larry, Jay, and Bob, right now," I told her.

∽

JENNIFER

I PASSED THROUGH THE LOBBY, AND EVERYTHING LOOKED AS IT HAD YESTERDAY.

The elevator disgorged passengers at several floors before reaching the fourteenth, where I got off. Turning right into finance, I could see and hear the hum of gossip as people stopped at each other's cubicles to share what they'd heard, or read, or just guessed at.

I unlocked the drawers in my cubicle and dropped my purse in the bottom one after taking out my phone and putting it on the charger. A dead phone was a useless phone, and mine was losing charge faster these days. I needed to take it in for a battery replacement when I got the time—if I ever got the time. Time and money always seemed to be in short supply for me.

I pushed the power button, and my computer slowly came to life.

"Did you see the news?" Vanessa asked breathlessly from behind me.

I turned. "No, what news?"

"You have to check the *Times* website."

"Is it good? We're due for some good coverage about now."

"This is the opposite. You gotta read it."

"Okay." I turned back to my monitor and logged in. "We're having the worst luck with those guys." I selected the browser and navigated to the *Times* site.

The story was still third from the top. "Oh my God," I said as I read the words I knew so well. I put my hand to my mouth. "Oh my God," I repeated.

"It's terrible."

I kept my hand over my mouth to hide the smile that grew as I read. The article took the Bensons and this company down a notch. They deserved that, and much more.

I composed myself. "Is this true?"

"I don't know for sure, but Leo thinks it is."

Leo had been here the longest, and everyone approached him as if he held all knowledge related to the company.

Vanessa left, and I busied myself with work.

Three other people stopped by throughout the morning to see what I thought of the news. Each time I expressed horror and said it probably wasn't true, or that I hoped for all our sakes it wasn't.

This story had amped up the company gossip mill even more than the last one.

My cell buzzed. It was my sister, Ramona.

"I might have to stay late," she started.

"I can't talk right now," I answered. "Things are kinda busy here."

"I'll text you if I have to stay."

"Sure. No problem," I said.

We hung up, and I went back to the spreadsheet torture in front of me.

Vanessa wandered by a little later. "Sixteen percent," she muttered before she made a throat-slashing motion across her neck and left.

The upside was that the stock slide was hitting my target, Dennis Benson, where it hurt the most, and it couldn't happen to a more deserving toad.

Emailing Hydra, the one person I could share this with, was also off the table. No emails from work—that had been a firm rule from the beginning. I couldn't share the reaction until I got home, another reason to hope this day went quickly. While I attacked my spreadsheets, I had to keep my glee to myself. Nobody here could know I was the source behind these damaging news stories.

Fuck you, Dennis Benson. Someday I'd be able to speak those words to his face. That would be a good day. No, that would be a great day. Vengeance would finally be mine.

I checked the stock price again. Down eighteen percent.

As Shakespeare wrote, "Revenge should have no bounds." And I had only just begun.

CHAPTER 4

DENNIS

BOB SHAPIRO, OUR COO, WAS THE FIRST OF THE THREE TO ARRIVE. "SORT OF AN ugly day today with that *Times* story."

"Yeah," I agreed. "That's what this is about."

He took a seat. "You know I wasn't even here when that stuff happened," he said.

"Nobody's blaming you, Bob. Just wait until the others get here."

He checked his phone. "Can I buy today? Or am I locked out?"

That was probably the one question I *hadn't* expected. Today nobody seemed to want our stock. "Not with what I'm about to tell you. Why?"

"The company's on sale; I just thought I'd add a few shares. When hamburger goes on sale, everybody stocks up. People just don't react rationally to a stock going on sale."

"Yeah, well, I hope to take it off sale, so given what I'm about to tell you, you're locked out."

His impulse had been a good one. Baron Rothschild had become immensely wealthy buying when fear was prevalent, and his belief that "the time to buy is when there is blood in the streets" was still taught in business schools today. The MBA weenies, however, never took it to heart.

They all followed the crowd down the path of panic, which only amplified the fear.

When the previous two Sigurd articles had come out, I'd taken the opportunities to buy a significant chunk of company stock and come out way ahead so far. Hamburger had been on sale those days. The difference today was that I had a counterattack, and knowing that, I couldn't take advantage of the situation and buy.

Bob settled in, and I gave him a quick overview of my plan.

A wide smile grew on his face. This was going to be a good day for him.

Jay walked in a minute later.

Larry was the last. He looked askance at Bob. The two had never seen much use for the other.

"I have Citibank calling in a half hour," Larry announced. "Can't this wait, whatever it is?" He didn't bother to move past the doorway.

I pointed at the empty chair. "Have a seat, and close the door." I looked between them. "Ever heard the saying, you can't make lemonade more sour, but you can make it sweeter?"

All I got were blank stares and shaking heads. Apparently, we were all from the wrong generation.

"Well, we're going to add sugar to today's lemonade." I turned to Jay. "What are the projection ranges for the brake division spin-off to our net?"

Jay rubbed his chin. "You mean to our bottom line?"

I nodded. "Exactly."

He shifted in his seat, apparently unsure if I was setting him up. "They're not final, but twenty-two to thirty-cents positive."

"Good. We're announcing the spin-off today."

Bob smiled, the other two went slack jawed.

"But we're not ready," Jay complained. "The plans Bob and I put together are only preliminary."

"They're final now," I told him. "Larry, we're announcing the spin-off, and use thirty cents as the projected effect."

Larry's face went from confusion to elation as he absorbed this new ammunition to counter the article's negativity. "When can I use this?"

Jay was the only unhappy one of the group. "We should always go with a middle-of-the-road projection, and thirty cents is an optimistic upper limit."

I shrugged. "Then you and Bob need to figure out how to make it happen."

Bob was all smiles. "We'll make it happen."

He would be going with the spin-off and have his own show to run for a change. It was a serious step up for his career. I could count on Bob to push this through in record time.

Jay was the one with hard work to do based on my pronouncement, and his furrowed brow showed his apprehension. "This is awfully short notice."

"That's it," I told them. "Let's get cracking."

The other two left, but Jay dawdled. He shut the door. "Can we talk about this a minute?"

"Sure."

"This isn't going to be easy," he cautioned.

"It never is, but we have all quarter to make it work."

"A lot more goes into a transaction like this than you realize. Bob needs a finance and marketing staff set up right away to handle things on his end, not to mention HR."

I nodded. "Yeah, we'll have to power through it. Today we need sugar to add to the lemonade."

"Are you absolutely certain you don't want to take a few days to discuss it? We can always add your sugar to the news cycle next week. Sometimes unintended consequences crop up in things like this."

"I'm sure."

"This can only be done if Bob and I have the authority to make the hard decisions on personnel and such without other departments coming to you to complain and muck up the plans."

"That won't be a problem," I assured him.

After he left, I turned to my best thinking position: facing the window without a desk or papers or a computer crowding me. Jay was right—caution could be useful at times, but this wasn't one of them.

The market had been down significantly already, and these things had a tendency to snowball out of control if left untended. We were under attack by Sigurd, whoever he was, and giving him a chance to get another blow in before we reacted to this one didn't fit my style.

The benefit of splitting off from the family company was that I got to set the rules and make my own decisions, right or wrong. And I knew this one was right. Hell, leaving Benson Corp. hadn't even cut me off from Dad's advice.

The only difference was that this morning Dad had *suggested* what he thought I should do instead of telling me, and that was a thousand-percent improvement.

~

JENNIFER

VANESSA STOPPED BY AFTER LUNCH. "WE HAVE AN ALL-HANDS FINANCE MEETING at three."

"What about?"

"No idea," she said as she moved on to pass the word.

It was a typical big-company move. We'd had one after the last bomb hit the papers, too. Departmental meetings would rally the troops, explain the company's biased point of view, and rescue morale from the abyss it was falling into.

Most of the people I worked with had drunk the Kool-Aid at the last meeting and come out happier than when they'd gone in.

This time I had a plan. I'd made a list of what I expected the PR points from management would be, and I had a few embarrassing questions to pose regarding the facts of the article—nothing that would put me in the enemy camp, just clarification questions that were guaranteed to give them fits and raise a good number of queries from the audience.

I reviewed my questions before the meeting time. I just had to wait for the question-and-answer portion that would follow the rah-rah bullshit speech our boss, Jay Fisher, certainly had planned. I knew his background. He'd come out of public accounting, worked his way up at Benson Corp., and become the CFO here under Dennis Benson when Vipersoft was spun-out. Facts and numbers were king with him. His reputation was his stock in trade. He wouldn't sully it by continuing to spout the company line when the facts were on my side. Fisher was the perfect foil. His answers, or non-answers, would show everybody there how heartless Benson had been.

I left for lunch with my question list in my purse. Last time I'd made the mistake of forgetting it, and I'd failed to ask my two most killer questions. The rush of adrenaline from challenging Fisher had made me nervous and had cost me my best opportunity to score points. I wasn't letting that happen today.

At street level, I removed the lanyard displaying my company badge. Advertising that I worked for the soon-to-be universally hated Vipersoft wasn't wise.

After two blocks, that same odd itch at the back of my neck bothered me. I turned, but didn't see anybody following me. My late-night hide and seek in our building had made me paranoid.

I walked an extra few blocks to avoid any company people and chose Tina's Tacos as the recipient of my meager lunch spending today. Several nice tables near the window were available, so I got in line and made my mental choice from the overhead menu.

The tables filled up quickly, as none of the people in front of me chose takeout. By the time I collected my change, the only table left was in the back corner next to the restrooms, right behind two suit-types I didn't recognize.

As I munched my two tacos, I overheard talk of local companies, and the lingo of stock traders drifted my way. They weren't quiet about it either. The taller one was arguing the bullish case for Intel, and not getting far convincing the shorter one. They reminded me of a lot of my classmates at biz school—all numbers and no concept of the people and products behind the real world of the companies. To them, a company was a stock symbol with a number attached and no more. They didn't make money by producing anything. The stock market was just a casino to them, and if they could beat the other suckers by hearing gossip first, they'd call that an honest day's work.

I ignored them and read over my third question again and again, until I could visualize the words if I closed my eyes.

Q3: The paper said thirty-three deaths have been attributed to defects in our products so far. How many do you think the total will rise to by the end of the year?

That should get the room buzzing. It was a killer question, but maybe it could be shortened somehow…

Tall Guy changed the subject. "Did you see that latest from Gumpert? He thinks Cartwright is going to take down Vipersoft."

I stopped chewing to listen to their conversation. I'd seen negative comments in the press from Carson Cartwright about our company, but hadn't paid them much heed. If this guy could damage the company, I was all for it. He might even warrant reaching out to anonymously to provide data. I'd helped Hydra; why not another aligned interest?

Tall Guy switched topics again, and I went back to my questions after losing interest. Unfortunately they were loud. Harleys revving their engines on the street would be less distracting than the jabbering of those two.

I finished my lunch quickly, and back on the street, my phone chirped with a text.

RAMONA: I have to stay late can you pick up Billy pls pls pls

I moved to the building side of the sidewalk, stopped, and typed my reply.

ME: Sure

This would work out well, because I didn't want to stay late today anyway.

~

THE AFTERNOON STARTED SLOWLY AS I TRUDGED THROUGH MY WORK AND avoided the groups gathering to gossip about the afternoon's all-hands department meeting.

I took the long way to the break room for some tea. Fisher and several others were huddled in a conference room going over something, and they were still at it two hours later when I went by again.

The sight of them still in there lightened my step on the way back to my cubicle. It evidently took a long time to figure out enough lies to explain away the misdeeds.

When the appointed time came, we assembled, and I took a position near the back. When I asked my questions, my voice would carry over the crowd, and everyone would hear. Last time, I'd been near the front, and I'd found out afterward that the people in the back couldn't hear me.

It was a few minutes after three when Fisher stopped exchanging pleasantries with the people up front and the group quieted to hear him speak.

"I know it's been a rollercoaster day for everyone, and I'll be brief," he said.

Rollercoaster, my ass. The market was already closed, and the stock had finished down twenty-two percent. Rollercoasters go up and down to end up back where they started. This had been a one-way trip down.

He cleared his throat. "I have a rather large announcement to make. The company has been exploring a reorganization transaction for some time."

Murmurs began in the crowd. *Reorganization* was usually a codeword for layoffs—*downsizing* in corporate jargon.

The article's effect had been even more than I'd anticipated if they were downsizing already to save the company.

"The management has decided that the best way to enhance shareholder value is to spin off the automotive brake division as a standalone business."

A number of heads in front of me cocked to the side. They were as confused as I was.

A spin-off?

"This is going to be a very rapid transition. The production people will be moving, naturally, but this will also affect support departments such as ours."

People looked at each other with questioning faces. Nobody had seen this coming, apparently.

If it had been on the company grapevine, Vanessa would have told me. She was as plugged in as anybody could be.

"As a result, several of us will be transferring with Bob to the new company."

That brought a few gasps.

"Don't worry, those of you who are moving on will be getting what I think are rather substantial stock-option packages for the inconvenience."

With that, the mood of the group improved. Stock options were a favorite topic in finance. They weren't worth anything in the short run, but could be quite valuable years in the future.

"As I said, this will be a rapid transaction. The people going with new organization will be…"

He started listing names, and the seventh and last name was a surprise.

"And Jennifer Hanley."

My heart skipped a beat. Without so much as a discussion, I was being shuttled off to a new company.

"If you seven could join me in the conference room after this, I'll fill you in. HR has your new packages to go over as well."

26

A hand went up.

"Yes?" Fisher said.

"Who will be running the new company?"

"Bob Shapiro will be going over as the new CEO."

Shapiro was the current COO, second in command, so that made sense, and he seemed like a nice-enough guy.

This was all too much to process.

"When will this be announced?" someone else asked.

"It was put on the wire just as we started this meeting," Fisher answered.

Another hand went up, and Fisher pointed to Vanessa.

"Can any of the rest of us apply to go with them?"

"Not at this time, but when they have openings in the future, I'm sure we'll be kept in the loop."

"Who will be running finance?" asked one of the other conscripts assigned to leave.

"Mark Timlin will be the CFO," Fisher answered.

After that there were one or two other questions I didn't follow. My head was spinning.

The group dispersed, and I wandered into the conference room on autopilot to hear my fate. The condemned walking herself to the guillotine, that was me.

Changing companies screwed up my entire plan. I'd lose access to the records I needed in this building. I wouldn't be able to complete my revenge.

Fucking Benson had found a way to thwart me.

This couldn't be happening. *Poof.* All my plans had gone up in smoke.

CHAPTER 5

DENNIS

JAY FISHER WAS BACK AT MY DOOR BEFORE THE DAY WAS OUT. "GOT A MINUTE?"

"Sure."

He closed the door behind him and took a chair. "This isn't going to be easy."

"It never is, but like I told you this morning, we have all quarter to make it work."

"A lot more goes into a transaction than you realize. Bob needs a finance staff right away to handle things on his end."

I nodded. "Yeah."

He took a breath and peered at me over his glasses. "This is going to affect you as well. Remember, your acquisition analyst, Mark, was my pick for Bob's CFO."

"And I said I'd support that. I'll find a replacement." Mark Timlin deserved the promotion opportunity.

The hint of a smile on Jay's face telegraphed a *gotcha* line coming. "Well, he needs to move right away. He's meeting right now with his new team. He has to hit the ground running if this is going to get done."

I wasn't prepared for that. I'd planned on having a few months to locate someone to fill his shoes. "I need him for a few months part time, then."

"You didn't ask me ahead of time about the ramifications of this decision. This is one of those ramifications. You can call Larry and pull back the announcement, or lose Mark starting tomorrow. We don't have time to find another qualified CFO candidate for Bob, and you can't do the spin-off without a CFO in place. If this isn't done right, the SEC will come down on us like a ton of bricks, and it won't be pretty."

I took a breath, but didn't see any alternative. "We go ahead. You can have Mark. And, Jay, I'm sorry I didn't prep you ahead of time on this."

He stood. "Water under the bridge." He stopped at the door. "By the way, who gave you that lemonade-and-sugar quote? Was it Lloyd?"

"Yup, Dad's full of them."

He reached for the door. "That he is."

"Just a minute, Jay."

He turned. "Yes?"

I was still the boss here, and that gave me some prerogatives. "I need someone to fill in for a month while I interview replacements."

"I'll have Denise in HR get someone for you from the temp agency I use."

"I have a better idea. Send me somebody qualified from your group, and *you* get a temp to fill in."

"Yes, sir." He shook his head and left.

After the door closed behind him, I turned to the window and chuckled. This would cost him a good guy. He wouldn't dare send me a turd.

Jay had insisted on teaching me a lesson about being rash, and I'd just taught him a lesson about how shit had a tendency to run down hill, which in this case was his direction.

Dad's suggestion hadn't been a bad one, but Jay had just pointed out—without rubbing my nose in it too much—that I'd made a rookie move. I could have taken a day or two to make this decision, and not huddling with him and others had just caused my first unintended consequence and bitten me in the ass. And the day wasn't over yet. The decision might cost me more in the future than I'd stopped to anticipate. Something more middle-of-the-road—between Larry's instant-action philosophy and Jay's conservatism—might have been better. A thought for next time.

I looked out over the expanse of the LA area. My office was this high up because I was willing to take risks, and sometimes those came with costs.

~

JENNIFER

THE OTHER SIX WHOSE NAMES HAD BEEN CALLED TO GO WITH THE SPIN-OFF WERE already in the conference room when I shuffled in—happy faces on all of them as they mumbled about stock options. This greedy group had no other questions apparently, like where we would be working.

I returned their smiles as I contemplated the abundant empty space on the lower floors of this building. The company had been trying to lease that out. The possibility that I might keep a badge that gained access to this building brightened my outlook. My vengeance could stay on track.

Fisher introduced Mark Timlin, the CEO's acquisitions analyst, as our new boss and left the room.

Timlin took a seat at the head of the table. "Look around. This merry group will comprise the nucleus of the finance team we're taking over to Hydrocom—that'll be the name of our new company. Jay has told me wonderful things about all of you, and I look forward to helping you staff our team for success."

It was just my luck to end up working for someone who had spent the last two years at the right hand of the devil himself.

He was energetic in his description of the opportunities for all of us with the new venture. As the new CFO, it made sense that he would be.

I concentrated on the wood grain of the table in front of me as he went on too long for my taste about how excited he was.

He then went around the table, getting names from those he didn't know and telling us our new positions.

"Jennifer, you'll be the new General Ledger Supervisor," he said when he got to me.

My mouth might have dropped open, but with the fog in my brain I wasn't sure. It sounded like he'd said *supervisor*.

"You'll have two open reqs, one for a senior accountant, and a junior as soon as you can recruit candidates," he continued.

He had meant it when he said *supervisor*.

I nodded. Minions working for me was a serious step up career-wise. And a supervisor position had to mean more money—a promotion.

A godsend.

After Mark moved on to the next person, Ernesto leaned over. "Congrats. You deserve it."

The praise sent a tingle sent up my spine. Ernesto was right. I did deserve it. I'd worked hard here—not because I was devoted to the company, but because that was the way I was wired. Giving a hundred percent was the way I'd been raised, and there wasn't any alternative.

"Thanks," I whispered back.

"Now, HR has new packages to go over with each of you downstairs before you leave for the day. Also, we'll be moving into our new digs in Pasadena over the weekend." He slid a pile of papers down the table, and we each grabbed one. "That's the address of our offices starting next week."

Pasadena was not too far, but it would add more than an extra half-hour each way for me and half the people in the room. So much for keeping my access to this building.

Ernesto grinned. Pasadena wasn't far from his home in the valley—a win for him.

I couldn't help but slump in my seat. An extra hour-plus of daily commute torture in my car was going to be one cost of the promotion. The other would be an end to my quest for revenge on Benson, and that was the worst of all.

A series of meaningless questions from the others followed as I concentrated on the paper in front of me. Without access to this building, I'd never be able to feed Hydra the material that would make Dennis Benson pay. And who knew how many other families would have to pay the price in the coming years if he wasn't brought down.

"Any more questions?" Mark asked.

I had one I couldn't ask.

"Very well then, welcome aboard. HR is expecting you downstairs. And we'll start off right back here tomorrow morning at seven-thirty." He stood, and the happy group followed him out.

"Jenn, you okay?" Ernesto asked as we passed through the door.

"Oh, sure. I'm just thinking about the commute is all."

"Yeah, that can be a drag, but you made supervisor."

He and I took the second elevator down to HR.

A half hour later, I sat across the table from an HR specialist with a written compensation letter in front of me.

"The salary increase will be fourteen thousand a year," she said.

I could hardly believe it as I read along. Over a thousand a month extra gross pay would go a long way toward making life livable for all of us. Between my student debt and helping with Ramona's schooling, I'd been getting further behind on my credit cards every month.

"The option package is twenty thousand shares vested over four years," she added.

That was huge as well. I'd only been awarded two thousand when I started.

Everybody in finance knew how valuable the options could be over time. Nobody in her right mind would pass on a deal like this, despite the extra commute.

I sat back. "How long do I have to consider this?"

Her brow shot up. "It's quite an opportunity, Jennifer. I can check, but as I understand it, these transfers are mandatory."

"What if I don't want to drive all the way to Pasadena?"

"If you're not satisfied, I suggest you talk to Mark. He might be willing to sweeten it a bit. But I'll tell you right now, this is quite generous." She shrugged.

I'd obviously thrown an unexpected wrench in the works by not jumping at the opportunity.

"Mark?" I asked.

"Yes. I'd start there. We weren't given much time to work on these, so I'm sorry if it's not what you were expecting."

She didn't get it. She was talking money, and I was thinking of not going at all.

"I just don't make decisions like this on the spur of the moment."

"We were told to have you sign this afternoon."

She was obviously not the one to be having this discussion with.

"I'll go talk to Mark, then, and be back later."

She didn't seem thrilled that I'd messed up the schedule.

I excused myself and stood by the elevator, rereading the paper.

Ernesto passed by me, all smiles. "See ya tomorrow, Jenn."

I waved and decided to press the *up* button on the elevator. Only one person in our department was likely to be able to override this, and it wasn't Mark.

Jay Fisher was in his office when I approached. It was just after five, and his assistant, Margie, no longer guarded the door.

He waved me inside. "Jennifer, come on in."

I closed the door after me.

His brow lowered at my attempt at privacy. "Is everything all right?"

"I wanted to talk about the move."

He nodded and looked over his glasses at me. "Okay?"

I took a seat opposite him and folded my hands, unsure how to put it. "I'm not sure going with Hydrocom is the right thing for me."

He steepled his hands and leaned forward. "I see. It's a promotion, and frankly, Jennifer, I think you're ready."

I couldn't possibly explain my real motivations. "I'd like to stay here with this team."

He sat back. "But your position here becomes redundant with the move." *Redundant* was a nice way of saying my job was going away.

"I understand. I'm open to changing areas, but I'd like to stay here with you, rather than go with them."

"Do you have some particular issue with Mark or someone else in the group?"

That was my opening.

"Well, there was this... I'd rather not say."

He seemed to be buying it. "If you stay, are you up for a challenge?"

"Yes. Certainly."

He took a deep breath. "The hours may not be what you're used to, and your new role can be a little demanding at times."

"Not a problem," I assured him. I needed something, anything that would let me stay in this building.

"I only have one place I can put you right now, and it will be difficult but like I said, I think you're ready."

I waited.

"You'd be replacing Mark, working for Mr. Benson on acquisitions."

In spite of my efforts, my face must have fallen. Working for the devil himself was never part of the plan. "Is there anything else I could move into? Maybe Vanessa could do the acquisitions work."

The corners of his mouth turned up. He thought that was as unlikely a solution as I knew it to be. "Jennifer, think about it overnight, and let me know tomorrow. Those are your two choices." His eyes held mine.

"Would there be a raise involved with the acquisitions position?"

His head tilted. "It's not a supervisory position, but perhaps I could suggest some adjustment. That's really a discussion you'd need to have with Mr. Benson at the end of your probationary period."

Three months to find out would be an eternity working for the devil.

I tried to keep eye contact and discern if there was any way I could get another alternative out of him with more pleading. I settled on *no*. "Thank you. I'll think about it."

"They're both good opportunities," he said as I left.

I thanked him again and headed to my desk. I didn't have a lot of time before I needed to retrieve Billy from daycare.

Before I turned off my computer, I checked the stock price for the dose of good news I needed after these meetings. The stock had closed down twenty-two percent, but I couldn't believe my eyes. The after-hours quote was up five percent. The spin-off headlines had overpowered the *Times* article.

I'd had such high hopes for today, and now I was faced with two awful choices. Benson had pulled a rabbit out of a hat and dodged the news bullet.

How was that possible?

I stopped on the floor for HR on the way down.

Her door was closed. I'd have to get with her in the morning and explain my discussion with our CFO.

CHAPTER 6

JENNIFER

RAMONA HELPED ME CLEAN UP THE DINNER DISHES. "WHAT ARE YOU MOPING about?"

My eyes darted to Billy. "Later." He was still finishing the last of the broccoli his mother had insisted he eat.

The television news was on, and it was something about a little girl gone missing this afternoon on her way back from school. An Amber Alert had been issued.

Ramona rushed to get the remote and changed the channel. "That's depressing."

Billy left his plate and went to the couch.

"Hey, little guy. Let's see your homework first," his mother told him.

"I did it already," he said as he picked up the DVR controller.

"Then I want to see it already," she said.

He gave in more easily than usual and brought it to the table from his backpack. "It was spelling, which is easy."

Ramona checked the paper and nodded. "Good job, little guy."

Billy stiffened at the comment. "I told you I did it. And I'm not little. Jeremy is little."

Jeremy was another kid in his class, and Billy had it right that Jeremy was tiny for a seven-year-old.

"You'll always be my little guy," Ramona said as she tousled his hair. "Why don't you go into the bedroom to watch so I can talk to your auntie Jenn."

"Okay." He got up, but stopped at the hallway. "When do I get my own room?" He'd lodged the complaint before, but it was becoming more frequent.

"When we can afford it. Not just yet," Ramona answered.

Financially, things were tight, even with this two-bedroom place, and when we'd last looked, getting a place with a room for him would have meant a neighborhood neither of us felt comfortable with, and Billy wouldn't have been able to stay at his current school either.

He shrugged, retreated to their bedroom, and closed the door behind him.

Ramona shut the dishwasher after loading the last dish. "I know pretty soon sleeping in the same room as Mom is going to be a giant embarrassment for him, but it's scary out there, and I feel safe here."

True to form, she hadn't addressed the crimp it put in *her* life to not have a room of her own, but rather how it affected her *little guy*.

"He won't stay this age forever, you know."

She shrugged. "Doesn't make it any easier." She walked to the couch and sat. "So what's the big news you couldn't tell me?"

I brought my glass of water and also took a seat on the couch. "Did you see the news today?"

"No, did you and your sick accomplice put out another hit piece?"

Ramona hadn't embraced my desire for revenge against Dennis Benson and his family.

I smiled. "This morning." I felt for Mom's ring on my finger.

She shook her head. "This isn't healthy. You know there's a name for what you're doing, and it's not a pretty one."

"I'm avenging Mom and Dad," I shot back.

"No, you're getting pleasure from hurting someone else, and that's not right. Two wrongs don't make a right, and none of this will bring him back." She'd long ago made her opinion of my crusade clear. "And Mom killed herself."

"It was Dad's accident that caused her drinking."

Mom had taken to the bottle and driven drunk, going off the road into a telephone pole. At least she hadn't taken anyone else with her.

Ramona huffed. "It was her drinking that killed her."

"And that was because of Dad's accident."

Ramona shook her finger at me. "She was a drinker before, and you know it."

She had me there, because Dad had always been on her about it, and his persistence had kept it to a minimum.

It wasn't worth the argument. I'd given up trying to convince Ramona to see it my way. "That's not what I wanted to talk about."

She glared across the space between us. She wasn't giving up. "When is enough going to be enough?"

It wasn't a question I'd spent much time thinking about. "I don't know yet."

"Then you're just doing it for spite."

"Can we drop it? I have a problem."

She waited for me to explain.

"The company is shifting me to a new job. Actually, it's sort of a choice between two jobs."

She sat up. "That sounds interesting."

I put my water down. "This afternoon they told seven of us that we were leaving the company with a spin-off."

"Those things happen, I guess. Does that mean we have to move?"

I ignored the question to start with. "If I go with that one, it's a promotion to supervisor."

She stood and gave me a high five as she passed me on her way to the kitchen. "That deserves a toast. I knew sooner or later they'd see how hard you work."

Her pride warmed me. She was the most supportive sister anyone could ask for.

She opened the fridge and pulled out the bottle of cheap red wine we'd used for cooking yesterday.

"If I went with them, it would be a raise and stock options."

She unscrewed the cap and pulled down two glasses. "How much of a raise?"

I sat up. "Fourteen thousand."

"Fourteen? That's fucking fantastic." She put down the bottle and screwed the cap back on. "That calls for the good stuff."

I agreed.

She pulled our special bottle of cabernet from the back of the cabinet.

"No! That one's for when you graduate." We'd been saving it.

She started to unwrap the foil over the cork. It was our only bottle of wine that wasn't screw top.

"We can get another," she said.

Giving in, I located the corkscrew in the drawer. "And, I'd get two minions working for me."

She handed me the bottle. "That's a real supervisor job, then. Next thing you know, you'll be a manager."

I worked the corkscrew into the cork, pushed down the levers, and pulled it free. "Let's not get ahead of ourselves."

She held out a glass for me to pour. "What's the other opportunity?"

"Working for the CEO."

She pulled the glass back. "You mean *him*?"

I took the other glass from the counter and poured. "The one and only."

She put her glass forward, and I poured.

"To you, sis." She raised her glass.

I raised mine as well. "Thanks."

We both sipped.

The wine wasn't as sweet as what we usually had, but then I had no experience with good wine—and it hadn't been chilled either. The wine snobs all had cellars or separate wine coolers, didn't they? It had to make a difference.

Ramona followed me back to the couch. "It sounds like the second one is also a step up."

I sat and nodded. "It probably is, but I would have to work with him, and I don't know if I could stomach that."

"Have you ever considered that you could be wrong about him?"

I ignored her comment. She wasn't going to dissuade me from my goal. "And, I'm not sure there's much of a raise involved." There certainly wasn't a bird in the hand the way there was if I went with the group to Pasadena. Knowing Benson, he'd probably delight in not giving me a raise, especially if he knew my lineage.

But he probably didn't. He was likely cold enough to not remember the names of the people he'd hurt. *Don't know* went along with *don't care* in my experience.

"Are you sure about that? You said they were both promotions."

I finished the sip of wine I'd taken before answering. "Not one hundred percent, but if I stay here it's not a supervisory position."

I still thought this wine wasn't worth the price, but then, was a Ferrari that cost ten times as much as a Chevy ten times the car?

With the likelihood that I would ever own a Ferrari at dead zero, that was a question I'd never know the answer to. They did look good though.

"What are you smiling about?" Ramona asked, pulling me from my internal deliberations.

"Nothing. Just wondering if we could afford a three bedroom after my raise."

"Fourteen K sounds good enough to me."

I nodded. Even after taxes, it should allow us to get Billy his own room.

She worked the remote. "Sandra Bullock okay?" She'd stopped on *Two Weeks Notice.*

"Sure."

The movie was funny, and I couldn't help but compare it to my situation. The heroine ended up working for the guy she didn't like and didn't have anything in common with. He betrayed her for corporate greed. Then the movie took a weird turn and he reformed for her—so unrealistic in the real world. In real life, the bad guys got a way with it most of the time, got caught some of the time, and never turned over a new leaf.

My phone chirped that a text had arrived.

EB: Call when u have time

Ramona shot me a quizzical look, so I pointed the screen her way. She rolled her eyes. "Screw that."

I turned the phone off. Ed didn't deserve my time.

At the end of the movie, the rich guy made a joke about how small Sandra's parents' apartment was. That brought me back to the choice I had to make.

Ramona and Billy deserved a bigger place with separate bedrooms. The

Pasadena option made the most sense, even though I'd have to give up my access to the files that held Vipersoft's dirty laundry.

I could handle the commute; giving up justice for Dad was the hard part.

When the movie ended and Ramona and Billy had gone to bed, I poured myself another glass of wine to contemplate my decision.

CHAPTER 7

DENNIS

TUESDAY MORNING I WOKE EARLY. ACTUALLY, I'D BEEN SO NERVOUS ABOUT THIS morning's market opening that I kept waking and checking the clock.

I gave up and dressed for a run when my latest clock check showed five thirty. I made a long loop of it, but was still back with plenty of time to shower before the market opened at six thirty Pacific Time. This was one of those times where it helped that the New York types were lazy and didn't start work till nine thirty their time.

I finished my cantaloupe and toast and had my laptop open to the trading software I used.

Promptly at six thirty, the trades for Vipersoft started scrolling down the screen. They were all green, and the little daily chart gapped up from yesterday's terrible close. It had already crossed above where it had been before the *Times* story.

"Yeah," I yelled to the empty house. "Take that, you asshole."

Sigurd's latest attempt to torpedo me had failed.

Dad's advice had been spot on, and I'd won this battle. We still didn't have a clue who was behind this, but secrets like that didn't withstand the test of time.

The first rule of secrets was not to tell anyone. Keep the secret to yourself, and you only had yourself to blame if it was discovered. But since Sigurd clearly had an accomplice, the circle of those in the know was already beyond one, and a slip up was just a matter of time.

Melissa's envelope from yesterday sat next to my computer where I'd left it last night. I picked it up, but decided to let it rest unopened again today. Why give her the satisfaction of annoying me? My lawyer could give me the short version later after he'd digested it and had a plan for how to deal with her.

As if she had surveillance in my house, my cell burst to life with her ugly mug on the screen.

I hit the decline button, and the face disappeared. The picture of her wasn't actually ugly; it was just that I had seen through the facade.

Beneath the pretty face, embellished with too much makeup, was an ugly soul, one intent on inflicting pain and misery. She also had less common sense than a squirrel. She had insisted more than once that we give it another try, but that would be like pissing into the wind—after all the effort I'd come out even worse than before I started.

It had been my fault for rushing into the wedding, but maybe more time wouldn't have changed the outcome. She was, or had been, an actress, after all. And her performance had been good enough to fool me.

The phone beeped, and the screen showed she'd left a voicemail.

I navigated to the voicemail page and deleted the message without listening to it. I'd had enough aggravation yesterday to last me a month.

THIS MORNING, I SKIPPED MY NORMAL STOP AT STARBUCKS AND WENT DIRECTLY to work.

The elevator doors opened, and I was ready for a better day than yesterday.

When I opened the door to Mahogany Row, as some called it, Cindy was already at her desk.

Her smile was even perkier than usual. "I thought today might be a busy one," she said, answering my unasked question. She handed me several pink message slips. "They started calling early."

"Thanks, Cin." All three messages were from analysts. I handed them back. "Larry can handle these. He'll enjoy it."

The analysts were always trying to get past Larry and talk directly to me, hoping to get something beyond the standard info dump he gave all the analysts access to. They were looking for an angle, an advantage over the next guy.

She held one slip up. "All except Gumpert. He was mad yesterday that he hadn't gotten a heads up."

"He deserves Larry."

Inside my office, I spotted a cup of coffee already on my desk.

"Thanks for the coffee," I called.

"I figured you could use it," Cindy replied from my door. "Also, Jay was already by this morning."

After his attempt to lecture me yesterday on being rash, I would look forward to pointing out how well the spin-off strategy had worked at turning around our stock price.

I powered up my computer and clicked on the stock price bookmark. Up another two percent.

Yes, it would be a good discussion.

I took off my jacket and hung it on the antique coat rack in the corner, a gift from my brother Zack, who was into antiques. Even the car he drove was old.

"Hey, Cin, would you mind fetching Jay for me? I'd like to have that chat."

She agreed and was off. If she called, there was a chance he'd be busy. When she went personally, she never failed to return with him in tow.

Jay had worked directly for my dad back at the family company. He'd never said as much, but I wondered if he didn't think working here for me represented a step down for him.

My desk phone rang, and I answered it.

"Glad I caught you," Michael Gumpert said when I picked up.

"Morning, Michael. I'm on my way to a meeting." It wouldn't be wise to hang up on him the way I wanted to.

"Dennis, I won't take much of your time. I wanted to ask for your take on the revised EPS projections Larry is handing out. They seem a bit aggressive to me given the current climate."

The question was a trap.

Things had moved so fast yesterday that I hadn't gotten a copy of the notes Larry had written up for his analyst calls. But I couldn't say I didn't know exactly what Larry was feeding the analyst community—that would be suicide.

"I don't have anything to add to Larry's comments," I said.

"I get that, Dennis. I do. I was just looking for your take on the aggressiveness of the numbers."

Another trap. He would use any tilt I offered in his forecasts. If I were optimistic, he'd set a high bar of expectations, and the market would punish us if we missed. If I didn't show confidence, he'd move them down right away in a surprise move, the other analysts would follow, and the market would punish us.

Managing their expectations had to be done slowly, not the day after a major announcement, and he knew that.

"The numbers he gave you are our numbers. There's been no change."

"And the bottom-line benefit next quarter of the Hydrocom spin-off?"

"Michael, I'm late for my meeting. Get with Larry on your questions. He'll be happy to help you."

"I'm going to have to move down my forecasts, then."

His threat might not be an idle one, but it was for Larry to handle.

"And also, do you have any rebuttal to Cartwright's comments yesterday afternoon about the spin-off?"

I didn't pay attention to Cartwright's barbs anymore. He could go fuck himself. I took a moment to control my anger. "No, I don't have any comment. Bye, Michael." I hung up on him.

Not the best way to curry favor with the financial community, but he was supposed to be calling Larry, not me.

Besides, Gumpert was an arrogant ass and needed to be taken down a notch or two. He carried around a handkerchief embroidered with his family coat of arms, as if that should mean something in this day and age.

Cartwright was another thorn in my side. With a history of attacking companies such as ours—and extorting them—he was a financial low-life. His plan of attack followed a standard path. He'd publicly attack a company while buying stock and increasing his position. If the company became vulnerable enough, he'd demand seats on the board to "help" them.

That's when his targets often paid him off to go away, and where he made most of his money. Wall Street had even invented the term *greenmail* for this approach. Occasionally he'd go further in his attacks and attempt to gain control of the board.

I had to wonder if this was payback for the run-in I'd had with his son, Adam, years ago. Regardless, I had no intention of paying the blood-sucking scum.

~

JENNIFER

MY ALARM MADE THE FATAL MISTAKE OF BUZZING AT ME FROM THE NIGHTSTAND.

It took me two tries to whack it hard enough to get the devilish thing to shut up. The noise it made hitting the floor didn't sound good. One of these days it wouldn't survive the abuse.

Ramona had suggested I use my phone, but I was deathly afraid I'd break it the way I had my last two alarm clocks. At less than twenty bucks, they were expendable, and my phone wasn't.

I rolled out of bed having gotten almost no real sleep last night. But I needed to get up. Tuesday was my day to use the bathroom first.

The warm water of the shower slowly rinsed the grogginess out of my brain.

It should have been a soothing night after seeing Dennis Benson take the beating he deserved. Instead, *my* world had taken the beating, and my sleep had suffered.

It was so unfair that Benson had found a way to thwart me. He'd come out on top and put me in the position of having to choose between Dad and Ramona.

How would Ramona feel if I stayed at Vipersoft and cost us the income we needed? She and Billy would suffer the most.

How would I feel putting them through that?

She'd never supported my revenge project, and this would turn her even more against me. I'd tried to reason with her about it, but there was no bridging the gap of our views on the subject

Usually I found the shower a calming place to think through a problem, but today I climbed out no more sure of my path forward than when I'd entered. If anything, I was more mixed up.

Billy was already eating his cereal, Cocoa Puffs again, by the time I finished dressing and got out to the kitchen.

"It's Tuesday today," he announced.

I poured a glass of grapefruit juice for myself. "That's right. Want some juice?"

"It's hamburger day." His tone was more dejected than excited. He didn't answer my juice question.

His school served burgers at lunch on Tuesdays like clockwork. One of the parents owned a local burger place and sold patties at a discount to the school.

"If you want, I can make you a sandwich instead." I poured him a small glass of juice.

"No, I want a cheeseburger, but last week they only had ones without cheese left, and I didn't want the pickle either."

I brought the glasses over. "You were late?"

"Yeah, a little, but they know I always want a cheeseburger and no pickle."

I sat opposite him and drank from my juice. "Sometimes the early bird gets the worm."

He pushed his cereal around in his bowl. "Mommy told me not to complain."

"She's right about that. You don't want to be labeled as a complainer. You could always take the pickle off and get almost what you wanted."

He gulped down the juice I'd poured him. His cereal didn't merit the same attention.

"It's your turn," he said.

I stood to get some cereal for myself. "For what?"

"It's Tuesday. You take me to school, and Mommy said we could have pizza night tonight."

I checked the time on the microwave.

Shit.

This would mean no breakfast for me today. "Get your backpack. We have to go." I quickly moved the ball of pizza dough I'd made last week from the freezer to the refrigerator.

Ramona hadn't shown her face yet. If I'd wanted to switch, I should've arranged it with her last night.

I hustled him out and we made the drive to school. Unfortunately, work was in the opposite direction.

Take off the pickle. I needed to talk to the man who could change the options—the man who could take off the pickle. That was the solution to my problem.

Billy exited the car with a quick goodbye. I didn't pull away from the curb until I saw him make it safely inside the school.

I needed the new position with the big raise *and* to negotiate access back into the Vipersoft building. With seven people moving over, that had to leave holes somewhere in finance that I could help with after hours or on weekends, thereby keeping my badge with access to the building. Part-time weekend work would also ease my access to the file rooms.

I made a U-turn at the light, and the sun broke through the clouds—a definite omen that things were improving.

My skills were broad enough that there had to be something I could help with at headquarters—something between take it or leave it. I refined my sales pitch to Fisher as I drove in to work.

CHAPTER 8

JENNIFER

THE GROUP WAITING FOR THE ELEVATORS AS I ENTERED THE LOBBY WAS LARGER than usual.

Ben sat at his normal station behind the desk. As I approached, he tilted his head toward the crowd. "One of the elevators is down for maintenance."

I nodded. "Thanks."

I shuffled closer with each opening of the polished stainless doors, but I didn't make it on until the third filling of the little car.

Sweat was already threatening to soak my blouse when the door closed and it instantly got warmer. Packed between marketing people complaining about not being chosen to go with the spin-off, I counted the floors as the doors opened and disgorged a person or two at each stop.

Getting off at the finance floor, I dropped my purse at my desk before making my way to the conference room.

Through the glass I saw the meeting had already begun. I smoothed down my skirt and opened the door.

Mark looked up. His forehead creased. "I'll be with you in a minute, Jennifer."

I stopped. It was as if he knew I wanted to talk to him about doing after-hours work back here.

"Outside," he added.

I retreated to the hallway, but not before noticing the group had increased by one since yesterday.

Vanessa sat on the far side of the table, concentrating on the paper in front of her.

I silently rehearsed the lines I'd come up with in the car.

Mark came out and closed the door behind him. "Let's talk in number three."

I followed him into the adjoining empty conference room.

He didn't sit, so neither did I.

"You didn't sign your paperwork yesterday afternoon the way I asked you all to."

My shoulders slumped. "I went back, but they'd closed the office early." I backed up a bit. This wasn't the conversation I'd envisioned. This was all wrong.

"Everyone else managed to, and Jay told me you had misgivings about joining us based on the commute."

My throat went instantly dry. *Those two have already talked this morning?* "I can make the commute work." I couldn't start with my new boss thinking I didn't appreciate the opportunity. How often would I get a chance like this?

He held up a hand to stop me. "Vanessa expressed an interest yesterday in joining Hydrocom." He took a breath. "So she will be filling the general ledger supervisor role."

"But—"

"I have a meeting to get back to. You can apply for a transfer in the future if you like, when you're more certain of your situation." He left, and the door closed behind him.

Tears threatened, and my knees wobbled. The room became cold, and I slumped into the closest chair. I'd totally screwed this up. I'd let Ramona and Billy down. Vanessa had aced me out of my chance at the raise we needed.

After a few minutes, I took a deep breath and sat up straight. My current job was being eliminated, and I needed to work. The only thing left to do was to put on my brave front and face the music. What alternative did I have? Short answer, none.

After a stop in the ladies room to check my eyes, I turned right toward Fisher's office.

His assistant, Margie, appraised me with cold eyes as I walked up. She helped his productivity by protecting his time, as she saw it. Nobody got past her without an appointment.

I stopped and prepared to argue my case, but was cut off with a hand gesture. "He asked for you to join him in Mr. Benson's office." She checked her watch. "That was four minutes ago."

"Thank you," I said as I turned for the elevator.

"You should take your purse," she said.

I reversed course and gathered my purse before heading once more for the elevator that would transport me to my doom.

The door closed, and a line from *Alice in Wonderland* popped into my brain: "*Off with her head!*" That's exactly how it would go if Benson got an inkling of how I felt about him. I practiced the smile I planned to hide behind. It didn't look half bad in the polished stainless of the elevator door.

As I entered the executive offices, I heard voices and stopped short of the door with Dennis Benson's nameplate beside it.

"I need a guy with an MBA, and experience," Benson said.

"No, you don't. I have someone who can provide the support you need," Fisher said from inside the office.

"Are you deliberately trying to jam me up for moving fast on the spin-off?"

"I just said these kinds of trade-offs wouldn't have been necessary if we'd taken the time to plan properly."

"We had to move quickly. You know that."

"If you want to go outside, you can start interviewing next week to fill Mark's position. It shouldn't take longer than a month or two."

My God, they were arguing about me. Not only did I not want to work for the devil; he didn't want me either. Suddenly the prospect of losing this job too became a real possibility, and then where would I be? Unemployed, on top of all the other things I stood to lose.

I smoothed my skirt, took a deep, composing breath, knocked on the door frame, and then moved into the open door.

"There you are," Fisher said.

"Dennis, I'd like you to meet Jennifer Hanley."

I pasted on my fake, I-don't-hate-you smile and entered the devil's lair.

~

DENNIS

SHE WALKED INTO MY OFFICE.

Jennifer Hanley—now I had a name to go with the face, the body, the fantasies.

"I think she'll be just what you need," Jay said with a sly grin.

Could he know what he'd just done to me?

My mind raced. I caught myself before my jaw dropped very far. I hadn't been expecting a girl, much less this girl—my Starbucks girl. Jay stood and made his way to the door. "I'll be downstairs if you need me," he said as he left, leaving her behind.

I composed myself and rounded the desk to shake her extended hand.

It was warm and soft as I'd always imagined, but with a firm grip—a grip I'd imagine every time I closed my eyes in the shower to stroke myself.

She looked down at our joined hands before I realized I'd held hers too long, enjoying the warmth, the electric touch I'd imagined for months.

I let her go. "Please take a seat, Jennifer." Returning to my chair, I scooted close to the desk, a position that hid my stirring cock. "Where did you get your MBA?"

She looked down. "I have a BS in Accounting and Business Administration from Pepperdine, not an MBA."

I noticed the rise and fall of her chest as she talked. No way was having her just down the hall going to work.

This was totally fucked up. Her working under me couldn't possibly end well. She didn't have an MBA, and she was the face I saw every morning as I closed my eyes and jerked off—the one keeping me sane during my enforced period of abstinence leading up to the court date with Melissa.

"Mr. Benson?" she asked.

Her voice pulled me back to the moment. "Dennis, please." I tried in vain to look away from those luscious lips I wanted on my dick every morning when I woke up, but looking any lower would probably break my zipper.

She shifted in her seat. "How should we start? Would you like to explain the position I'm going to be in?"

I had barely enough working brain cells to keep from explaining ten different positions I'd like her to assume.

Her face had softened from the distressed, forced smile of a minute ago to something more neutral. She might have overheard my complaints to Jay.

I cleared my throat. "Just a second."

I buzzed Cindy to come in. I had to get this girl out of here and make a plan, any plan.

I'd meant what I'd told Jay, even before I knew he'd picked this girl to saddle me with. Now my concerns were tripled at least. Working this close to her could, or most likely *would*, lead to something that would unravel everything with Melissa.

She was supposed to be an after-Melissa treat, not a fuck-up-the-negotiation indulgence. The plan had always been to pursue her after the Melissa legal skirmish was done.

Cindy opened the door and popped her head in with her usual speed. "Yes?"

"Jennifer here will be taking over Mark's position. Would you please get her situated in the office?"

"Sure thing," Cindy responded with a smile. "Jennifer you said?" She extended her hand.

Jennifer stood and greeted Cindy. "Yes, Jennifer Hanley from downstairs in finance."

"Oh," I added. "Get her the Talbot paperwork. Jennifer, get up to speed on them for the two o'clock meeting."

"Of course," Jennifer responded as they left, and Cindy thankfully closed the door.

I'd made the decision to send her back to Jay's floor the moment I laid eyes on her. He needed to be taught a lesson about messing with me this way, but to make it sink in, she had to help me by screwing up in a documented fashion.

JENNIFER

ALTHOUGH HE'D ACTED AS IF HE DIDN'T KNOW ME, A HINT OF RECOGNITION HAD flashed across Dennis Benson's face when we met. What were the chances that he knew me and what I was up to? Could this be a scheme to fire me and later paint me as a disgruntled former employee? My mind raced a thousand miles a minute.

Cindy led the way. "Don't let his gruff exterior scare you. He's a softie underneath."

Easy for her to say. He hadn't ruined her life.

I followed, checking my hand for all five fingers. I'd survived my first encounter with him.

"I'm sure he keeps plenty of things hidden," I said, attempting a light tone. "How long have you worked for him?"

She stopped at the final office door on the row. "Long enough to know where the bodies are buried."

"You'll have to tell me some day."

She smiled. "We should do lunch soon."

She didn't realize how literally I meant what I'd said.

She handed me a key. "The key to this office. I hope you find it comfortable, and I'm sure you'll enjoy working for Dennis."

That last part I couldn't agree with.

I used the key and opened the dark wooden door. My mouth must have dropped. It was smaller than Benson's office—or rather Dennis's—but not by a lot. It was easily as large as Fisher's, and he was the CFO, for Christ's sake.

"Are you sure this is the one?" I asked.

"Dennis doesn't believe in squabbling over rank, so the offices of all the people reporting to him are the same size."

The statement made sense, but at the same time it didn't. I was a lowly analyst, just out of business school with no staff, and my office was two floors above Fisher's *and* the same size?

The view out the window was magnificent, looking over the city and toward the Pacific beyond. I wasn't in real-ville anymore, that much was certain. Ramona wasn't going to believe this.

"Nice view, huh?" Cindy remarked.

"I was just thinking that." I ventured in and felt the polished mahogany of the desk, another step up from cubicle-land.

"I'll get you the Talbot paperwork," she said. "Take an inventory, and let me know if you need anything else."

"Sure."

"Your system login should be the same, but with upgraded access. Give me your cell number, and I'll send you all the office contacts."

I wrote the number down for her. "Thanks. I'll need a few minutes to get my bearings. And where will the meeting be?"

She pointed toward where we'd come from. "The boardroom. Second door past Dennis's office."

It was odd to hear her call him Dennis, as if he were just another guy, a normal occupant of this floor, instead of the creature from hell I knew him to be. How would she feel about him when the truth was revealed?

She left me alone in the space that was now *my* office.

I opened one of the short lateral files, which was mahogany like everything else in sight. The top drawer was sparsely filled, and its files were alphabetized. The second-drawer files were numerically coded—the same system as in the file rooms I'd burgled.

The numeric coding made it impossible to find something unless you knew the code it has been stored under, and only Hydra had access to that information somehow. But even he had been wrong twice and sent me after files that didn't seem helpful in bringing down Benson.

As promised, my phone chirped with Cindy's message, which contained a bunch of office and cell numbers. I added them to my contacts.

A few minutes later, Cindy reappeared with an armload of papers. "This is everything on Talbot—at least everything I could find." She set them down on the small, circular conference table near the door.

I had an office with a couch, a meeting table, a monster desk, and a view to kill for. What a life.

The sheer height of the stack Cindy had arranged changed my perspective quickly.

"Two o'clock? Is that right?" I asked.

"That's right. It's the final meeting to sign, as I understand it."

"Sign?"

"Didn't he tell you? We're purchasing a Talbot division. It's been in the works for a few months now."

I sighed. "By two o'clock?"

"If you want to tell him you need more time, you better do it right away. The Talbot team is flying in from Oregon."

I followed her down to Mr. Benson's, *Dennis's*, office. I had to remember to use his first name if I wanted to fit in.

I knocked, and he called for me to enter.

He looked up as I stopped just inside the door. "Yes?"

"The Talbot files are massive. What would you like me to concentrate on for this afternoon?"

His brow knit as if that was a stupid question. "The entire file, of course. This is the final meeting with them. We should be signed by tonight."

"It's just that it's so—"

He put up a hand to stop me. "Should I get someone else?"

I pasted on a smile, finally understanding the game. "Not at all. I'll be ready."

This was his way of getting me to fire myself because he and Fisher had some power play going on, and I was the pawn.

"Good. I'm counting on you, Jennifer." He looked down at his desk, a non-verbal cue that our discussion was done.

I departed and closed the door behind me.

Cindy raised an eyebrow, but didn't say anything.

I merely smiled in return. Internally, I called bullshit on him being a softie.

Being unprepared for the meeting was one way to point out my inadequacy, but I didn't plan on playing along. I would not be the pawn in their tug-of-war.

I returned to my office and shut the door to concentrate.

The term sheet and contract papers were in the first folder I opened. Five hours to go to finish this stack and attend a corporate merger closing meeting. It was worse than cramming for finals.

By noon, I'd made good progress and dialed Cindy to inquire about lunch.

She offered help. "I'll order for you. Chinese, Thai, pizza, or a sandwich?"

I chose Chinese.

CHAPTER 9

DENNIS

I SAT IN THE BOOTH AT THE BACK OF THE RESTAURANT. LARRY HAD AGREED TO meet for lunch, but as always, he was late.

I'd ordered his usual and changed mine up as I tended to do. I couldn't see getting the same thing every time.

He called it controlling the variables; I called it boring.

Finally he slid in across from me. "I see you let Mark get away from you. Who's the new girl?"

I took a sip of my hot tea. "Jennifer. Jennifer Hanley."

"She's cute."

"Give me a break. Jay stole Mark and sent her up in his place. This is Jay trying to teach me a lesson."

"What kind of lesson?"

"He thinks I should have gotten the group together to decide the Hydrocom spin-off instead of just announcing it."

"He's right. You should have."

"I thought at least you'd back me up."

"Shoot the messenger, why don't ya? I agree with Jay on this one."

"We needed good news, so I pulled the trigger and moved up the spin-off. Big deal. We were doing it at the end of the year anyway."

"Asking for help from the group isn't a sign of weakness."

I'd heard that lecture before.

"Anyway, she's got no experience and no MBA," I lamented.

"Maybe she's better than you think."

The waiter interrupted with our plates.

My kung pao chicken smelled delicious.

The broccoli beef on his plate was the same as always: boring.

Larry spooned some rice onto his plate and offered it to me. "Give her some time and see how she does."

"I don't have the time to find out. I'm going to see to it that she hates the job and wants to move back downstairs."

Larry thought about that for another few bites. "How?"

"Easy. I'll be the impossible boss."

He shrugged. "Not like it's hard for you."

∾

JENNIFER

IT WAS A FEW MINUTES BEFORE TWO WHEN I CLOSED THE FINAL FOLDER OF THE Talbot paperwork tower Cindy had brought me. My brain swam with numbers, contracts, and a million details.

How had he ever expected me to absorb all this in one day and go into the meeting prepared? I knew he hadn't. He counted on me not finishing, not being prepared, and not knowing what was in these. He expected me to make a fool of myself and prove I wasn't ready. He expected a quick exit from Mahogany Row for me.

I felt the smooth, cool, real-wood surface of the table I sat at and looked over my shoulder at the cityscape out my window—my top-floor office window.

Screw him. He wasn't getting an easy win today

I pushed away the carton of Chinese I'd barely had time to touch. Twisting the top off my Diet Coke bottle, I wet my parched mouth with two gulps. A quick time check showed I had just enough time for a trip to the bathroom before the meeting.

The restroom door seemed heavier than the one downstairs, but that was probably my imagination. Inside, I almost dropped my purse. The difference was stark. The sinks were set into a granite counter, and the stalls weren't the standard beige, airport-style metal structures found on my floor. Here, solid-wood partitions provided the elegant privacy top-floor ladies deserved while they peed. Everything about life on the top floor was evidently different.

After washing up and refreshing my lip gloss, I was ready to learn what a signing meeting was all about.

As I approached, four men were standing about between Cindy's desk and the conference room door, which was open—the Talbot team, apparently.

I ducked into my office to grab a pad of paper and my phone. It had a good calculator and was better than doing things in my head.

I put on my brave face and approached the group. I stopped at Cindy's desk, unsure if I should introduce myself.

The oldest among them looked at me. "Honey, I'll take a coffee. Two sugars."

I froze.

"Gentlemen, you can set up in the conference room," Cindy said. "Mr. Benson will join you as soon as he's off the phone."

The group followed Mr. Coffee through the door.

"I'll get it," Cindy said to me. "Wait for Dennis and go in with him. It may be a few minutes." She headed off to the coffee room. I'd stumbled upon it on my way to the bathroom.

Glancing at her desk, I noticed neither of Dennis's phone lines were lit.

I laid my things down, my phone on top, and headed back for my Diet Coke in case I needed the caffeine. After finishing most of the bottle and releasing a quick burp, I was back at Cindy's desk.

She pointed at my phone. "You got a message while you were gone."

The phone was face up with the awful text on the screen.

EB: We should talk

I shook my head. "My ex. I wish he would stop texting." I picked up the phone, cleared the screen, and put it on silent.

Cindy shrugged. "Surely he'll give up after a while."

It was another several minutes before Dennis emerged from his office. A forced smile crossed his face as he saw me. At least it wasn't a frown.

"You ready?"

I nodded. "As ready as I'm going to be."

He closed his office door and stepped toward the room with our guests.

I put my arm out. "Stop." The word escaped before I could come up with a nicer one. I stepped in front of him and reached up to straighten his tie.

His eyes met mine, and the smile was no longer forced. "Thank you."

"I want you looking your best." My brain-word filter was malfunctioning this afternoon. I'd meant to say *we*, not *I*.

He turned for the door. "Your job is not to grill them, but let me know if they say anything that's off."

I followed him and closed the door behind us. *Don't grill them?* That should be no problem. I'd just been thrown in the deep end without a life preserver.

The group of four stood and one by one started introducing themselves and shaking hands with Dennis.

I came next.

Mr. Coffee was the first to reach me. He extended his hands, a business card in one and the other open to shake. "James Talbot the third."

I accepted his card and shook with him. "Jennifer Hanley. Sorry, I don't have a card yet. I'm new."

His hand fell away quickly. "Are you by any chance related to Senator Hanley?"

"Sadly, no."

"You look like her. You must get that a lot." It was the first time I'd ever been compared to the senator. The comparison made me smile. The old man was a top-notch bullshitter.

"Not often enough." I smiled.

The name-handshake-business card exchange, minus my card, repeated three more times with the others. Sweaty Palms was their CFO, Baldy their marketing VP, and Beak Nose their general counsel.

I collected their cards while still clutching my legal pad, phone, and pen in one hand.

Dennis had his hands free. He'd pre-placed his notepad and pen on the table before they arrived, claiming his seat: one chair down from the head of the table and on the side facing the window.

I obviously had things to learn about the power dynamics of these meetings.

I took my seat to the right of Dennis after he sat.

The Talbot group had helped themselves to refreshments from the drink cart Cindy must've supplied—all except Talbot himself, who waited for the coffee he'd ordered from me.

The others had chosen Pellegrinos.

I retrieved a fresh Diet Coke bottle and unscrewed the lid. Before I sat, I noticed my faux pas. They'd all poured their drinks into glass tumblers.

I retrieved a glass from the cart and took my seat, feeling like a child at the adults' table.

Then I noticed Dennis didn't have a glass either and took a sip directly from his plastic bottle.

I also took note that Dennis was also coatless, versus suits for the opposing side.

I definitely had yet to understand the dynamics.

Dennis and Talbot were saying something about the weather when Cindy entered and placed a coffee cup on a saucer in front of Talbot.

He nodded, without a verbal thank you to her. Jerk.

Before she left, another of our team came in and went through the handshake ritual with the other side.

I learned he was Pembroke, our general counsel.

He took a seat next to me. "Syd," he whispered, sliding me his card.

I leaned and whispered back, "Jennifer." I arranged my cards in front of me in the order of their seating.

"Shall we get started?" Talbot asked.

"Let's," Dennis responded. The pad in front of him was blank. He lifted the top sheet to read from the next page. "My note says you were going to give us a quarter update."

I glanced sideways. The page he read from was also blank.

Sweaty Palms gave Talbot a sideways glance.

"I don't remember that," Beak Nose said.

Dennis lifted his Coke. "Let's start there anyway."

Sweaty Palms shuffled through his pile of papers, pulled out a folder, and opened his laptop to start the presentation..

Syd got up and flipped a switch on the wall that brought down a screen from the ceiling, and then adjusted the vertical blinds on the far wall to darken the room a bit.

Sweaty Palms started talking to the first slide.

"Can we get a copy of that for Jennifer?" Dennis asked.

Sweaty Palms glanced at Talbot, who nodded before he pulled out a stapled set.

I rose and thanked him before reclaiming my seat. Following along, the numbers were similar, but not the same as what I'd seen, but without the folder in front of me, I couldn't be certain. I fidgeted, but decided not to leave to get the folder.

Then Dennis started asking me if I had any questions for Sweaty Palms after every few sentences their CFO got out.

Each time, I was question-less, and now my palms were sweaty as well.

Dennis was testing me, and I was failing at my new job.

By the fourth page of Sweaty Palms's presentation, Dennis had given up asking me and had taken to grilling Baldy and Sweaty Palms himself about projections down the line.

Turning back to the second page, something had seemed odd at the time, but I hadn't connected the dots.

I opened my phone's calculator and had the answer in a few seconds. I raised my hand like a schoolgirl asking a question.

Talbot started talking over Baldy about the new product line and ignored me.

"Excuse me," I inserted at a pause in their conversation. "I want to go back to the receivables for a moment."

Talbot dismissed me with a wave. "We're past that. George, let's hit the next slide."

"George, let's not," Dennis said in a tone that froze the man at the projector. "I'd like to see the receivables again."

Talbot sent me a sneer.

Sweaty Palms complied and went back to the receivables page.

"The footnote on the bad-debts reserve seems to have been left off of my copy," I said. "Could you slide that up so we can see it?"

Talbot huffed. "Are we going to go backwards and get into footnotes here? I thought this was going to be a signing meeting."

"George, slide that up, please," Dennis said.

He did. The footnote was at the bottom of the slide, but omitted from my printed copy.

I read it out loud. "Subject to revision. How big a revision?"

Sweaty Palms looked to Talbot for guidance but got none. "Double digit millions." The blood drained from his face.

"Can you be more specific?" I asked.

"Eighty-ish," was his reply. The man looked like he wanted to melt into the carpet.

I had him on the ropes. "Eighty what?"

"Eighty-nine."

"It'll be resolved before the end of the quarter," Talbot said loudly. "Right, Malcolm?"

Baldy was a deer caught in the headlights. "Sure. It's just a small disagreement in China."

Dennis turned to me. "Does that answer your question?"

I swallowed hard and hoped my memory was good enough. "George, if it doesn't get resolved, doesn't that put you in violation of your bank-debt covenants?"

Sweaty Palms turned even whiter than before, but didn't answer.

"Does it?" I asked Talbot.

"Technically, but I don't like your insinuation," he answered.

Dennis stood. "Syd, you can hold down the fort. Jenn, a word." He grabbed his note pad and walked to the door.

I gathered my things and followed. I'd found the flaw in their numbers Dennis wanted me to find.

Talbot's mouth hung open as I closed the door behind us.

Dennis went to his office door and motioned for me to follow him, which I did.

"Shut it," he said.

I did.

He walked behind his desk. "I should fire you right now. That's a two-month negotiation you just blew up. I wanted that division, and now you've insulted the hell out of old man Talbot."

I sat and shrunk into the chair, my mouth instantly parched. "You weren't clear about what you expected of me. I'm sorry. I thought you wanted me to point out discrepancies."

"You don't get it. We're past that stage. We were supposed to exchange pleasantries and sign today. You just made us look like assholes."

"They're the ones who were hiding something."

"Everyone is hiding something," he shot back.

He didn't know how true that statement was.

"We need to close this deal today. We don't have any time left before the end of the quarter."

My heart was pounding so hard his words barely registered. "Can we slow down a second and talk about what they hid?"

"Are you trying to blow up months of work, or are you just stupid?"

"You told me to flag anything they said that was off. That's what I did."

He ignored me. "I knew you were too junior. You don't get it. This acquisition is already baked into this quarter's numbers. We need to close."

I stated the obvious. "You were going to fire me today no matter what. You've already made up your mind."

I was clearly a goner. No promotion, no raise, and now no job. The conversation I'd overheard made it pretty clear what this was. It hadn't mattered how prepared I was, if I'd asked too few questions or too many— either way the outcome had been predetermined: a quick chewing out and a summary execution.

He didn't deny it. "You've got ten minutes. Go back in there. Apologize, kiss ass, suck dick, or whatever you have to do, just fix the damage. We have to sign today."

His tone was not joking. Suck Talbot's dick? I almost puked at the thought. Wobbly legs carried me to the door.

"Ten minutes," he repeated.

My blood boiled as I closed the door to his office behind me.

The cocksucker had ruined my family, and now I'd be forced to leave the company with *my* reputation in tatters instead of his.

The unfairness of it was staggering. The rich made the rules, and the rules determined the outcome—an outcome that always favored them over the rest of us.

CHAPTER 10

DENNIS

I waited a minute after Jennifer left to cool down before calling Jay.

"How did the Talbot closing go?" he asked.

"You went too far this time, Jay. Saddling me with a rookie may have blown up the whole deal."

"Slow down a second. What happened?"

I worked to control my breathing. "I took her into the meeting, and she blew the thing up with some questions about their accounting."

"Then it's on you," he said.

"Fuck that. She screwed the pooch."

"You shouldn't have been in such a hurry to take someone new into a meeting like that, then. I warned you. Slow down. If you hadn't moved so aggressively on the Hydrocom spin-off, you wouldn't be in this predicament."

"Let's not go there again," I said.

"Lloyd wouldn't have made that mistake."

Another thing I didn't need today was a father-son comparison.

"Get me somebody better for tomorrow."

"I don't have anybody better."

I had the retort for that. "Find someone by tomorrow, or you come up and do the job yourself."

"Let's talk in the morning when you've had a chance to cool off." He hung up.

I didn't call back and berate him because I didn't need the blood-pressure spike.

I couldn't fantasize about my Starbucks girl anymore, the Talbot transaction was going sideways, and I was on the verge of pushing Jay too far. Everything about today sucked.

I wanted to rewind to two days ago where I could jerk off to visions of Jennifer, I hadn't gotten the latest nastygram from Melissa, Sigurd hadn't written another hit piece, and Talbot was within my grasp.

This week sucked big time.

JENNIFER

AFTER CLOSING THE DOOR TO DENNIS'S OFFICE, I LEANED BACK AGAINST THE wall to catch my breath. He'd chewed me a new one, and I didn't deserve it. It was so unfair.

Cindy wasn't at her desk, so I could stand here and contemplate the path he'd laid out: kiss ass and suck dick. My God, the man was crude, but above all *mean*. It didn't matter to him how demeaning it was—or whether they were cheating him—so long as he got his stupid deal.

It only made my blood boil hotter to think of how he'd ravaged my family and was now killing my career. At the next job, they'd want a reference from here, and there was no way I was getting a good one after pissing off the CEO.

I felt for Mom's ring on my finger and counted to ten in my head before I opened the conference room door. If I was leaving, it wouldn't be with my tail between my legs. The parting shot would be mine.

The conversation stopped, and all eyes went to me when I closed the door behind me and moved to the beverage cart.

"When is Dennis joining us again?" Talbot asked.

I unscrewed the top of a second Diet Coke and downed two swallows, this time directly from the bottle, before answering him. "He's not."

Talbot's eyes widened. "Pardon?"

The other suits were speechless, and even Syd's brow knit with confusion.

I retook my seat. "He put me in charge of this negotiation."

"That's absurd," Talbot said with a huff.

"Do you have a problem with a woman being in charge, James?" I asked. "Because I'm the one you're talking with now, not Dennis. If you don't like it, you're free to leave."

He didn't budge, at least not yet. "Now you remind me of his father."

I fixed Talbot with my coldest stare and ignored the comment. "He told me to handle it, and I am. End of story."

Syd looked like he might have a heart attack any second.

If Benson thought I was screwing up his negotiation, he had no idea how bad I could make it for him. I would gladly fuck him over with these idiots.

"You four are the ones who waltzed in here trying to hide material information."

Sweaty Palms and Baldy cringed. Only Beak Nose held his head high. Lawyers had no compunctions about trying to cheat. I'd learned that years ago.

I took the agreement Talbot had pushed our way earlier and slid it back to him. "You tried to cheat. We're not signing this. You insulted me. You insulted my boss, and our entire organization."

"But..." was all Talbot had to say for himself.

I stood and walked out.

Fuck them. Fuck Benson, fuck 'em all. Benson wanted this deal, and I'd just nuked for him. Take that asshole.

I passed Cindy on the way to my office. "I'm going home," I told her.

"Are you okay?"

I turned. "I don't get paid enough to put up with this shit." I spun and continued to the temporary sanctuary of my office.

After closing the door behind me, I let out the yell I'd been holding in. "Fuck!" It was the most coherent thing I could manage. It summed up my whole horrible day.

Take that, *Dennis fucking Benson*. I'm not kissing anybody's ass, and there goes your precious little deal.

Collapsing into the chair behind my desk-for-a-day, my eyes closed with the weight of my failure. I would have to be satisfied with torching the deal, along with his relationship with Talbot. It was all that could be salvaged out of this miserable day.

Tomorrow I'd have no job, no paycheck, and no entry back into this building to get the files to take down Benson once and for all.

He had no idea I was his personal nemesis, but somehow he'd dodged the bad news bullet *and* gotten rid of me, all in two days. The man had some super-lucky charm.

As my eyes reopened, I took one last look around the sumptuous office. "I guess you win."

He'd won, I'd lost, and it was time to find another job. The rent would still be due.

How long would it take to get on unemployment? That was something I didn't know.

The karma of this was all wrong, dead wrong.

A knock sounded at the door.

"Come in."

It was old man Talbot.

I straightened up, and hid my surprise. "What can I do for you James?"

"We'd, like… I'd like another chance to talk this through." The man was fresh out of bravado.

"Okay, I'll join you in a minute."

He shut the door, and I gathered up my nerve.

The deal was harder than a cockroach to kill, but where there was a will, there was a way, and I sure as hell had the will.

I'd make sure Benson and Talbot didn't talk to each other for a fucking year.

CHAPTER 11

DENNIS

I'D BEEN MENTALLY SWEARING AT MY BAD LUCK THIS WEEK FOR TEN MINUTES when the knock came.

Cindy popped her head in. "They're ready for you now."

That meant Jennifer had finished kissing ass enough for me to try to recover the deal.

Later I would have to apologize to Jay. He'd been right that I should have known better than to take a rookie into a meeting like that. I'd eat the crow I deserved for jumping down his throat earlier.

"You better give her a raise before you lose her," Cindy said as I passed by.

"Right." No way was that happening. It didn't matter how distasteful apologizing to Talbot had been.

As I entered, Syd was sliding paperwork across to Talbot. "I made the changes we agreed on, and we're ready now," he said.

I had no idea what changes Syd had agreed to, but right now closing the deal was the imperative.

Syd was too smart to give away the store.

Talbot finished initialing all the pages and signed on the back page of the first copy before sliding it over to me. He started on the second copy.

I took my seat and started initialing as if I knew what was going on. Never let them see you sweat, Dad had taught me. Letting them see me as indecisive or uninformed was also not in the cards.

Talbot finished the second copy just before I completed the first and slid it down to Syd.

The second copy went to their lawyer after I signed the last page.

Their entire entourage stood, looking happy to escape the room Jennifer had turned into an insult party.

I shook each of their hands on the way out.

Talbot was the last.

I pumped his hand. "I apologize for her rudeness."

"She's quite a spitfire, that Hanley girl. Reminds me of doing business with your father." He patted me on the back, and in a few seconds Cindy was showing them out.

Syd closed the door as I gathered my pad and special signing pen. His grin was ear to ear. "I'm sure glad you chose her."

I spun my pen on the table. "Huh?"

"She's packing a set of brass ones. I've never seen anything like it."

I wasn't following him, but the rule about them not seeing me confused was still in effect.

"When she told him she had full authority and since she didn't like the deal, it was off. She walked out. Their side had a heart attack. Talbot had to go chasing after her himself. Then she told him you wouldn't sign unless they took double the accounting slip-up off the price, and then she walked out a second time. Talbot folded like a wet napkin, and I had Cindy make the changes to the contract. You two concocted one hell of a plan, and she executed it like she's been doing this for years. That was the best good cop-bad cop routine I've ever seen."

"Pretty good, huh?" was all I could say at this point.

Syd thought I was in on it, and I wasn't bursting that bubble today.

He shook his head. "She had them shitting in their drawers. All I can say is I wouldn't want to get on her bad side. Ballsiest move I ever saw."

Syd took the signed contract and left me alone in the conference room with the door open to figure out what the fuck had just happened.

I was watching my pen spin on the polished surface of the table when Cindy walked in.

"You should call."

"Call who?" I looked up and corrected myself. "Excuse me, call whom?"

"Jennifer. Syd told me what happened while I was typing up the contract changes. She didn't deserve what you said to her."

"You heard that?"

"You were pretty loud."

"Where'd she go?"

"She wasn't a happy camper. She left. And I quote, '*I don't get paid enough to put up with this shit.*'"

"That bad, huh?"

"Worse. She's a nice girl, and that thing you told her to do. I won't repeat the words, well… If you don't fix it with her, don't be surprised to find salt in your morning coffee."

Cindy wouldn't have any problem making my life miserable, and maybe I had been a little too graphic.

"For an entire year," she added.

I nodded. "Can you get me her cell number?"

She put a sticky note on the table and waited.

This new girl was a lot more capable and complicated than I'd guessed.

Now I owed Jay an even bigger apology.

I dialed the number on the sticky note. It rang twice, and then my phone died. The apple logo appeared on the screen again as it restarted.

"I gotta get this fixed." I turned the screen to face Cindy. The damned phone did this once a week and wanted to reset itself.

"We have a guy down in IT that's a real whiz with those. I could give it to him."

I checked my watch. I was already running late for my dinner meeting. "Not tonight." I handed her back the sticky note. "This will have to wait till the morning. Text her and have her meet me at Starbucks first thing."

"Which one?"

"The regular. She'll know which one."

JENNIFER

. . .

I MIGHT BE UNEMPLOYED NOW, BUT I'D FINALLY GOTTEN BENSON WHERE IT HURT —in his wallet. I'd shoved Talbot's underhandedness in the old man's face, sure it would screw the deal and have him walking out.

It would have served both those snakes right. Talbot had tried to pull a fast one, and well, Benson deserved to have what was important to him taken away, and today that was the Talbot deal.

Then Talbot had backed down, and I gave him one right between the eyes. I'd upped the stakes and walked out a second time. With that, Talbot was sure to never return Benson's calls again. With two torpedoes like that, the deal was going down.

Take that, you arrogant jerks. Both of you.

I would have preferred to keep my job and the ability to hurt Benson some more, but at least I'd gotten a good parting shot in and screwed his plans. That would cost him in the stock market when he had to admit the Talbot transaction wasn't happening.

My phone rang on the car seat beside me.

Glancing over, the screen showed it was Dennis. I ignored it, and the ringing stopped. I reached over to turn it off.

Eventually I reached our apartment and let myself in.

"You're home early," Ramona said.

"Yeah." I didn't elaborate.

"What's wrong? First day as supervisor not go well?"

I shrugged and went to change out of my work clothes, particularly these diabolical heels.

"I'm just trying to help," she said before I closed the door behind me.

I sat on the edge of the bed and unbuckled my shoes. It felt good to curl my toes in the carpet. The feeling grounded me. The soft carpeting protected me from the cold floor the way the walls protected me from the meanness of the world. This was my safe space. Dad's picture was on my dresser alongside pictures of the rest of my family, as if he were still with us.

Ramona yelled from the other room. "I'm going to pick up Billy."

"Okay," I yelled back.

She meant well, and I'd have to level with her tonight about the situation. I laid back on the bed and closed my eyes.

I'd have to move to the backup plan.

Vipersoft contracted with an outside cleaning crew, and I knew their routine. In time I'd find a way onto their crew and gain access to the building again. It would take time, but good things came to those with patience and persistence—two qualities I possessed.

I opened my eyes. It was time to stop whining, get changed, and start dinner.

Once in my sandals, shorts, and T-shirt, I started pulling together the ingredients for tonight's dinner. Billy expected homemade pizza.

By the time Ramona returned with him, I'd preheated the pizza stone in the oven, rolled out the crust, and we were ready for toppings.

Cooking for the three of us was good therapy. It got my mind off my work, or lack thereof, and back to the basics in life: food and family.

Billy put down his backpack. "Mommy said you get to be the boss."

I shot Ramona a you-shouldn't-have look.

"What? I'm proud of you," she said.

"Salami or hot dog slices on your pizza?" I asked.

"Salami and no olives. I don't want olives."

Ramona shot him a scowl. "Yes on the olives. They're good for you."

He'd been getting really picky about his eating lately.

"But I don't like them."

Ramona didn't back down. "Then you can have green soup tonight, and Auntie Jenn and I will have the pizza."

His shoulders slumped. "Okay. But I don't like olives."

The split pea soup she'd threatened was at the absolute bottom of Billy's food list.

I added the toppings, including the black olive slices Ramona liked, and slid the pie into the oven.

Billy had already turned on the TV when Ramona wandered my way and braced herself against the counter.

"What happened?" She plugged one charging cable into her phone, and the other into mine, which I'd left on the counter.

I slid sideways to get the plates. "Huh?"

"You can't hide your bad mood behind a pizza."

She was probably right about that. The cooking was only a temporary distraction. "Work didn't go very well. I didn't get the supervisor job."

"How come? You said they offered it to you yesterday."

I pulled napkins from the counter. "I screwed up by asking about staying, and the new CFO decided he wanted somebody more committed to the new company."

"I'm sorry. Something better will come along soon. I'm sure of it."

She should have been mad, knowing I'd screwed up the raise that would have allowed us to move, but she didn't focus on that. Ramona was the most supportive sister a girl could ask for.

"There's more," I added, preparing to tell her that instead of getting a promotion, I was about to get fired.

My phone chirped the arrival of a text when it powered up.

Ramona picked up my phone. "Who's Cindy?"

"Assistant to the big boss. Why?"

"She says you have a meeting tomorrow morning." She held up the phone for me to read.

Cindy: Meeting at Starbucks at 7:30

"What's that about?" Ramona asked.

My gut tightened. "Probably my exit interview. I screwed up pretty badly today."

She took silverware to the table. "I doubt that."

"Trust me, it was worse than anything you could imagine."

Cindy's text must have been sent earlier while my phone was off. I composed the most polite reply I could come up with and sent it.

ME: Not feeling well might not be in tomorrow

The timer went off, and I extracted the pizza.

Ramona had the cutting wheel ready, and we had it sliced on our plates in minutes.

I'd only taken a few bites when my phone chirped again.

Ramona quickly lunged for it and handed it to me with a smile.

Cindy: You don't want to miss this

"Probably not as bad as you thought, huh?" Ramona asked.

Billy chowed down on his pizza, picking the olives off when he didn't think Ramona was looking. He slid them under an uneaten slice.

I texted back.

ME: Which Starbucks

Her reply was immediate.

Cindy: Your normal one

How the hell could she know where my normal Starbucks was?

I didn't bother asking that question, or the more important one of what the meeting was for. I didn't know her well, but I had to trust her.

Ramona grabbed for my phone as soon as I set it down. "It's good news. I can feel it."

Her feelings always went to the positive, and it was pretty much a coin flip whether she was right or not. She gave up on interrogating me.

It was just as well. I could tell her about my need to find a new job tomorrow after my exit interview.

A few minutes later, Billy pushed his chair back and picked up his plate. "I've got homework to do."

He was halfway to the sink before Ramona finished chewing enough to say, "No you don't, little guy. Come back here and eat your olives."

She hadn't missed his trick.

He slouched back to the table. "I don't like them."

"And I don't like paying for food you don't eat. They're good for you. They have a special oil that's healthy."

After retaking his seat, it took Billy a full ten minutes to push them around on his plate and eventually force them down. He made a face for his mother's benefit with every one.

"That wasn't so bad, was it?" Ramona asked.

I knew the answer before Billy mouthed it.

"Yuck. I don't want pizza again if we have to have olives."

"Then you can have green soup next time," Ramona replied.

He didn't say anything, which promised a repeat on next week's pizza night.

As I watched these confrontations grow, I wondered how I would handle them with my children.

Ramona had a difficult situation raising Billy by herself, but it was certainly better than when her ex, Stanley, had been around.

An unintended pregnancy followed by marrying the jerk hadn't left Ramona with a lot of options. Loser couldn't be spelled in big enough letters to describe Stanley.

She'd thought she could marry him and fix him, but from day one, I'd known the odds of that were less than zero.

My sister's positive attitude often had its redeeming qualities, but it had led her to stick with a bad situation for too long—way too long.

CHAPTER 12

JENNIFER

I STOOD UNDER THE HOT WATER LONGER THAN USUAL THE NEXT MORNING, because I was still groggy from lack of sleep.

I'd stayed up late after Ramona and I had finished the movie, perusing the online job listings for accounting types like me. There had been several openings that might work, but each one had a large salary range listed, which extended quite a bit below what I was making now, and only a little above.

That didn't bode well for finding a better-paying position.

One listing had been in Pomona, and that was even farther than the Hydrocom location I hadn't liked.

Once I went to bed, I'd tossed and turned, wondering how I was going to get out of this mess. It seemed I hadn't gotten to sleep until just before my infernal alarm clock had demanded I get up.

I made it to Starbucks a few minutes before seven-thirty. Even if I only worked at Vipersoft another few minutes, I would be on time for this meeting. I was a professional, and a professional was always on time.

A quick scan of the tables didn't reveal Cindy anywhere. The M&M girls were already in our usual spot, but they hadn't gotten their coffees yet.

"There you are," Mona exclaimed.

"Hi." I pulled out the chair facing the door, so I could see Cindy when she showed up.

"This is a treat," Martha told me.

I almost fell over when Dennis Benson appeared, tray in hand with four cups.

"Cinnamon latte for you," he said, putting the first cup in front of Mona. He proceeded to pass out the other drinks. He gave me a mocha—same as his, except for the extra shot, thankfully.

"He was just about to tell us what you did yesterday," Martha said.

I looked at Dennis, expecting wrath to show in his eyes, but all I got back from him was a smile.

He finished his sip. "Why don't you tell them?" He raised his cup to me.

I'd been ambushed. "I don't think I should."

Dennis put his mocha down. "We had this very important meeting yesterday."

The girls leaned in to hear.

He pointed at me. "The other side tried to gloss over a very large issue, money-wise, but Jennifer caught it and threw it back in their faces."

"Not very nicely," I added.

"True," Dennis said. "So I took her aside and instructed her to apologize so we could sign the deal as it was."

I slid down in my chair.

"But," he continued, "she had a different idea."

"What was that?" Mona asked.

Dennis looked to me for an answer.

It couldn't get much worse, so I told them. "I told them we weren't doing a deal with a group like them."

"You tell 'em, girl," Martha chimed in.

Martha crossed herself. "That's what my Marty—God bless his soul—would always say. To win the negotiation, you have to be willing to walk away."

Her husband had been a salesman at a car dealership forever.

I picked up my drink and sipped to keep from talking.

"You know what happened?" Dennis asked.

The girls didn't offer a guess. They didn't understand that I'd screwed the whole thing up.

Dennis's eyes held mine captive, perhaps daring me to admit my failure in front of my friends?

I waited for the *you're fired* sentence to arrive.

He grinned. "She demanded better terms, they agreed, and that's what we signed. This lady here talked them down one hundred and seventy-eight million dollars in a few minutes." His smile brightened even more. "That's why she's getting a raise today."

I choked on my coffee. "What?" I asked through a coughing fit.

He reached across to touch my hand. "Jay told me you turned down a raise for the chance to work with me, and after yesterday, you certainly deserve one."

His touch sent an uncomfortable tingle up my arm. My brain was misfiring. I blinked hard.

He was still here, his fingers over mine.

I pulled away and lifted my coffee to my lips to hide my speechlessness.

"You're my kind of boss," Mona said.

Dennis gave her a warm smile. "I try."

My heart had almost returned to a normal pace, but my head was spinning. I had attempted twice yesterday to screw up his deal with Talbot, and somehow I'd only made it better. Why on Earth would Talbot have gone for that? Everything was working out backwards. I was helping Benson instead of taking him down.

On top of that, now I had to continue working with him, though it was good to still be employed. Then his words registered—I was getting a raise.

"How much?" I asked.

He stood. "We'll talk about it at the office. I'm going to run along now. You girls have a wonderful day."

"Can't you stay just a little while?" Mona asked.

"Sorry, not today," he replied. "Jennifer, I'll see you at work."

His words were more command than prediction. He was off in a flash, despite another plea from Mona to stay.

"I think he likes you," Martha said.

"And you didn't tell us you'd already met him," Mona said.

"I hadn't, not until yesterday."

Martha twisted her cup. "You made quite the impression on your first day."

"It didn't work out the way I expected," I told them.

An understatement by a mile.

I scooted my chair back. "I need to get going. I don't want to be late."

Martha pointed to the table. "Sit back down. You should stay a while and make him wait. That always works better with men."

"I agree," Mona said. "You don't want to seem too eager. Right now you have that man right where you want him."

Martha giggled. "Not quite where I'd want him."

"You're not helping," Mona shot back.

Martha pointed her finger a Mona. "Just because you're too old to get any action doesn't mean I can't dream."

Mona put her chin up. "And who had the most recent date?"

I stayed quiet; they could go like this for an hour.

"But that was Harold, and you had to ask him. That doesn't count," Martha said.

Mona huffed. "It does too, but we should be concentrating on Jennifer's dilemma."

"What dilemma?" I asked.

"Whether you should wait for him to ask you out, or if you ask him," Mona replied.

"He doesn't want to go out with me," I said.

Martha giggled. "Are you blind? I saw the way he looked at you. That man's engine is revving for you, sweetie."

At her age, she shouldn't be smoking whatever was giving her these delusions.

"No way," I protested. "He's just feeling bad that I showed him up." I sipped my mocha.

For sure, and he had to atone for what I'd caught him saying to Fisher yesterday about wanting somebody more senior.

"I'm with Martha," Mona said. "Mark my words, you're sharing a meal, and soon. It's in his eyes. I remember the first time I saw that look in Marty's eyes." She sighed loudly. "Things certainly got more complicated after that— complicated in a good way."

These two didn't understand what I knew about Benson, about his true character and how incompatible we were. "He's not my type."

Mona shook her head. "And that's why you watch for him every morning? You're so transparent, Jenn. Don't think for a minute I didn't see your reaction when he touched your hand."

"And the way your face lights up every time he comes in," Martha added. "You can't hide that from us, you know."

"You have it all wrong," I said.

"Tell me you don't think he's good looking," Mona demanded.

"I'd say yes to him in a flash," Martha said.

"I wasn't asking you," Mona said. "Your definition of the right man is any man with a pulse."

"At least I didn't go out with Harold," Martha replied. "Now, Jennie, answer the question. Hot or not?"

I shook my head. "That's not it."

"Hot or not?" Martha repeated.

I took in a breath. "Okay, I admit he's kinda good looking."

That was putting it mildly. Dennis was movie-star handsome—tall, with an athletic build, and richer than sin. He was every girl's dream, and he would be mine if he weren't a monster underneath.

Mona gasped. "You're not… Are you gay?"

I laughed. "That's not it. I just know he's not right for me."

Martha shook her head. "You hadn't even spoken to him before yesterday. You can't possibly know that."

"Now that I've met him, I know we're not a good fit," I replied.

"Trust me. I speak from experience," Mona said. "If he's a tight fit, that's even better." She laughed.

Martha laughed as well. "You're incorrigible. I can't take you anywhere."

"Well, it's true," Mona said.

I stood. "It's time for me to go to work."

Mona lifted her cup. "Till next time. Go get that raise."

"I intend to," I told her.

"Not so fast, honey," Martha said. "You should negotiate a bigger raise. Don't take his first offer."

"Yeah, hold out for more," Mona agreed.

"And walk slow," Martha added. "Make him wait."

After saying goodbye and depositing my cup in the trash, I left them to bicker between themselves.

A little while later I caught myself walking quickly down the sidewalk and slowed my pace.

He could wait.

∼

Dennis

I'D REACHED FOR JENNIFER'S HAND OUT OF INSTINCT, AND IT HAD BEEN A mistake. Only sheer force of will had kept me from jerking mine back like a frightened kid. I'd left the Starbucks as quickly as I could after that, lest I drool or babble incoherently and make a complete fool of myself.

All the way to work, my hand had tingled as I walked—from the spark of touching Jennifer. I'd wiped it on my trousers, but I couldn't rid myself of the feeling. It was as if she wore some damned skin cream laced with pheromones, and the chemicals had leached into my skin.

The woman was beautiful, but there was much more to her than that. The shock of hearing Syd's description of her closing the Talbot deal, followed by old man Talbot's comments had solidified that she was not the meek junior accountant I'd taken her for. All night, I'd played back my scolding of her and realized how wrong I'd been. I was rarely wrong, and never a hundred and seventy-eight fucking million wrong—never. She was a puzzle wrapped in an enigma, she was.

And a force of nature. Jennifer had saved me triple-digit millions yesterday, and today she'd given me a jolt like she was wired with electricity.

I stopped outside our building to take a few calming breaths.

Upstairs, when I opened the door to the executive area, Jay was seated by Cindy's desk, chatting.

I could hear Larry on the speakerphone in his office.

"Am I putting salt in your coffee today?" Cindy asked.

I passed Jay, who cocked a brow.

"No. I expect her in later," I responded.

Jay rose from his chair. "I want to hear the real story about Talbot."

Cindy tilted her head. "He doesn't believe me."

I opened my office door. "I don't know why not."

"Well?" Jay asked.

I entered and waved him in as well. "We closed the deal on better terms than expected."

He followed. "I won't believe it until I see it in black and white."

I picked up the signed contract on my desk and handed it to him. "By the way, I owe you an apology."

He accepted the papers and sat. "Cindy, could you come in here, please?"

She appeared at the door.

"Would you repeat that?" Jay asked me. "I want it on the record."

I shook my head. "I owe Jay an apology for underestimating Jennifer, and you can write that down for him."

"I could make a plaque, if you want," she said to Jay, before addressing me. "But I would say you're apologizing to the wrong person."

She was right. The apology needed to go to Jennifer.

Jay ignored her comment.

Cindy retreated to her station.

Jay sucked in a breath when he got to the critical page in the contract. "I told you she would do fine. Where do you think she learned negotiating?"

I leafed through my messages. "No idea. Maybe her father is a used-car salesman." I meant it as a joke, but realized I knew absolutely nothing about her beyond her name—and that she'd worked in Jay's department before yesterday.

"Maybe." He finished and stood, taking the contract with him. "I'll get this back to you after I make a copy."

I waved him off and picked up the phone to return the first of my calls for the morning.

A half hour later, I spied Jennifer through my open door, walking by on the way to her office.

She didn't look in my direction.

~

JENNIFER

I WALKED INTO WORK WITH A SPRING IN MY STEP THAT HAD BEEN MISSING FOR FAR too long.

Once on Mahogany Row, I carefully avoided looking toward Dennis's office as I passed Cindy and moved to my office.

Cindy followed me a few seconds later. "How did it go?"

I unlocked my door and slid inside. "Fine, I guess."

It had been two days of contradictions, with everything happening the opposite of the way it was supposed to.

"Did he do right by you?"

I shrugged. "I don't know yet. There were other people at the table. He said we'd talk when I got in."

"Well, then go on in and ask."

I didn't feel comfortable about this. It was too surreal to be reality. "Is this your doing?"

"Absolutely not. You're the one who pulled the rabbit out of the hat."

That praise got a smile out of me.

She lingered by the door. "He tests people when they're new, and you passed. He tried to call you after you left."

"I know. My phone was dead." Not true, but that was my story.

"He told me he'd decided to give you a raise, but you'd already left. Pretty good for your first day, I'd say."

My smile grew. By her measure, I had done well, even if it was by accident. And a boss that showed he appreciated me—that was a new feeling. "Yeah. It didn't go quite as I'd expected."

"It never does. Go down there and get the good news. You deserve it." The sound of a phone ringing pulled her away.

I touched up my lip gloss before marching the few steps to Dennis's office.

He was on the phone. "Sure, Dad, I won't forget." His voice didn't carry any of the harshness I'd heard from him yesterday, but then it shouldn't when he was talking with his family. He noticed me and held up a finger to indicate a delay.

I wondered what he wasn't supposed to forget, but then I was always too curious about Dennis, and for all the wrong reasons. I leaned against the wall, and it occurred to me that in all my plotting to take him down, not once had I considered that he had a family.

To me he had always been the devil, the cause of pain in *my* family. But he had a family too, and I hadn't considered the effects my actions might have on them. However, he hadn't either a few years ago.

He hung up and urged me in. "Close the door."

As I walked in to take a seat, I caught him scanning me—and not just my face.

For a moment, his eyes held mine with a laser-like focus.

I returned his gaze without a blink. "You said we should talk."

Surreal wasn't a good enough word for this situation. Yesterday I'd helped the man who killed my stepfather, and now he'd expect me to thank him for a raise. That wasn't happening.

CHAPTER 13

DENNIS

WHEN I HUNG UP AND MOTIONED HER IN, I COULDN'T HELP BUT SEE A DIFFERENT girl than the one I'd met yesterday.

She didn't break eye contact—very interesting.

"You said we should talk." She returned my gaze with intensity.

I motioned to the chair. "Have a seat."

"Is that an order?"

Attitude radiated off her like waves of heat.

"An offer."

"I'd rather stand."

I finally looked down and opened the folder in front of me. "Jennifer, I want to start with an apology."

That was not something I said lightly. Dad had taught us to be careful, because apologies could be turned against us as a sign of weakness. But this merited an exception to his rule.

The smile left her face, "Yes, you do. Before you met me, you decided I wasn't who you wanted for this job, and you set me up for failure." Her tone conveyed even more anger than the words.

I shifted in my seat. I'd never had to sit and take backtalk of any kind from an employee before—hell, from anyone outside the family. If an employee had ever felt this strongly, they hadn't had the guts to say it to my face.

Spitfire was the word Talbot had used, and this was a firsthand taste of what he meant.

"You're a bastard," she continued. "You didn't tell me what you expected of me, and then berated me for not knowing what you wanted. It wasn't fair."

I leaned forward. "You are right. I was entirely wrong about you and your capabilities. I treated you poorly, and for that I'm sorry."

Her eyes thawed.

My words had hit home. "I'm not used to being this wrong, and I'm… I'm not very good at apologizing, but I'm truly sorry."

Her eyes narrowed, but only momentarily before her face softened to a smile. "You do suck at it, but apology accepted."

I let out the breath I'd been holding and took in the sight of her.

She broke the silence. "Cindy said you decided yesterday afternoon that you wanted to review my compensation."

I'd have to thank Cindy later. It was just like her to change things around and give me more credit than I deserved.

I looked down at the personnel-change form I hadn't filled out yet. "I'm giving you a fifteen-thousand-dollar raise, effective immediately."

Her head cocked as if she was calculating. "Did you call me in here to insult me again?"

The words set me back. I'd never had someone react badly to getting a raise. "No. Not at all." This girl had me completely off balance.

"I was offered fourteen to move to the Pasadena job, and you're offering me fifteen? That's insulting." She huffed and turned.

I should have checked what Mark had had planned for her at Hydrocom before this discussion. I made a quick correction. "You've got it all wrong, Jennifer. I meant fifteen on top of the fourteen they offered." I'd had no idea about the Pasadena job, but surely this would rescue the situation.

She turned back and this time decided to take the seat I'd offered, crossing her legs slowly.

My mind was playing tricks on me this morning. Everything she did looked like slow motion in a movie.

A stray hair fell forward across her cheek.

I wanted to tuck it behind her ear.

As if she'd read my thoughts, she swiped it to the side with a slow finger. "That will be acceptable, on one condition."

"Yes?"

"You make it retroactive to the first of the month."

The request seemed inconsequential compared to her bargaining power at this point.

"Done."

"Thank you, Mr. Benson."

We'd moved back a step from Dennis to Mr. Benson.

"Dennis," I corrected her.

"Very well, Dennis. What do you have for me to do today?"

I couldn't give her any of the lewd answers that came instantly to mind. "Familiarize yourself with the Stoner transaction."

My cell phone rang. Bill Covington's name appeared on the screen.

She stood. "Anything else?"

"No, that's it to start with."

I realized I'd just had a taste of the treatment she'd given Talbot yesterday. She knew she had the leverage, and she'd used it to get a better deal. This morning she'd had the leverage on me, but that would change.

She stood and turned to leave.

I reached for the phone while admiring her ass. My cock stirred at the sight of her hips swaying. I blinked back the mental image of that ass bouncing on my cock. I would grab those hips and give her a ride she wouldn't forget. I blinked and the image of me spearing her burned itself into my brain.

She reached the door and looked back, breaking my mental image of her naked. Her mouth twitched, and she bit her lower lip. Could she feel it too?

I cast my eyes down and answered the phone.

JENNIFER

I TURNED AT THE DOOR AND CAUGHT HIM LOOKING. I SMILED AS I LEFT.

He'd averted his eyes, but he'd definitely been checking me out. He'd studiously stayed focused on my face during our talk, our negotiation—but then I'd turned my back.

Men.

"Sure, Bill, I haven't forgotten. I'll be there early Friday," I heard him say into the phone. It was the second time I'd heard him promise not to forget.

The man had a weakness after all. The master of the universe was forgetful.

I reached Cindy's desk. "Thank you," I said softly.

She looked up from her typing. "Did it go well?"

"Satisfactory, I'd say."

I didn't need her to know how over-the-top happy I was about the outcome. The M&M girls had been right about rejecting his first offer, and it had netted me a raise that definitely put a three-bedroom place in our future.

"That's good, because sometimes he can be a little clueless about how tight money is for the rest of us."

"He wants me to look over the Stoner deal. Where do I find those files?"

"I'll get them for you in a moment—as soon as I'm done with this one thing for Larry." She pointed to the notes she was working from.

I backed away toward the restroom. This morning's coffee was getting to me. "I'll be in my office."

Cindy nodded, still typing away.

Ten minutes later, I was at my desk, and I turned to face the view of the city and the ocean beyond. Things had changed so much from last week, my life was unrecognizable. I had a top-floor, window office, and I was working for the CEO after a twenty-nine-thousand-dollar raise—two things that would burnish my resume when I left for greener pastures, even if I did have to work for *him* in the meantime.

Karma had taken an odd few turns this week, but I'd come out in a better position to wreak my vengeance. I could more easily get the files for Hydra that he'd assured me would take down my nemesis, and I had a position that would keep people from questioning my access to any part of the facility, or any file I wanted. Long term, that was the definition of success.

Later, I would quietly slip off to another company, my mission accomplished, and restart my life—a normal life, happy in the knowledge I'd righted a wrong, justice had prevailed, and the guilty party had been punished, even if not through the legal system.

In the end, nobody except Hydra and my sister would know of my involvement in Benson's destruction.

Cindy arrived with an armload of files. "This is the first batch."

"There's more?"

She set the files down on my circular table. "This is about a third of it."

I wondered if this could be another test, but discarded that idea. "Where do I start?"

She stopped at the door. "You got me. That's why we pay you the big bucks."

This was going to take forever, but I moved to the table and sat. The first file I opened was from a year ago.

When Cindy returned I asked, "How long has this been in the works?"

"About a year." She set down a second stack of files bigger than the first.

"Do they normally take that long?"

She thought for a moment. "No. This is probably the longest. Three months or so is more normal. I'll get you the last stack."

"This is going to take forever," I lamented. "When are we meeting with them?"

"I'll check, but two weeks or so, I think."

I started my notes as I paged through the first document.

By eleven, I was going batty with the Stoner files. This job was going to bore me to death if I spent all day, every day with crap like this.

After a trip to the bathroom, I stopped by Cindy's desk for a chat. "Did Mark spend all day, every day reading files?"

"Not every day."

That was little consolation.

CHAPTER 14

JENNIFER

FRIDAY MORNING, AFTER READING BORING MATERIAL ON STONER FOR THE umpteenth hour, I had three questions for Dennis about this purchase: why, why, and another why. The company didn't seem to fit at all with what we were doing. Not that we couldn't branch out a little, but livestock feed, with an emphasis on poultry, didn't move the excitement meter for me.

I'd tried to get a minute with him yesterday, but he'd put me off.

Larry poked his head into my office. "Having fun yet?"

My eyes were going blurry, so his interruption was a welcome one. I waved my hand over the stack of papers. "Tell me why we're talking to Stoner about livestock feed. I don't get it."

Larry leaned against the door jamb. "He's a good friend of Dennis's dad. I guess he doesn't want to make him feel bad by telling him to shove it."

"Was Talbot also one of his dad's friends?"

"Yeah, but that one made sense. Especially after you knocked the price down."

"Thanks." Things were a little clearer now.

"Any time." Larry waved and wandered off.

I gathered up the relevant files. Dennis wasn't going to avoid me any longer. He needed to tell me if he was serious about this or not.

When I made my way down the hall, I found Dennis's office empty.

Before I could ask Cindy where he'd gone, her phone rang. "Uh-huh. How many? I'm not sure my car will hold all that. Just a sec." She removed the phone from her ear. "Jenn, do you have a car?"

I nodded. "Not much of one, but it runs."

"Could you spare some time to help me with a delivery?"

"Of course."

She got back on the phone. "Jenn and I will leave right now." She hung up. "That was Dennis. At least he's in a better mood today. Whatever he had for dinner last night, he needs more of it."

I met her at the elevator with my purse. "What are we delivering?"

The doors opened, and we entered.

She pressed the button for the parking level. "Chickens. You know where Costco is?"

"Yeah, one of my favorites." Having to watch pennies meant things like breakfast cereal in bulk. If it wasn't at Costco, sometimes it wasn't on the menu.

The numbers clicked down, and the doors opened onto the parking garage.

"I'll meet you there. We need to pick up some food for Dennis," she said as she walked to a small four-door.

It seemed big enough for most people's Costco runs, so I wasn't sure why she needed me.

The drive to Costco wasn't a long one.

Cindy was waiting with one of those flatbed push carts when I walked up. "We'll need a second cart."

I followed her in with another flatbed. Mine had a wheel problem that made it want to veer left.

She walked quickly to the meat department at the back of the store, where she started loading rotisserie chickens onto her cart.

I grabbed one. "How many do we need?"

"Fifty."

"Fifty?" I repeated.

"Let's make it sixty to be on the safe side."

I piled the warm plastic containers on my cart. Thirty chickens was going to to be a serious stacking project on this sucker. I stopped after I counted the thirtieth and hoped they wouldn't all tumble off halfway to the register. That would make one hell of a mess.

"Why so many?" I asked.

"A lot of mouths to feed." She counted the stack on her cart. "I've got thirty. How about you?"

"Same."

She started off to the registers.

I pushed my squeaky cart behind her, careful to go slow enough not to lose one of the birds off the top.

The cashier counted the containers and rang us up like it was no big deal that we'd wiped out nearly their entire supply of pre-cooked chickens.

"Who is this for?"

She paid with her credit card. "Dennis. We're going to meet him on Laurel. Do you know where that is?"

"Pretty much. Where on Laurel?"

"Near the south end. You can follow me."

We split up at the door. After loading the birds and backing out, I found her idling by the front of the store, waiting for me.

The traffic-signal gods were merciful, and I didn't lose her on the way to Laurel Street. I still hadn't gotten an explanation of who we were feeding, and on the drive over, nothing rational came to mind.

When we reached Saint Helena's, Cindy signaled and turned into the parking lot. The sign outside explained that they served food to the poor and homeless here. A soup kitchen, you might call it, but today we were providing chicken.

Dennis was outside waiting for us.

The bazillionaire was donating food to a soup kitchen.

The thought made me smile. It was a nice gesture—better and more personal than just sending a check.

A good deed from a bad man was still a good deed.

～

JENNIFER

. . .

A LARGE GROUP WAS GATHERED BY THE FRONT DOOR.

I followed Cindy, who parked by the side door.

Dennis waved over several guys after we stopped, and they grabbed armfuls of chickens and took them inside.

"How many did you get?" Dennis asked Cindy.

"Sixty."

He gave her a thumbs up. "Good call. The crowd looks bigger than normal."

Moments later, the original helpers were back for more birds, along with a few more helping hands.

I waited quietly by my car as it was being unloaded, unsure what to do next.

Dennis said goodbye to Cindy and walked my way. "Want to stay and help?"

The question was a simple one. My answer was the hard part.

Staying with him made me uneasy, but leaving would mark me as a jerk. "Sure."

He pointed back toward the front. "Park in the lot, and then meet me inside."

I closed up my car and moved it to the parking lot. The question of how to get inside loomed. The front door had a line of people slowly entering, and I didn't want to look like I was cutting in, so I walked around to the side door where the chickens and Dennis had disappeared.

The aromas of warm food hit me the second I passed through the door. Our dozens of chickens were now stacked behind the counter, and in front of me were several people—including Dennis—serving delicious-smelling plates.

He looked back and noticed me. His hands were full. A jerk of his head asked me to join him. "Wanna help slice?"

When I reached where he was serving, the immensity of the operation hit me. "Sure."

"Gloves are on the table."

I donned a pair and realized I'd been wrong about Dennis. He wasn't just donating the food, he was donating his time as well. I'd always thought the rich massaged their guilty consciences by writing checks at the end of the year to a charity here and a charity there. This was a different level of giving. I hadn't suspected this aspect of Dennis Benson at all.

"White or dark?" he asked the next woman in line.

"A little of both," she answered.

He cut the last of the useful meat off the carcass he was working.

I retrieved another for him from the stack on the counter, and one for myself.

He slipped the finished one into the garbage. "Thanks."

"White or dark?" I asked the man in front of me.

"White. I like breasts."

There was no hint of an insinuating smirk. He just preferred chicken breast meat to drumsticks or thighs.

The hall had filled with people at tables, eating away.

The two servers to my right, a man and a woman, both in suits, were also doling out chicken.

Farther down the line, ladies offered mashed potatoes, green beans, and peas. At the very last station, a lady was serving brownies and reminding each guest that the limit was one, which she enforced, regardless of the diner's protests. By and large, the group was better mannered than the clientele at some restaurants.

To my left, it sounded like the peas weren't faring as well as the green beans.

Several times Dennis's shoulder brushed mine, and each time I succeeded in controlling the gasp that threatened to overcome me. I was going all high school just working next to the man, even without conversation or emotion-filled glances. Just a guy and a girl standing next to each other serving food.

It should have been easy. The touches were innocent enough, but his touch transferred electricity each time.

I looked up and decided his profile would have been one a Greek sculptor might have chosen.

"White, please," the slight old lady in front of me said, jerking me back to reality.

"Sure. I've got extra dark meat, if you'd like some of that as well."

"Extra?" she asked.

"Sure."

She nodded vigorously as I added more to her plate.

The exchange brought out what we were doing here. This wasn't bonus food, or a social outing, this was food they wouldn't otherwise get to eat. Food they probably couldn't afford.

The group ranged from the obviously homeless to those who seemed merely down on their luck. They were young and old, a few with young children, but not many.

"Thanks," she said as she moved down the line.

My next customer asked for dark meat, preferably a drumstick. He was in luck. All the people here today were in luck, thanks to Cindy.

If she hadn't decided on the extra ten chickens, we would have run out before serving the final person in a line, a middle-aged man in an old army jacket.

Dennis helped him. "Joe, have a little extra, if you want it."

He knew the man's name.

Joe's jacket had *Mason* stitched on the name tag. His eyes darted around, and he wiped his hands on his jeans more than once.

"Sure, but white meat only. I don't eat the greasy stuff."

Dennis cut off some extra for him. "Take care now, Joe."

"Thanks, Mr. B."

Not only did Dennis know Joe's name, but Dennis had been here often enough for Joe to know his name as well.

Joe limped down to the mashed potatoes.

"That's a wrap," said the guy in the suit to my right.

"Joe is always our last customer," Dennis explained.

"Is he always late?"

Dennis continued to carve his bird. "No, but he waits for everyone else to go first." That painted Joe in a different light. "Would you do me the honor of lunching with me?"

His question meant Martha's prediction of sharing a meal with him had come true.

I didn't have to think twice. "Sure."

He sliced more from the chicken he was working on. "White or dark?" he asked me, just as he had all of his guests.

There was more dark left on his bird. "Dark will be fine."

"Good, because I'm a breast man myself." He smiled as he looked up.

No doubt there was a double meaning to his statement.

I stifled my laugh, but couldn't resist poking him. "I would have taken you for a leg man."

He moved the chicken slices onto a plate for me. "It's a close call at times, but I find the breast…" His tongue darted out to wet his upper lip. "…more succulent."

The wickedness of his smile sent a tingle through me. I couldn't believe I was standing here trading sexual innuendos with him. I took my plate and walked down the counter to add mashed potatoes and green beans. The thought of a man's tongue, his tongue, on my nipples sent heat to my core.

Farther down the counter, the brownie plate was almost empty.

He plucked two brownies from the plate, and placed one on each of our plates. "Unless you don't like chocolate."

I smiled back at him. "Who doesn't like chocolate?"

He picked up his plate and motioned toward the tables.

I moved out of the way. "You saved yourself two? I thought one was the rule."

He led the way toward an empty table. "The second was for you."

He nodded at several of the people we passed as they acknowledged him as "Mr. B."

I took a seat on the bench across from him.

He was already chewing a bite of his brownie. The man and woman who'd been serving next to him walked our way. The way the man guided the woman with a hand at her back made it obvious they were a couple, and a gorgeous one at that.

When he got closer, and with his apron now off, it was easy to tell his suit wasn't off the rack.

"Thanks for the help, Dennis," he said. "Lauren and I are going to head out."

Dennis looked back and stood. "Any time. I'd like you to meet Jennifer Hanley. Jennifer, this is Bill Covington and his lovely wife, Lauren. She's the brains of the pair."

The name rang a bell, but I didn't immediately place it.

Bill scowled in response to Dennis's ribbing, but only briefly. He extended his hand, which I stood and shook with my mouth still full of food.

Lauren's broad smile showed how much she appreciated Dennis's compliment, even at her husband's expense.

She offered her hand as well. "Be careful with this one. He's a silver-tongued devil."

"Nice to meet you both, and thank you for the warning."

They were gone with a quick wave.

Only then did I place the name. "I visited UCLA, and there were Covington buildings there. Are they related to—"

Dennis nodded. "His grandfather."

I'd pictured bazillionaires lunching on exotic dishes with unpronounceable French names over white linen tablecloths, washing it all down with bottles of wine that cost a month's rent while discussing their Mediterranean yachting plans for the summer. Instead I sat across from one—on a wobbly folding chair with no padding—eating the same food we'd just served the homeless on a worn wooden table. Then there were the Covingtons, husband and wife both taking the time to volunteer here.

The producers of *Lifestyles of the Rich and Famous* weren't about to be filming this scene.

I took a sip of my water. "Do you help out here often?"

He had to finish chewing before answering. "Roughly every two weeks, but Wednesday Bill called to say they expected to be short staffed." He motioned to the retreating Covingtons. "It's one of the ways we give back to the community that has given us so much."

"And he, they, come down here often?"

"About the same frequency, and his restaurant brings leftover food every morning as well. But today that got gobbled up before you arrived. It always does. It's an incentive to be early."

The Covingtons brought food every day? That was a shocker.

A man's voice boomed from behind me. "Thank you for the chickens. They were a great help."

Dennis waved. "My pleasure, Father Dan."

I looked over as Father Dan sat with a couple behind us.

I turned back to my lunch partner. "Do you always bring food with you?"

Dennis shook his head. "No. The Carmelos' truck broke down. They were scheduled to bring turkey. I was just helping out." He shrugged as if it was normal to wipe out Costco's chicken supply to feed a few hundred people on a moment's notice.

He stabbed another bite of meat. "You look surprised."

I closed my mouth, realizing it had fallen open. "It's just…"

He waved his fork at me. "You're prejudiced, I get it."

"About what?"

"You don't like rich people. It's typical, but I'm proud of my family, and I'm not going to apologize for being born a Benson."

"How can I not like them when I don't know any?"

He pointed at one of the other men who'd been serving with us. "If it's okay for Stan to volunteer here, why can't I?"

I looked at Stan without an answer for him.

He looked like a retired...well, anybody, in faded jeans and polo with a slight rip on the sleeve.

"Stan," he continued, "has done a lot of things in his life. He was a waiter, a painter, a handyman, a hardware store clerk, and you know what he would tell you?"

I shook my head.

"He told me once that he never got hired by a poor person. He always worked for someone richer than himself. My family employs tens of thousands of people. That's how many families we support. I'm not apologizing."

I'd gotten myself into a hole here. "I'm sorry. I didn't mean—"

"You probably think people with money drink expensive wine with every meal."

Can he read my thoughts?

"I do not. I just thought you were...too busy for this."

He sighed. "We should never be too busy to care."

He finally put the chicken he'd been waving at me in his mouth to chew.

I felt ashamed and wished we'd stuck to the back and forth about breast meat and legs.

He finished chewing. "Since we're on the subject of applying labels to people and misjudging them, I want to apologize again for underestimating you because you don't have an MBA."

"I understand."

"It wasn't fair of me, and we haven't gotten much time together since you started, but I want to say I'm very happy to have you working for me."

"Well..." For a moment my revenge-focused brain didn't know what to do with this information, but then I managed a heartfelt smile. "Thanks, I'm glad you think I'm doing a good job."

I meant it, and I hoped to get off the topic of my surprise at his generosity and caring. It wasn't a comfortable conversation.

He swallowed and pointed his fork at me. "And I look forward to having you under me for a long time." A wicked grin grew over his face.

I blushed at the dirty innuendo.

Confusion gripped my rational brain. He was the devil who deserved my vengeance, after all. The death, the pain he'd caused had been real, and it couldn't be papered over with a few dozen chickens. None of this brought my dad back.

But the primitive, cavewoman side of my brain sent heat to my core as it signaled its desire. I had to blink back the image of his face over mine with the ceiling in the background—or would it be outdoors with the sky in the background? I averted my eyes to my plate and forked some green beans.

Had he meant it the way I'd taken it? I couldn't tell, as his face quickly went back to the passive mask he often wore. I could hope though, couldn't I? But why would I *want* to hope?

It was wrong to be attracted to him, one side said. *I don't care. I want to feel good and be wanted*, the other side replied. I should've known better than to dance with the devil.

I crossed my legs. The cavewoman was winning this argument. When I looked up, we locked eyes. I hadn't verbally responded to him.

As a smile tugged at the corners of his lips, I could sense my eyes had betrayed me and telegraphed my desire.

My phone chose that moment to come alive and chirp on the table.

Turning it over, I found what I didn't need.

EB: We really need to talk

I put the phone back down.

Dennis glanced at the phone, which still displayed the message. "It's okay if you need to answer that."

"No way. It's my ex. He doesn't know when to give up."

"Tell me who EB is, and I'm sure I can convince him."

I ignored the offer, flipped the phone over, and looked away. "Do they serve here every day?"

Dennis's impassive face returned. "Six days a week. On Sunday Father Dan is busy with some other things."

The moment had passed. He was back in boss mode.

Our meal concluded as he gave me a quick history of Father Dan's mission to feed the poor in this part of town.

He stood and took his plate and glass with him.

I followed to add mine to the dirty dish stack. Somebody had a monumental task this afternoon.

He touched my shoulder. "Thank you for helping."

The shock of the touch unwired my brain for a second. "It was my pleasure."

"See you back at the office," he said before turning for the door.

Father Dan intercepted me. "Jennifer, isn't it?"

I nodded.

"Thank you for helping us today. It makes a world of difference to those we feed here to have the support of caring people such as yourself."

"You do good work here. It was my pleasure."

As I walked to my car, his thanks gave me an internal warmth I hadn't felt in a long time. I'd spent much of the last months and years worried about Ramona, Billy, and myself, without stopping to realize we were luckier than some. We had food to eat and a roof over our heads, even if it was only a two-bedroom apartment.

As I drove back to the building, I had trouble making sense of today's experience.

Yesterday I'd known Dennis Benson to have an evil heart, bent on profit over safety, but this episode completely muddled my image.

"We should never be too busy to care," he'd said. The simple sentence tugged at my heart strings in a way that made me tear up. He'd shown me *two* sides of himself I hadn't seen before, and they didn't fit my previous view at all. The puzzle of Dennis Benson was no longer as simple as a devil hiding behind a suit.

Although I knew beyond a doubt he was guilty in Dad's death, the man had compassion for others that I couldn't square with that knowledge. He also had pride in his family and himself for what they contributed to the community. I'd have to leave that part of the equation in the enigma column for now. This was more than I could handle today.

Then there was the sheer animal magnetism when he looked at me. It was a pull I couldn't deny. It was a force I couldn't wish away.

Last week, my objective had been clear. Now Dennis Benson was messing with my ordered view of the world, and nothing made sense.

CHAPTER 15

JENNIFER
   (Two Weeks Later)

I'D BEEN WORKING UPSTAIRS WITH DENNIS FOR JUST OVER TWO WEEKS NOW. IT had been odd at first to call him Dennis instead of Mr. Benson—or the devil, as I'd always named him before—but the day at Saint Helena's had changed that.

Since then, I'd seen more instances of the man who was giving enough to volunteer at a soup kitchen, more of the boss who cared about his employees, and none of who I'd thought he was. When I looked at him, I was seeing more suit and less devil every day.

This morning, my before-breakfast email check revealed my first message from Hydra in weeks. Not that previous communications had been frequent, but I hadn't gotten any feedback from him after the disastrous day Dennis's spin-off announcement had nullified our "bad news balloon," as Hydra liked to call them. I'd expected a reaction of some kind, given how shitty I'd felt about Dennis escaping the wrath of the market that day. Hydra had to have been pissed as well, but his radio silence had been deafening.

To: Nemesis666

From: HYDRA157
Number 89461 is next.
It may have moved upstairs.

As usual, the message was businesslike and to the point. I'd asked once before how he knew what file numbers I should get, and been told merely that he had his sources. Clearly I wasn't the only one in the company in league with Hydra. Someone else had to have access to the file number cross-reference—it was the only way to find these.

The fact that I'd gotten another file number from Hydra should have cheered me up. But now that I'd met the man and knew him as *Dennis*, this morning's message hadn't had its normal effect on my mood. Had I gotten too close? Was my judgment impaired, or getting clearer? My two views of him didn't mesh, and my hold on the truth was getting murkier by the day.

Nevertheless, I needed to focus on the task at hand. I'd promised Mom I'd get the proof. I wouldn't let her down, and for that I had to follow Hydra's instructions and not ask questions. My vow to her to make him pay was a promise I had to keep. I might not enjoy it the way I'd thought I would, but it had to be done.

I'd been clear about my motivations, and Hydra had been clear that I would have to wait until I'd retrieved all the files he was interested in. It wasn't a surprise, since once I had what I wanted, we both knew I could blow off Hydra and stop my high-risk, nighttime sneaking around.

I would need to pull this file one night this week. The quicker I got what he needed, the quicker I would get what I wanted.

My attempt at creating a problem for Dennis had failed so spectacularly that I clearly needed to leave the bad news to Hydra. And I had a part to play in that—small, but essential.

I wrote the file number on a Post-it note, folded it, and stashed it in my wallet before heading off to work. A month ago, I would have been eager to get the file. Today, it was an obligation.

I'd helped Dennis with the Zarniger transaction last week and earned a bonus, in addition to the gigantic raise he'd given me. His interest in my analysis of the Zarniger deal had led to a change in our strategy when they came to visit. His adopting my view had done more to build my self esteem than even the day I'd graduated from Pepperdine.

It was an odd feeling to be appreciating his comments, even his praise, given what I knew he'd done. But I'd decided right now good news was welcome from any front, even from him.

Ramona had been getting more excited by the day, and she planned to start the hunt for a suitable three-bedroom this weekend. She and Billy deserved rooms of their own.

My drive into work was uneventful, and uneventful was good. Overall, life had improved. I could see financial daylight for us, and my new normal with less stress was a welcome change.

Upstairs, when I passed through the door leading to Mahogany Row, I didn't feel the apprehension I had those first few days. The unease of entering the devil's lair had been replaced by a feeling of calm. This was a safe place, a place I belonged, more importantly, a place I'd earned.

At first, the denizens of these offices had been standoffish, but Dennis's public praise for my efforts in the Talbot and Zarniger transactions had changed that. These people worked on a higher floor than others in the company, but they weren't the stuck-up jerks I'd expected. Even Larry was nice.

At eleven, I gathered up my notes on the huge Stoner purchase and made my way to Dennis's office for our scheduled meeting.

Dennis waved to me and motioned to the small conference table while he continued a phone call.

I closed the door behind me and took my normal seat facing the window —a seat that allowed me to watch him at his desk while also viewing the ocean.

He finished up his call and joined me at the table. "Where should we start?"

"I've done a quick analysis of their last three years of financials, if you want to start there."

"Sure. That sounds..." He stopped mid-sentence. His eyes went to the door.

A woman walked in without so much as a rap on the door frame.

I knew the face instantly from my research on my target.

Her choice of a dress—more appropriate for going to the opera than anything work-related—was almost laughable. She wore it well, but a plunging neckline of obviously braless cleavage and a thigh-high slit didn't fit in the office environment.

She gave me a flit of her hand as if she were shooing away a bug. "You can go. We'd like privacy."

I had no desire to make her acquaintance and stood.

Dennis stood as well, and his hand on my arm was a command to stay instead. As much as I wanted to get the hell out of here, I was the pawn in this war of wills, and I was Dennis's pawn.

"Dennis, we need to talk." She cast a glance my way. "In private."

"Melissa, this is Jennifer Hanley. Jennifer, Melissa."

"A pleasure," I said, offering my hand.

She huffed, shaking off the introduction as if it were beneath her to respond in kind. "Melissa Benson, his wife."

I pulled my hand back when she didn't accept the offer to shake.

Dennis stiffened. "Ex-wife."

I waited for the inevitable verbal artillery barrage.

If break-ups were on a continuum from cordial to murderous, the papers had categorized theirs as one step short of bloodshed, and the legal aftermath still raged, with her claiming he'd misrepresented the situation and hidden assets. Her demands for more were still ongoing, I'd gathered from the news sites.

Her glare at me was cold enough to freeze a cup of coffee. "Dennis, I said *in private.*"

Dennis moved his gaze to the table. "I'm in a meeting, Melissa. If you want to talk, make an appointment with Cindy on your way out." He made a point of not looking at her. "For next month."

She ignored the put-off. "I'm on the organizing committee for the museum fundraiser, and think you and I should go to your father's gala together. It's what he would want." Her voice had a fake sweetness so syrupy it would have attracted flies if we'd been outside.

Dennis's jaw clenched. "Not in a million years."

The insult bounced right off her. "Don't be impetuous, Dennis. You know that's your weakness. We should both do it for Lloyd. We did it last year."

The woman's eyes were cold as death. It was abundantly clear why she was now the *ex* Mrs. Benson. She was the kind of bitch who deserved to be kicked out of the female category for giving the rest of us a bad reputation.

Maybe I couldn't screw up Dennis's life today, but it sure seemed this woman could.

I knew his father, Lloyd Benson, was the chairman of the museum, but she was insinuating a deeper backstory than that.

Dennis shifted, clearly off balance with this woman. "And last year was the last time. I'll be taking someone else this year." His jaw twitched.

She rolled her eyes. "Don't be silly. You're married to this job—you always have been—and I checked the seating chart. You're not going with anyone."

Perhaps *witch* was a better description for her.

"You're going with me," she concluded.

Dennis didn't say anything. He wasn't a good liar, and she seemed to know it.

Melissa was here to create trouble, and if she was trying to ruin his bank account, and I was out to ruin his reputation, we were aligned, in an odd way. I didn't like her, but we had the same end goal.

The witch advanced a step.

Dennis was quiet, seeming to search for an answer.

She'd unnerved the great Dennis Benson, not an easy feat.

I saw my opportunity to strike a blow and took it. "*I'm* going with him."

I slid close to Dennis and put my arm around his waist. An even-more pissed off ex-wife would certainly screw up Dennis's day. Mom would have been proud of me.

I chalked the icy stare I got from her up as a win. She was steaming mad, the kind of mad that would make her dangerous if there were sharp objects handy.

Dennis snaked a hand around my waist and moved me closer yet. When he looked down at me, his smile was oddly warm and appreciative.

I didn't flinch. Instead I upped the ante against his ex. I welded myself to his side. "Isn't that right, Denny?"

Melissa's face went red with fury.

Dennis looked down at me. "And I'm so glad you said yes, Angel." He gave me a squeeze.

Calling me Angel? I hadn't seen that coming. But it was my signal to smile up at him.

"I'm so looking forward to it." I turned to her. "I've heard so much about it, but this will be my first time."

Her Witchiness huffed audibly. "I don't believe it for a second."

Dennis spun me toward him, and his mouth came down to mine in a kiss clearly meant as payback for his ex.

He pulled me close, my breasts pillowed firmly against the hardness of his chest. A hand behind my head held me in place.

His tongue sought entrance, and suddenly this was anything but acting.

My eyes slammed shut, and my heart thundered in my chest as his hand fell to my ass and squeezed. He tasted like coffee, desire, and *passion*. As his tongue swept over mine, I breathed in the woodsy scent of his hair or his aftershave—I couldn't tell which, and it didn't matter. All rational thought halted.

Logically, I should have pushed the ogre away, but logic wasn't in charge any longer. All that mattered was that I'd tasted the predator, the king of the jungle, and my body wanted more. It needed more. Hormones, instinct, and desire won the day.

My fingers speared through his hair, and I pulled myself up to meet his passion.

His hand moved to my breast, stroking the underside through my clothes, before a thumb smoothed over the pebbled nipple straining to puncture my bra and meet his touch.

The witch huffed.

The door slammed.

He didn't stop. For what seemed like an eternity, he held me there, kissing me, caressing me, like we belonged together, like I belonged to him. And for this moment, I did.

He shifted, and the unmistakable bar of his erection pushed against me. This embrace wasn't fake for him either. His reaction couldn't be hidden.

I surrendered entirely to my animal brain. The instructions it sent to my tongue, my mouth, and my hands said to pull him close and not let him get away. In my core, I wanted him to desire me as much as my body desired his.

In the end, I didn't pull away. He did.

Catching my breath, I smoothed my clothes and looked to the space Her Witchiness had vacated at some point. "She's gone."

Dennis smoothed the hair I'd messed up. "Good riddance."

"Is she always like that?"

"You caught her on a good day." His hand went into his pocket, probably in an effort to hide the bulge in his trousers—it didn't work. "Will you accompany me to the museum fundraiser?"

It wasn't clear if that was an actual question or a rhetorical one at this point.

"Please," he added.

I took a deep breath and willed my logical brain to save me from myself. My tongue darted out to trace my still-tingling upper lip. "Will it piss her off?"

He chuckled. "Incredibly." It was the answer I'd hoped for—the witch would be working extra hard to destroy him now.

But of course I'd already made up my mind. "I'd love to." Going to the party with him was sure to frost her ass even more. Fantastic kisser or not, he needed to pay. My family deserved to be avenged.

He shifted nervously. "Thank you for that. I wasn't prepared for the question." He looked away. "We should get back to Stoner later."

With my rational brain back in charge, I agreed. I was hot, aroused, and completely unable to concentrate in my current state. Hormones could be such a bitch. After another deep, calming breath, I walked to the door and turned. "Later, Denny."

His eyes narrowed at my audacity, before the smirk he tried to hide showed itself. "Later, Angel."

I closed the door behind me and rested against it for a second.

Cindy rolled her eyes with a chuckle. "A piece of work, isn't she?"

"You heard that?"

"Hard not to."

"Not somebody I want to spend any time with."

Melissa and I might both be working against Dennis, but that didn't mean I had to like her.

Cindy went back to her computer, and I headed to my office.

After I closed the door behind me, I took the seat and swiveled to face the ocean.

The man had scrambled my brain. Rational Jennifer knew he was dangerous, unpredictable, and exactly what I didn't need. Emotional me, hormonal me, said he was exactly what I wanted—dangerous, predatory, the king of the jungle and all he surveyed. His kiss had been everything I hadn't experienced before—sensual in a new and different way I couldn't put a name to. Not a boy's kiss, not even a man's kiss, something more animal than that, primal even.

The ancient cavewoman genes in me had reacted to him as the caveman I instinctively craved—the biggest, baddest one around, the one who would keep me safe.

My tongue still tingled with the aftereffects. I closed my eyes, and a smile overcame me. Our brief touches while volunteering in the lunch line a few weeks ago had hinted at what the kiss had proven. Dennis was my kryptonite. There was no denying it. I'd melted in his arms, completely at his mercy.

I told myself I'd impulsively claimed to be his date to piss off his ex. If she was trouble for him, our goals were aligned, and I expected an angry Melissa would cause him extra-serious grief. But I don't think that was the whole truth.

What the hell was wrong with me? Which was reality and which was illusion? Had I snuggled close to him and accepted the kiss merely to piss her off, or because of the magnetic attraction he held for me?

And for him, what part of it was play acting to piss her off? Any of it, or all of it?

He called me Angel.

I could live with that. In time, he would learn I was an avenging angel

CHAPTER 16

DENNIS

MELISSA'S VISIT HAD COME OUT OF THE BLUE, AND CLAIMING TO HAVE ARRANGED to go to Dad's museum fundraiser with Jennifer had gotten rid of her.

But that had undone a lot of work, on my part. I'd been careful to avoid any improper contact with Jennifer since our visit to Saint Helena's.

She'd been temptingly close that day, and just brushing against her had almost stirred me to act on my fantasies. I'd considered asking her to join me for dinner more than once since then, but I'd pulled back each time. I couldn't risk it.

Melissa's motion to modify our divorce decree had been assigned to Judge White. My lawyer, Birkman, had been complaining about that turn of events ever since.

Judge White had married into money, and after her husband dumped her for a younger trophy wife, she'd become the most husband-unfriendly judge in the district.

Birkman had warned me that any hint I was involved with another woman, even now, would allow Melissa's side to play to the judge's prejudices and hurt me in the end. I would be painted as the rich guy trading the poor first wife in for a newer model, and the result could be very expensive.

As a result, I'd not even been on a date in a long while. I'd hooked up with a woman in Vegas, but that hardly counted as a date.

When Jennifer had claimed to be going to the gala with me, the shock had served its purpose of getting Melissa the hell out of my office. But what I hadn't counted on was the reaction I got from Jennifer, or my reaction to her when I'd upped the ante with a kiss.

She'd more than played along. Her kiss had consumed me and taken me down a road not recently traveled. A road called desire, where logic didn't register, where impulses took over, and I did what felt right. Kissing her felt right. The heat of her against me had made it difficult to avoid stripping her on the spot once Melissa stormed out.

It hadn't been smart. It hadn't been logical, but now that it was done, it felt natural. It felt right. Denying that it felt good—better than good, *great*—wouldn't be honest. I still felt her as I ran a finger over my bottom lip. Her peach scent lingered with me. *Great* might not even be a strong enough word.

But now I had to deal with the consequences of being impulsive once again. If I called Melissa right away and apologized, I could probably avoid the court fallout of what I'd just done. I considered that for a moment. I would have to tell Jennifer I wasn't taking her after all *and* endure the evening with Melissa.

How long would Melissa hold it over me? Probably forever.

Jennifer had already saved me a hundred and seventy-eight million on Talbot alone. And she was still doing great work.

Screw Melissa.

I was taking Jennifer to the fundraiser. If I was going to piss off Melissa, I was doing it right. The Talbot savings had already paid for it, but beyond that, it's what I wanted. I was done letting Melissa ruin so much as one more day of my life.

A knock sounded at the door, and Larry popped his head in. "Got a sec?"

Larry didn't often waste my time, so I motioned him in. "Sure."

He closed the door behind him. "It's about Gumpert."

Gumpert was always asking for a little something extra. "What's he want now?"

Larry leaned on the chair back instead of taking a seat. "He's really pissed about the spin-off."

"He's the one who wanted to paint the news story that day as a death knell."

I'd overstated it a bit, but Gumpert had gone out on his own limb on that one.

"Rumor is he lost half a mill."

"The stock was up the next day. All he had to do was not panic."

"It's worse than that. He shorted us in the afternoon, and he thinks you stiffed him on purpose by not giving him a hint."

I shook my head. "All I did was refuse to give him anything we weren't giving everyone else. He's a twerp."

Larry cocked his head. "A very powerful twerp. I'm giving you a heads up that he's out to get us. It's personal for him now, so I wouldn't advise talking to him at all. And don't be surprised when he writes a hit piece on us next quarter."

I wasn't sure what Larry wanted me to do with this information. "Do you want me to call him and try to square it?"

Larry's eyes widened—I'd guessed wrong. "No way. I think it's beyond repair. This is just the price of being publicly traded."

Yep, I knew it was one of the big trade offs, probably the biggest. "It just burns me that these guys get to critique us, when most of them couldn't run a profitable lemonade stand."

Larry straightened up, ready to leave. "Life's not fair. Anyway, you've been warned."

This visit had been to put a stake in the ground for the future when Gumpert caused trouble. Larry didn't want me blaming him.

"Got it. Give me a heads up if you see it coming."

He waved a salute as he backed toward the door. "Will do."

Life certainly wasn't fair, and not all shit ran downhill either. The Melissa and Gumpert vendettas weren't problems I could delegate away.

JENNIFER

As I TURNED ON TO MY STREET, I CHECKED MY REARVIEW MIRROR, BUT I DIDN'T see the gray car I thought had followed me. Paranoia was a bitch.

Upstairs, I busied myself with dinner to control my urge to tell my sister everything. It had been such a confusing whirlwind of a day. I downed a glass of wine while cooking to calm myself.

"And whose canary did you swallow?" Ramona finally asked me after we'd eaten.

I closed and started the dishwasher, then crossed the room to settle on the couch, smiling wordlessly.

Billy was at the kitchen table doing his homework. "Eww. That's gross. Jeremy ate a salamander once. Do the feathers tickle?"

"It's just a saying that means she looks like she's hiding something," his mother explained.

"Oh." He went back to his paper.

I didn't think the discussion was Billy-appropriate. "Maybe you should finish your homework in the bedroom."

"I like it out here."

I had another idea. "You'll like it better in the bedroom. We're going to talk about kissing boys."

That got him moving. "Eww."

Ramona let the door close before continuing her interrogation. "I knew you were holding something back at dinner."

I couldn't keep this from her. "He kissed me."

"Who exactly is *he*?"

"Dennis."

"But you hate that guy."

I nodded. "It happened so fast." It had been fast and surprising—wonderful and terrifying all at the same time.

"And you let him?"

I gave her the whole story about his haughty ex and how it had started as a fake kiss to piss her off but ended up so much more.

"So I gave her another reason to hate the guy and put him through the ringer," I concluded.

Ramona had been slack-jawed the entire time. "He's using you to piss off his ex."

"That's the point. She wants to ruin him, and so do I. Getting her more pissed off will damage him in the long run."

"That's sick."

"I know, but that's not all. He asked me to go with him to the museum fundraiser."

"But that's still using you to rub her nose in it."

"I said yes."

"I didn't ask what you said. Don't you get how this looks?"

"You weren't there."

"This is seriously screwed up. A few weeks ago you would have been shopping for cyanide-laced lipstick, and now you want his and hers bottles of lube?"

I knew she was kidding, but I had no idea how to answer. "It was just a kiss."

"Three seconds?"

I shook my head.

"How long then?"

"I don't remember."

"Was it good?"

I couldn't hide the grin. "Yes."

"See? You want him."

"Aren't you the one always telling me he might not be as bad as I think?"

"I always thought your obsession with getting back at him wasn't healthy, but that's not the same as instantly switching to wanting him in your bed."

"You're getting a little ahead of yourself."

She scoffed. "You know how guys think. He's gotten you to first base, and he'll be looking to round the bases and score pretty quickly. And besides, you've got horny written all over you."

I ignored the horny comment—not that she was wrong, but it wasn't the point. "You weren't there."

She shook her head. "I would have stopped you. I know you've had a dry spell. Hell, we both have, but wouldn't it make more sense to hook up with a guy you don't want to kill?"

"But I'm using him too."

"Are we back to poisoned lipstick now?"

"No, but getting close to him will give me better access to the company's files."

"So the poisoned lipstick comes later, *after* the bottles of his and hers lube."

"You're not helping."

"Only because you don't want to hear how fucked up this sounds. You have to make a choice. You can't be both lover and destroyer. You need to choose now."

I settled back and closed my eyes. I had to admit that how it felt and how it sounded were completely opposite. "I guess."

Ramona clicked on the DVR. "I don't want to see you get hurt. In the end you have to decide if he's your enemy or your love interest. He can't be both. You have to put him in one category and bury the other. You can't let it pull you apart."

I mulled that for a moment. I didn't have to decide tonight, but eventually it would come to that, and she had it right. I would have to decide.

She scrolled through the movie selections. "Hey, go spend time with him, and in the end you might decide you were wrong about him all along. But you have to figure it out before you round the bases." She punched a button to check out a movie's description.

I'd hoped talking to her would help me make sense of the situation, but it hadn't. I knew what I knew, and I knew how I felt, and the two were polar opposites.

Ramona wasn't done with me yet. "You know, the biggest problem I have with this obsession of yours is that you can't really hate a person you don't know. So go full Mata Hari on him and decide if you still hate the guy later. Just understand going in that you're using him for sex and dump him." She clicked on another movie. "My God, I can't believe I just said that."

Billy didn't have a father because she'd realized too late that Trevor had only been "using her for sex," as she put it.

Perhaps the latest file Hydra had pointed me toward would provide clarity about who Dennis really was. In the meantime, color me both horny and confused.

The one thing I'd learned today was that Dennis Benson was dangerous in the extreme. He could be impulsive and demanding, a combination that could get me in over my head before I knew it—a tornado that could sweep me up in a vortex beyond my control.

Ramona started the movie, but I couldn't concentrate.

My thoughts kept coming back to the kiss. I hadn't read the kiss wrong, but what if my sister was right and he was only using me to spite Melissa? That was okay, wasn't it? It would make his life harder, and that was a good result.

Mom had always told me to trust my gut, but how did that translate to a situation like this? Was Ramona right that I was too horny to understand how I really felt about him? It *had* been a long dry spell; too long. Perhaps a drink from that well would clear things up. Even if it didn't, it would quench a thirst. And boy, was I thirsty for that man.

Just the thought of what it might be like sent a tingle to my lady parts. Ramona looked over. "You all right?"

I squeezed my legs together. "I will be."

He could use me for his purpose, and I could use him for mine. We'd both get what we wanted.

I smiled. That would be fair.

∼

DENNIS

I STOOD OUTSIDE CASCADA AZUL AT DINNERTIME WAITING FOR MY SISTER, WHO was late as always.

Serena and I got together about once a month for dinner, and she'd scheduled this one at her favorite Mexican restaurant.

Cascada Azul wasn't a hole in the wall, but it wasn't elegant either. The family-run restaurant had a loyal following and was as packed as usual.

I'd already told the hostess we wanted a booth in the back and was waiting for my name to be called.

The young hostess opened the door. "Dennis, party of two."

I raised my hand and followed her inside. "My sister will be along in just a bit."

She smiled, grabbed two menus, and started toward the rear. She stopped at a booth very near the back, as I'd requested.

I accepted the menu and pressed a bill into her hand, getting a warm smile in return. I'd only been seated long enough to receive the bowl of chips and the tray of bean dip and salsa when Serena waved from the front. I waved back and stood.

She rushed over and gave me a hug. "Dennis, sorry I'm late."

I'd long ago given up trying to get her to be on time. "No worries. You're looking good."

"Why, thank you. It's the Pilates."

Our waitress arrived to take our drink orders.

I chose my standard Luna Azul margarita on the rocks, no salt, and Serena asked for the same, only frozen. The blue curacao made it look similar to my favorite drink, a blue Hawaii.

Serena started in as soon as the waitress left. "I heard you got a visit from Maleficent today."

That had been Serena-speak for Melissa since shortly after we got married, and it fit.

I knew where she'd gotten the heads up, but I asked anyway. "Who told you that?"

She scooped a chip in the bean dip. "You know Cindy keeps me up to date. What did *she* want?"

She'd probably also gotten that from Cindy.

"She wanted to talk about the museum gala."

"Dad should kick her off the committee, if you ask me. She's just never-ending trouble."

I felt the same way, but it wasn't an argument worth having with Dad just yet. "That's Dad's cross to bear. Take it up with him." To help smooth over the divorce, Dad had promised to let Melissa stay on the committee. It had been another of her off-the-wall demands when we ended things.

It wasn't in writing, but Dad felt he had to honor it, even if Melissa never kept any of her promises.

Serena waved her chip at me. "Go on."

"Nothing much to tell. She wanted me to attend with her. I said no."

She continued to fish. "And what else?"

"Nothing else."

"I heard she blew her top, Mount Vesuvius style, so you must have said more than that."

"I told her I already had a date."

"Who?"

This is where it could get tricky. "Someone from the office."

"Really?"

Our waitress appeared to take our orders, chicken tacos for me and the enchilada suprema for Serena.

After the waitress left, Serena came at me nine different ways, trying to get more out of me, but all I gave up about Jennifer was her name.

I didn't mention the off-the-charts kiss, her incredible body, the fantastic smarts, or those green eyes that looked right through me—none of it.

I smiled, recalling the feel of her warm, soft tit under my hand, and the way she'd gasped when I'd squeezed her ass. It hadn't been a gasp of protest, rather a gasp of desire, of hunger for more.

Jennifer wanted more, and today I didn't give a shit about how it affected the legal negotiations with Melissa.

Serena eyed me as she finished chewing another chip. "I saw that."

I could play innocent with the best of them. "What?"

"That smirk." She pointed her finger at me. "You just thought of something you're holding back, and it made you smile. Now give."

"It was nothing. I liked the sound of the door slamming behind Melissa is all."

Serena set her drink down. "Liar."

Our dinners arrived. We got off the Jennifer-Melissa-fundraiser topic after I started probing Serena about her dating life.

She could dish it out, but she couldn't take it.

The rest of the meal was more sedate after we both abandoned the topics the other didn't want to discuss.

CHAPTER 17

JENNIFER
(Four Days Later)

MY ALARM CLOCK SCREAMED WAY TOO EARLY.

It stopped its diabolical racket when it hit the floor.

It was another Monday morning, and I dragged myself out of bed. I'd stayed up late last night to make another after-hours trip to the file rooms at work. It hadn't taken long to locate the file folder for Hydra. I still had to drop it off, but that could wait.

This file had contained a thumb drive in addition to papers. I'd made a copy of its contents to peruse later. The memos inside didn't look like anything important, but I wasn't privy to Hydra's full plan.

The hot water of the shower slowly cleared the cobwebs from my brain.

Things with Dennis had been completely businesslike in the days since that kiss. He'd taken to calling me Jenn on occasion instead of Jennifer, and I suppose that was something, but he hadn't used the Angel moniker again. In fact, he hadn't alluded to it in any way, as if it hadn't happened.

I hadn't been thinking of it as a kiss, but *The Kiss*. Maybe it hadn't been as spectacular for him as it was for me. But he'd grabbed my ass and cradled my breast with a passion that had surprised me.

Maybe I was supposed to reciprocate and squeeze his butt, or rub him through his pants. Guys liked that, didn't they? But we'd been standing in his office, for God's sake—with an audience for at least part of our performance.

By the time I finished with the conditioner, I'd replayed the scene a dozen times, and I had to turn the water temperature down to keep from overheating.

Had I misread him? Had it only been a good acting job to piss off his ex? I could have sworn it was real.

Getting out of the shower, I banished thoughts of Dennis and busied myself with my morning routine. I hurried and decided on a stop at Starbucks for a breakfast sandwich, instead of cereal here.

The M&M girls were at our usual table.

Martha saw me first and waved as I ordered.

As I approached with my sandwich and mocha, Mona pulled out a chair for me. "We haven't seen you for a while. Welcome back."

I told them the truth. "Work's been pretty hectic on the days I don't have to take Billy to school."

Martha twisted her cup. "Did you get a good raise?"

I nodded. "Sure did."

Martha smirked. "And did you hold out for more?"

"Yes, and it worked."

Martha nudged Mona. "I told you he was a good man."

Mona protested, "I never said he wasn't."

Martha lifted her cup. "Did my prediction come true yet?"

A blush rose in my face. I wasn't about to tell them everything. "Actually, yes. We did have lunch together, if Saint Helena's counts."

Mona cocked her head. "Mr. Moneybags couldn't splurge and buy you a meal himself?"

I smiled as I recalled my surprise as well. "That's not it. He was serving. Well, that and he supplied the chickens. I helped." I took a bite of my breakfast sandwich.

Martha looked back to me. "That's a good start. What's next? Dinner?"

I should have been prepared for the twenty questions. I hadn't seen them since the kiss. "He's taking me to a museum fundraiser." I followed it up with another bite.

Martha smiled.

Mona's mouth dropped open "That's pretty highbrow, like going to the MET in New York. What have you picked to wear?"

I was still chewing. Like an idiot, I hadn't considered the question until she asked it. "I dunno," I mumbled.

Martha added to the bad news. "That's a do-your-hair, mani-pedi kind of event, not something you just dash some lipstick on for."

I was way behind the power curve in getting ready for this. But I wouldn't give Melissa the pleasure of seeing me looking like the poor girl I was, as if I'd just moved out of a double-wide.

"I'll have to work on that."

Martha reached over to touch my arm. "You'll do just fine. Let us know if you need any advice. Mona here used to go to that."

She perked up. "My Harold took me. The highlight of my year."

This was sounding more and more ominous. I took one last bite of my breakfast and stood. "I gotta get to work."

We exchanged goodbyes, and outside, I turned toward work with more questions about this weekend than answers.

Upstairs, I made it to my office and a search of the internet came back with terrifying news: dozens of images of ladies that looked like they were dressed for the red carpet.

I'd thought this would be a simple dinner at a hotel ballroom, eating rubber chicken with men in suits and women in nice dresses, not men in tuxes and ladies in gowns.

Now I was totally screwed. There was no way anything in my wardrobe qualified as nice enough for this event. My best dress looked like it came from Goodwill compared to the pictures here.

I'd have to tell Ramona we were putting off the apartment search for a month or so. Buying something for this would use up the money I'd been saving for our first, last, and security deposit on the new place.

It was either that or tell Dennis I couldn't go, after all.

I'd been a complete idiot to agree to the invitation without thinking through the ramifications. But it had been too tempting to refuse, and now I was trapped. I didn't even know where to shop for something like this.

CHAPTER 18

DENNIS

IT WAS A NEW WEEK, AND I'D FINISHED OFF THE LAST ONE WITHOUT MAKING A fool of myself with Jennifer after the kiss to shut down Melissa.

It had taken all of my self control to not ask her to dinner—a dinner I would certainly have wanted to take further, with her as the dessert.

Just the thought made my dick swell. But that was dangerous.

We'd had sandwiches brought in for a few lunch meetings with just the two of us in my office. That had been tempting enough.

It had been impossible to tell how she'd felt about the kiss. She hadn't brought it up, or even hinted at it since, and I hadn't either.

Professional had been the watchword. No hand holding, no touching, and absolutely no kissing. I'd shortened her name to Jenn, but I hadn't slipped up and called her Angel again. The name fit her, though. She had been nothing but good luck since she'd started upstairs.

Cindy appeared at my open door, came in, and closed it behind her.

"You've created a problem," she said.

"What did I do now?"

"You asked Jennifer to go with you this weekend to your father's fundraiser for the museum."

She'd actually invited herself, but Cindy didn't need to know that. "Yes?"

"She doesn't have anything to wear. She's too proud to mention it, but I don't think you understand how big a problem it can be for someone in her financial situation."

This had been the first I'd heard of money problems for Jennifer.

"Thanks for letting me know." I picked up my phone and dialed Jennifer's extension. "Come down here. We have to go out."

"Where? What should I bring?" she asked.

"Nothing. Just make it quick." I hung up before she could ask another question.

Cindy opened the door. "Thank you."

"I'll take care of it. Please ask Karl to bring the car around."

She gave me a thumbs up.

Jennifer arrived a moment later.

JENNIFER

CINDY WINKED AT ME AS I WALKED UP.

When I got to his office, Dennis was slipping into his jacket.

"I thought we were meeting at three," I said.

"Change of plans. We're going out."

I couldn't keep my mouth shut. "Where?"

He didn't answer, just moved past me toward the elevator.

I hurried behind him.

The man was a perpetual-motion machine, never taking a break. When one task was complete, he immediately moved to the next.

After the elevator door closed, I tried again. "Where to?"

"You'll see."

I gave up trying to crack the shell. I shifted away. In the enclosed space, his scent reminded me of the kiss, the kiss I couldn't forget if I wanted to. I'd decided it had been an act on his part, since he'd not mentioned it and had studiously avoided getting anywhere near my personal space.

Downstairs on the street, he opened the door to a waiting town car.

I stood back. "This is yours?"

"The company's." He was all short answers today. He held the door for me.

I slid in and across to the other side, which I found out was a mistake when he rounded the back of the car and opened the street-side door to let himself in.

I slid back to the right. "Sorry."

He closed the door. "Apologies for the short notice, Karl."

Somehow it didn't strike me as odd that this particular billionaire apologized to his driver.

The driver nodded. "Anytime, sir." He pulled us out into traffic.

I decided against asking a third time about our destination and tried another tack. "Who are we meeting with?"

Dennis smiled. "Some very nice people. I think you'll like them."

He was enjoying this little game.

If he was going to be mum, I could be too.

We didn't speak for the rest of the trip.

Karl navigated to Santa Monica Boulevard, and I watched the buildings go by for a few minutes. I settled back in the seat, closed my eyes, and enjoyed the new-car scent of fine leather.

Karl finally pulled to the curb on a side street.

Dennis opened his door, and I followed his lead by opening mine. "Don't you move." He rushed around and held the door for me. "A gentleman holds the door for a lady."

I couldn't tell what had gotten into him, but it was cute. "I'm not always a lady." I accepted his hand climbing out, and instantly regretted it. That same electricity flowed between us that had scrambled my brain before.

He poked his head in the door. "Karl, I'll buzz you when we're done."

Done with what? I didn't bother to ask. Instead I looked around to get my bearings. The storefront said Bulgari, and the street sign on the pole read fucking *Rodeo Drive*. My mouth dropped. I hadn't recognized it because everybody knew you had to have a dozen zeros on your bank account to shop here, so I'd never even driven by.

I jumped at Dennis's touch. He had put a brain fog inducing hand to the small of my back.

"Let's start across the street."

Thankfully he removed his hand as I started to walk.

We crossed the street, and he guided me into the Vera Wang store on the other side.

I thought it was time to ask again. "What are we doing here?"

"I want you to look gorgeous when you walk into the gala."

I stopped.

"That came out wrong," he corrected himself. "You're gorgeous, and I want you to be wearing a dress worthy of you."

I wasn't comfortable with this. "I'm not your prize pony, you know." The objection escaped before I had a chance to play it in my head and hear how bitchy it sounded.

He locked eyes with me. "The party is my treat, and that includes the dress."

Some little birdie had been singing.

I'd confided in Cindy that the dress was going to be a problem. I hadn't meant it to pressure him. "You don't have to do that."

A saleslady started toward us.

He shrugged. "But I want to. You'll be representing the company, and we need to make the best impression possible."

That was almost a rational reason.

I only had a second to object before the saleslady glommed on to us. "But—"

He raised a finger to silence me the way he sometimes did. "Please, this is important to me."

The perceptive saleslady backed away to give us privacy.

I blew out a breath. "Okay. Because you asked nicely."

This was surreal. I was arguing with a guy who wanted to shower me with gifts. Why? Anybody else and I would have been falling all over myself to agree. But I'd trained myself that whatever Dennis wanted, I wanted the opposite.

"And shoes?" I asked.

"Shoes, handbag, the whole enchilada."

I was such an idiot. This was every girl's dream come true. A fully paid shopping trip to Rodeo Drive, and here I was arguing because it was him, and everything he wanted I seemed to end up resisting on principle. I should've been happy spending his money, the more the better.

The saleslady judged that it was finally safe to approach. "And what can I help you find today?"

Dennis took charge. "The lady is going to the museum gala this weekend, and we'd like to find a nice dress for the occasion."

Her smile moved up a few notches as she turned to me. "The gala. How nice. I'm sure we can find something you'll like." She motioned toward the rear of the store. "Let's see what we can find for you. My name's Kayla, by the way." She started off.

I followed her. "Jennifer."

"Lovely. Now, are we thinking a special color? I think a black would be particularly striking on you, and very appropriate for a function like that."

I looked back. "I wouldn't know. I've never been."

Dennis had taken a seat.

She walked on. "Neither have I, but we can always hope."

Kayla showed me several things, and one by one I tried them on.

A few didn't work well enough for me in the mirror, but two did, and I walked out to show Dennis.

It was my own little fashion show, walking and turning, but neither of them earned the glint in his eye I was looking for.

If I had volunteered for this as a way to make his life miserable by pissing off Melissa, I was going to do it right. The dress was going to be mouth-wateringly sexy. If it got Dennis's eyes to pop out, it would elicit the reaction I was aiming for from his ex: full-on, red-faced, homicidal anger.

I'd seen it in her eyes at the office. She'd stared daggers of jealousy at me. Turning my back on the crazy lady at the party would be dangerous.

Kayla wasn't happy when we decided to go a few doors down to the next store, but I wasn't settling for anything less than Dennis's eyes bulging when I came out of the dressing room.

He was patient, but his smile wavered when we walked out of a third store without a dress.

I'd had several more brain-fog incidents where he put a hand to my back to guide me into a store or down the street. Each time he touched me, the sensation was like the first time—an electric jolt that shook me to my core, a jolt I didn't want to admit meant something. My subconscious, my irrational animal brain, didn't understand the kind of man he was.

I'd avoided jumping, but only barely. One of these times, I was going to yelp like a little girl and embarrass us both. Twice I'd been about to object, but my animal brain had shut down my vocal cords.

I discarded the thought that he was being anything more than gentlemanly—that had to explain it. He couldn't help himself. Insisting on opening doors for me, always walking on the street side, he was just following the gentleman's code he'd been taught.

His words pulled me back to the present. "Should we try in here?"

"Sure."

On cue, he held the door open for me.

We were quickly met by Veronica, and he again explained my quest for a dress to wear this weekend.

I followed Veronica back to the racks while Dennis waited up front.

She pulled out several selections that were lukewarm at best. "These would be fitting for the museum event."

I looked them over briefly. "Not quite right."

She tilted her head in Dennis's direction. "You don't think he'd like these?"

Like wasn't the word I was going for. "He might, but I don't want him to *like* it, I want him to love it, or better yet, be shocked by it."

She moved down a rack. "Then this might be what you're looking for." She pulled out a bright red number.

I emerged from the dressing room. "How do I keep this from falling too open?" The neckline plunged almost to my navel.

"We have tape for that. Everybody uses it on the red carpet. I mean, if they didn't, they wouldn't be able to televise it, now would they?"

I turned around for her.

"You'll also need to go down the street to La Perla for something to wear under that." She pointed to where my panties were showing through the more than thigh-high slit. "They can also match this color for you."

I wiggled and pulled my underwear down to step out of them. I didn't want them ruining the effect when I showed this to Dennis.

DENNIS

HOW WOMEN COULD SPEND ALL DAY LOOKING FOR A SINGLE DRESS WAS beyond me.

We were at the fourth store, and I'd approved of everything she'd come out modeling. But after each one, she'd said it didn't feel right, whatever that meant.

Each of them had looked beautiful on her, but that was to be expected. Jennifer was a beautiful girl. She could make a T-shirt and jeans look sexy.

She appeared from around the corner. "What do you think of this one?" She twirled in front of me.

My mouth dropped.

She wore a bright red gown with a deep V front showing off her marvelous braless cleavage, and a slit that came almost to her waist, revealing a complete leg with each step, barely hiding what I guessed was her naked pussy. Each time she moved, my eyes darted to her thigh, hoping for a glimpse, but I was denied—just barely.

"Well?" she asked, breaking my stare.

I fumbled for the right word. "Breathtaking."

"You think so?"

"Absolutely. Every man in the room will be wondering…" I stopped myself and rephrased. "…how I got so lucky to have you as my date."

She would cast a spell on every pair of eyes in the room.

"You're going to make me blush."

"It'll just make the dress look better on you."

That extra line did draw a blush out of her, and it was cuter than I'd expected.

This latest saleslady was hovering, waiting on the verdict.

I stood and offered her my credit card. "We'll take it."

We had spent hours and only selected one thing so far.

When Jennifer came back, changed into her work clothes, all I could think of was how magnificently sexy she'd looked in that dress. My eyes drifted to her chest, imagining the luscious cleavage that had been on display, and that slit—my God that slit was like a pulse of aphrodisiac with each step, displaying her leg and all that skin.

I offered to carry the garment bag. "Shoes next?"

She tilted her head. "Among other things." She winked. "Just a few more stops, I promise."

Thankfully she knew where she wanted to go for shoes, and we accomplished that with only a single stop.

Next up was a handbag. The surprise after that was a visit to La Perla for lingerie.

I opened the door for her. "I hope you'll be modeling for me again?"

"Not a chance."

I didn't hide my disappointment well.

"I promise I won't be long." She held out her hand. "Card?"

I surrendered my black Amex card one more time and was relegated to wait by the front while she and one of the sales staff wandered off.

As additional female customers entered the store, I garnered a sideways glance from each that seemed to wonder if I was a pervert or just a guy too stupid to know this was a designated testosterone-free zone—no Y chromosomes allowed.

Jennifer reappeared with her purchase concealed in a bag.

"What'd you get?"

"I'm not telling." The vixen had me at her mercy.

CHAPTER 19

JENNIFER

Saturday evening had finally arrived: the big night.

The doorbell rang.

I glanced at the clock.

He was a half hour early.

Ramona closed the fridge. "Want me to get it?"

"Thanks. I'm almost ready." I closed the bathroom door to finish my eyes.

I could hear them in the other room.

"They're beautiful," Ramona said.

She introduced herself and offered him coffee while I touched up my eyeshadow.

The rest of the conversation was too muted for me to make out.

Moments later, there was a knock at the bathroom door. "Your boss man is here," Billy yelled.

"I know. I'll be right out."

When I opened the door, there Dennis was. I knew the man could wear the hell out of a suit, but the tuxedo took it to the next level. He looked like he'd walked straight off the set of a Bond movie.

He held out a bouquet to me.

I took the gorgeous red roses. "They're beautiful." I held them strategically to hide my cleavage. Now that I was wearing the dress for real, the neckline seemed even more daring than it had in the store. I'd expected it to make me feel empowered, but *vulnerable* better described my current state of mind. What the neckline didn't show was pretty evident behind the thin material. My nipples were hard and pokey.

"Not half as beautiful as you."

I contained my laugh at the corny comment. I was going as his arm candy, in an effort to unnerve his ex, nothing more.

"Stop that. There's no audience here." The words sounded harsher than I'd meant them.

His smile turned to a scowl, telling me I'd once again been too sassy— that was becoming a constant problem for me.

His mouth opened, then closed, as he apparently decided to keep his thoughts to himself.

Ramona came from around the counter. "Let me put those in some water for you." Ever the peacekeeper, she defused the argument.

I relinquished the bouquet, and his eyes went to my plunging neckline and back to my face with an approving smile. "You *do* look gorgeous this evening." His tone conveyed the don't-contradict-me message even louder than the words.

I tried not to squirm under his stare. "Should we get going?"

He swung his arm toward the door. "The lady's carriage awaits."

Billy scurried to open the door.

Dennis followed. "Thank you, Billy."

Ramona grabbed my arm. "Should I wait up?" she whispered.

I silently shook my head. I had no idea how late this would go.

Downstairs, Dennis held the door open for me as I exited the building.

At the curb, his driver, Karl, waited by the town car.

My neighbor, Mrs. Butterfield, stopped short and stared as I gathered up the long dress and slid into the car. Her glare made it obvious what she thought of my attire, and it wasn't complimentary.

Dennis climbed in the other side and closed the door. "Don't you dare do that again."

I jerked back. "What?"

"Refuse an honest compliment."

The man was impossible. "I didn't mean—"

"Yes, you did," he said, cutting me off. "A lady graciously accepts a compliment."

"I already told you I'm not a lady."

He pointed a finger. "That won't work with me. I won't tolerate anyone denigrating you. Not even you. Now, let's try this again. Angel, you look gorgeous this evening."

Angel disarmed me. "Thank you."

He fished into a bag on the floor and produced a small box. "These are for you."

I froze in place. It wasn't just any box. It was a small blue box with the initials HW on it. It was a fucking Harry Winston jewelry box.

"Go ahead, open it."

I took the box and after another nod from him, I opened it. Earrings with brilliant green emeralds and a pendant with a matching stone on a simple, white-gold chain sparkled in the late-day sunlight.

This was too much. "But I can't."

"What did I just finish telling you about arguments? These match your eyes perfectly."

This was completely over the top. Naturally the man shopped at the same place as the Prince of Wales and Hollywood elites.

I looked at him again. "Are you sure?"

"Have you ever known me to say something I didn't mean?"

I didn't answer, but started to remove the simple gold dangles I'd chosen for tonight. I swapped them out for the gemstone earrings.

He helped me with the necklace clasp, and then gave an approving smile. "They look good on you."

Paying attention to my training, I replied simply. "Thank you."

Dennis explained what to expect at this party. It sounded boring—a silent auction, dinner, and a bunch of old stiffs gaining social credibility by donating to a worthy local institution.

I took a guess. "And how many of these people are trying to curry favor with your father?"

Dennis took in a breath. "That's a crass way of putting it. But it's the way things work. Between Dad, Bill Covington, and the other board members, the attendees have a lot of interrelated interests."

I understood. "This is a rich people's mutual-admiration-society meeting —normal people need not apply."

His glare was cold. "It's not like that. Do you think the city is better off with or without a fine art museum?"

I hadn't meant to get into an argument, so I kept my mouth shut for a change.

"It's a simple question."

Art wasn't my thing, but I'd been to the museum once on a school field trip, and I had enjoyed it.

"With a museum, of course," I said.

"Dad insists on not charging admission, so he holds events like this to raise the money to keep it running. Normal people, as you call them, don't have money to spare for a cause like this. The people he invites do. At the end of the night, they feel better after having donated to the museum and getting the side benefit of rubbing shoulders with the other guests. In exchange, the city gets to keep its museum. Everybody wins."

Once again my smart mouth had gotten me into trouble. "I'm sorry. I didn't mean it was a bad thing."

"Sure you did. You let your prejudice show through. You think rich people should be punished for having money."

"No, I don't. I just…" I didn't know how to finish the sentence without getting deeper into trouble. I couldn't very well explain that I thought being rich let him get away with things normal people would go to jail for.

He reached over to take my hand. "Sorry for going off on you like that, Angel. I guess I'm a little sensitive."

WHEN WE ARRIVED, KARL STOPPED OUTSIDE THE MUSEUM ENTRANCE TO LET us out.

Once inside, I found Dennis's description hadn't prepared me for what awaited us. Walking through the museum's doors was like stepping onto a Disney fairytale set. *Wow* was the only description that came to mind.

I walked alongside Dennis past multiple ice sculptures, colorful bunting, and tall floral arrangements lining the entrance hall—an explosion of opulence in complete contrast to the drab exterior of the building.

Past that, waiters in white waistcoats weaved through the crowd, carrying silver platters of bubbly and hors d'oeuvres. We passed a fountain of liquid chocolate. Avoiding a stop to taste it was a supreme effort in self-control.

Dennis snatched two glasses of champagne for us as I followed him to the easels displaying the seating charts.

So far I hadn't seen any sign of Her Craziness, Melissa.

Dennis motioned toward a doorway to the side. "Let's check out the silent auction."

I nodded. "Sure."

On the way, he introduced me to his younger brother Josh and his sister Serena. In both cases he introduced me as his date.

I wanted to explain that we worked together, but thought better of it. After a quick, amiable chat, he dragged me into the other room with the auction items.

Tables stretched the length of the space, covered with expensive items for people to bid on, with proceeds going to the museum. Dennis put his name down on a week for two in Hawaii with a ridiculously high bid.

"Cindy said you don't take vacations."

He shrugged. "I don't."

I'd scoped out Hawaiian vacations—not that I could afford one, but internet browsing was free. "You know it doesn't cost that much, don't you?"

"It's for a good cause."

He intended to win this one. Apparently rich guys like him didn't mess around when they wanted something. I couldn't have afforded to bid on anything we had seen yet except an ugly chess set that hadn't gotten any bids.

"Why bid on something you're not going to use?"

"Hey, what's with the twenty questions?"

Appropriately chastised, I kept quiet as I followed him on a complete circuit of the tables.

In the end, he only bid on the Hawaii trip.

When dinner was called, we sat at a table with his sister and some others from work. Cindy was here with her husband, a nice guy who worked as a mechanic at the local Toyota dealership, as well as my old boss, Mr. Fisher, and his wife.

Just as I took my seat, I caught a glimpse of Melissa at a table on the far side of the room. She was looking the other way.

Larry, the marketing guy with the loud mouth, hadn't brought a date and took the seat on the other side of me before I could get Serena's attention to sit there.

She took the chair on the other side of Larry.

I expected Larry to chat me up, and he didn't disappoint.

"I'm glad you came," he said. "We haven't had much of a chance to talk."

I'd gathered from the other girls at lunch that Larry was a player and readied myself for the come-on lines.

"Dennis has kept me pretty busy," I said.

"Do you like dogs?"

I'd anticipated a more direct come-on. "Sure, who doesn't? But I can't have one in my apartment." I caught his quick look down my dress and was thankful the tape was holding. The unease of feeling naked caused a momentary shiver.

The dog question turned out to be just a delay. "How about lunch next week? I know a killer Thai place down the street." He shifted his chair an inch closer.

I sucked in a breath. "Thanks, but I generally like to eat in."

"My treat. I'd like to hear how you got old man Talbot to drop his drawers so quickly the other week. I'd been telling Dennis he was soft on the price, but he didn't listen."

"I really didn't do much."

He leaned even closer. "Still, I think you did great for being so new at this. Maybe we could spend a little time, and I could give you a few pointers. You could give me some dog advice."

I knew his kind, and there was only one pointy thing he wanted to give me. I nodded wordlessly as I sipped my water as noncommittally as possible.

"I see you didn't come with a date either."

His comments were becoming more obvious.

Dennis leaned forward before I could say anything. "She's *my* date."

The alpha lion had spoken.

His words shut Larry down like a blast of cold water from a fire hose. "I was just telling Jennifer how good a job she did with Talbot."

Dennis ignored him and went back to talking with Jay Fisher on the other side.

I listened to their conversation for a moment, and when I looked back, Serena was asking Larry to switch places with her so we could talk.

I didn't know if she was rescuing me from Larry, or wanting to size up Dennis's date, but in the end, I didn't care.

When dinner arrived, the choices were chicken or salmon.

Mrs. Fisher had received a plate of chicken and was having trouble cutting it. When the waiter got to me, I settled on salmon.

The conversations slowed a little as we ate, and Cindy, Serena, and I found common ground discussing Serena's passion for her vegetable garden.

She forked a tomato from the salad. "These are like cardboard compared to what comes out of my garden. Why can't they give us ones with some taste?"

I didn't have an answer for that, and we turned to the subject of rose pruning.

Serena struck me as very grounded for a rich girl, but then I remembered Dennis's comment about my rich-people prejudice. Maybe he had a point.

Larry seemed more likable after he mentioned his difficulty house training the puppy he'd recently gotten. "Binky just doesn't get it. I've followed what the book says, but it's not working."

I felt sorry for the poor mutt already. Not even a dog deserved a name like that. Asking how he chose that name got me a grumbled answer having something to do with Tina, who had left the critter with him two weeks ago and hadn't returned.

After hearing that, I felt sorry for Larry. But not sorry enough to have lunch with him.

"Try the training pads," I suggested.

"I've tried those, but he sleeps on them and pees on the carpet."

That garnered a muffled laugh from Cindy.

"The scent may not be right for him," I offered. "Wipe some of his piddle on the pad, so he thinks he's gone there before. That should work."

Larry shook his head. "The package says they're already scented like that."

Dennis got in on the action. "You should know better than to believe all the marketing bullshit on a package."

Larry looked crestfallen.

"What kind of dog is he?" Serena asked.

He lowered his voice. "Chinese crested."

I stifled a laugh. "Not your choice, I'm guessing." I'd seen pictures of the breed. They were hairless except around the head—definitely not a man's dog.

He shook his head and mumbled something less than complimentary about Tina.

Serena and I commiserated with him. Even Larry didn't deserve the likes of Tina.

An older man had been stopping at the tables to our left, seeming to be making the rounds. He resembled Colonel Sanders with his white hair, goatee, and cane.

"How are we doing at this table?" he asked as he arrived at our table. His tone was jovial.

Dennis spoke up first. "Great, Dad."

So this was the patriarch of the Benson family, Lloyd Benson himself.

He greeted each of the guests around the table by name, and then got to me. "You must be the great negotiator Dennis has told me about. Jennifer, isn't it?"

The man was charming and obviously good with names.

"I don't know about the great part. Pleasure to meet you, Mr. Benson."

He rounded the table to our side. "I want to shake your hand, young lady. Jimmy has needed to be taken down a few pegs for quite a while now."

Jimmy had to be James Talbot the third.

Lloyd extended his hand and gave mine a firm shake. "Good for you."

I couldn't help but like the friendly old man, even if he was a Benson.

Dennis interjected. "He certainly left with his tail between his legs."

The elder Benson laughed. "I'm sure he'll deny it next time I see him."

Without realizing it, I'd gotten myself in the middle of a pissing contest between two powerful families.

"Well, thank you all for coming and supporting our museum," Lloyd said. "Have a wonderful evening." With that he was off to the next table, once again greeting most of the guests there by name.

The waiters soon cleared our dinners, and the desserts arrived.

Cindy's husband was busy giving Larry housebreaking tips.

"He even peed on the top of my poker table," Larry complained.

That merited a round of laughs from all of us.

"The green felt probably looked like grass to him," Mrs. Fisher offered.

Larry shook his head. "Outside he refuses to go on the grass and pees on the concrete instead."

Dennis had an interesting question. "Where is he now?"

"Since he likes cement so much, he's in the garage till I get back."

The waiters were still clearing our dessert plates when the emcee took the stage. The crowd hushed with his announcement that the silent auction winners were about to be revealed.

Larry won a case of nice wine and jogged up to get his prize slip to a round of applause.

Fisher and his wife won a weekend trip to Las Vegas, which surprised me. Financial types were not usually gamblers, but maybe they were going for the shows.

And Dennis won the Hawaii trip he'd bid an outrageous sum for.

They reached the end of the auction, and music began playing through the loud speakers.

Dennis stood and held a hand out to me. "Dance?"

The question took me by surprise. I'd figured this was a dinner and boring conversation function, maybe with some awards or something.

He cocked his head. "Well?"

"Go ahead," Cindy urged.

I put my napkin on the table and stood to accept his hand, which quickly moved to my back to guide me to the open area rapidly filling with couples dancing—slow, intimate dancing. The heat of his touch was doing its brain-fog thing again.

I put my hands on his shoulders as we started to sway to the music.

He pulled me in. First our thighs touched, and then my chest met his.

I didn't push away.

The heat was unmistakable, a dangerous heat that threatened to weld me to him.

His mouth brushed by my ear. "Thank you for coming."

I looked up into his eyes. "Thank you for asking me."

How a week had changed everything. When I'd blurted out that I was his date, I'd meant to antagonize his ex-wife and cause him trouble. Tonight though, it didn't matter if I was using him, or he was using me. It felt good to be in his arms, and I was going to enjoy it.

His hand slipped lower on my back and pulled me tighter against him.

The warmth of his chest against mine, the heat of his breath against my ear made my cares drift away.

Right now I wanted this, and I definitely deserved it. Thinking could wait until tomorrow. The how and the why weren't important tonight, just the who and the where.

I closed my eyes. Him, me, the music and the motion on this dance floor. Nothing else mattered.

CHAPTER 20

DENNIS

HER WARMTH AGAINST ME AS WE SLOW DANCED WAS AN ELIXIR I NEEDED MORE of. The scent of peaches in her hair reminded me of the whiff I'd gotten during that kiss in my office, and I smiled to myself as I played the memory over again.

Having noticed her at Starbucks, I'd wondered what she might feel like in my arms, but I'd never imagined it could be as intoxicating as this.

After the thrashing from the latest article by Sigurd and the harried spin-off workaround, a night like tonight was a welcome break. Family, friends, music, and a warm woman in my arms brought back to me what I had been denying myself for too long.

She looked up at me with soft eyes. "What are you thinking about?"

The question caught me off guard. "Nothing in particular."

"You're not a good liar, Denny." It was the first time she'd used that nickname since the day of our kiss.

I went with at least a partial truth "Nothing, really. I was noticing the peach fragrance in your hair."

"You're deflecting. I can hear the gears turning."

I gave in. "I was thinking how nice it is to be here with you." Saying the words to her didn't feel as awkward as I'd expected, even though it was our first date.

Our first date. The words rattled around my head for a second. My subconscious was clearly voting for more time with her.

She stretched up and kissed my neck. "Me too."

I pulled her in tighter for a few steps and took a chance. "We should do this again."

Everything about her intrigued me. It wasn't just her surprising ability at work to see things from a different perspective, but also her simple grace with the people at the table.

She was a complete package of looks, brains, and class, with modesty to match, plus an extra helping of sass.

As we danced, I was certain of one thing. I had my arms around a woman I didn't want to let go of.

The song stopped and another started, and another followed that. Each song was a suitable slow dance for us, or a waltz for the few couples feeling more formal about their dancing.

Dad wasn't a fan of anything that engendered fast dancing at his gala event. He didn't think it was dignified, and tonight, with Jennifer in my arms, I agreed wholeheartedly.

Nothing that put distance between us was getting my vote, especially with the condition in my pants.

As the music went on, she melted more comfortably against me, if that was possible.

She had to notice my stiff cock pressing against her with every step, but she didn't push away, and she didn't show any alarm. If anything, her steps seemed intended to rub against me, or perhaps it was my imagination, or just the height difference.

The latest song ended and she pulled back, nodding toward a door leading to the courtyard. "Want to go cool off for a bit?"

I released her. "Sure." Backing away, I shoved a hand in my pocket to hide the bulge in my pants as I led her toward the courtyard at the center of the building.

It was chilly outside, and she wrapped an arm around me.

I reciprocated and pulled her around the back of the fountain where we would be shielded from those in the room we'd just left. Literal dancing had been fine, but I was done dancing around what was or wasn't between us. Stopping on the far side, I turned her toward me.

She let out the slightest gasp as I took her face in my hands and moved my head to within inches of hers. The light coming up from the water played on her face, a face that held not concern, but a question.

I hoped my question was the same. "Jenn, did I tell you how lovely you look tonight?'

"Four times."

She'd counted.

"I want..." The words halted as I searched for the right ones.

She wrapped a hand behind my neck, lifting up and closing the distance between us. Her lips did the talking as she took mine, and we resumed where we had left off in my office.

Arms intertwined, hands roamed, and the taste and feel of her mouth and tongue against mine was what I'd craved for days. We were on the same wavelength. I wanted her, and she wanted me.

She broke the kiss and put her hand on my chest. "What did you want to ask?" she said breathlessly.

It took me a second to organize my words, lest I tell her straight out I wanted to fuck her senseless tonight. "I want to take you on a date."

She giggled. "I think this qualifies."

"Then another date, just the two of us."

Her smile widened, transmitting her answer. "I'd like that." She lifted up to meet my lips again.

As we re-engaged our lip lock, her hand squeezed my butt, sending a clear signal of where this was heading later.

My fingers made their way to the slit in her dress and slid up her thigh, looking for the answer to the question that had haunted me since first seeing this dress. *Was she or wasn't she?*

The loud clack of heels on the cement and the yell came from behind her.

"Get the hell away from him, you slut." It was the unmistakable shriek of an angry Melissa.

Jennifer broke the kiss with alarm.

I guided her behind me, shielding her from the hellion that was my ex-wife on the war path.

Melissa's nonsensical yelling continued as she approached. "He's mine."

"Get a grip. We're divorced," I yelled back, holding Jennifer behind me. "Get the hell out of here before I have you thrown out."

"You wouldn't dare."

I stepped forward with a finger pointed at her. "It would be my pleasure." I pulled out my phone. "Are you going to make me call security?"

She hissed and fumed before backing away. "I'll ruin you both." She spun around and clacked off toward the doorway.

I didn't turn back to Jennifer until the door closed behind Melissa.

My girl was shivering. "She scares me."

The feeling was understandable, this being her first and hopefully last encounter with Melissa's hysterics.

"Don't let her get to you. That's what she wants. We should go inside where it's warmer."

Jennifer shook her head. "Not until we know she's gone. I don't need a repeat with everybody around."

"I'll tell security to not let her back in, and I'll bring more champagne so we can plan that date."

The mention of a date brought back her smile, and I gave her a peck of a kiss before marching inside.

The original three bartenders had dwindled down to one, and there was an uncharacteristic line. Eventually I received two flutes of bubbly and made my way to the front.

It was manned by Gus, one of the museum security guards and an LAPD cop. He looked up as I approached. "You shouldn't have. We can't drink on duty."

"Sorry, Gus, not for you."

The cop controlled his laugh.

I hadn't seen Melissa anywhere inside, or in the hallway leading here. "My ex-wife, Melissa Benson, is not to be readmitted under any circumstances."

Gus cocked a brow. "You got it, Mr. Benson, but I didn't see her leave yet."

Shit.

This was my father's party, but I made an executive decision. "Then radio the other guys to look for her and escort her out."

He pulled out his radio as I headed back to the tables.

My jacket was at our table, and I'd bring that out to Jennifer with the bubbly. Gus's guys could deal with Melissa.

~

JENNIFER

I'D MELTED INTO HIS ARMS FROM THE FIRST DANCE. THE SONGS WEREN'T MY favorite, but I had no complaints as he'd held me. I'd molded my body closer to his with each song, feeling the hard strength of his muscles beneath the fabric as he moved.

And that wasn't all that was hard. His reaction to me may have been easier to notice than the liquid heat pooled between my legs, but it was no more real than the arousal I felt enveloped in his arms.

Every shift of his weight brought me closer to demanding he take me someplace private. His suggestion of another date had my mind going to all kinds of naughty places.

All of that had made me forget the original plan for tonight—until his ex appeared, with all her full-throated anger.

Mission accomplished on that front, but oddly, it didn't give me the satisfaction I'd anticipated.

I held my arms tight around me to stay warm while I waited.

The man had thoroughly messed with my brain. I was having trouble meshing my previous view of him as the devil in a suit with the man who'd danced tenderly with me. My cavewoman brain wanted to be naked with him as clearly as he wanted me. The dress was meant to have that effect, and now that it had—and the ex had gotten angry—I could call off the charade and go back to hating him.

But it wasn't a charade, was it? Not once in the days I'd worked with him had I seen even an inkling of the deviousness, the cruelty, the inhumanity I knew he'd been responsible for. What did that mean? Why was he so different? Had he changed? Or had he been something other than I believed all along?

The push came from nowhere.

With a splash, I tumbled over the edge and into the frigid water of the fountain.

The shock of the cold stunned me. I pushed up from the rough bottom and swept the hair out of my eyes. "What the fuck?"

The angry, red face of Melissa Benson screamed at me. "I'll ruin you both. I promise."

CHAPTER 21

DENNIS

I WALKED BEHIND ONE OF THE GUARDS WITH THE CHAMPAGNE FLUTES. HE OPENED the door for me just as I heard Melissa scream again.

"I'll ruin you both. I promise."

She saw us and ran the other way.

"Stop," the guard yelled as he gave chase.

I couldn't see Jennifer anywhere, but splashing in the water got my attention.

It was her.

"My God, what happened?"

"Your psycho ex happened, that's what."

I put the glasses down and slid over the edge, finding my footing in the cold water and splashing my way to my girl.

"Here." I helped her up, and she hobbled with me to the edge.

I heard her dress rip as she struggled to get her leg over the edge.

"Fuck." She held on to me and luckily didn't fall again.

I followed her out and wrapped my coat around her. Pulling out my phone, I told Karl to meet us out front right away.

"Come with me," I urged.

She shivered, and her teeth were starting to chatter.

As we approached the door she asked, "Is there another way?"

"No. This is the only way."

She was clearly embarrassed to walk through the crowd like this, but it couldn't be helped, and she needed to get warm.

I hurried her through as quickly as I could, grabbing her clutch as I passed the table. She'd lost a shoe in the water and was hobbling on one heel.

Karl was out front, and I got her into the backseat.

"Home. Quickly," I told him.

"Yes, sir." He gunned the engine and we sped off.

The water had chilled my lower legs to the bone, and it had been much worse for Jennifer.

I held her tight and rubbed. "We'll get you warmed up in no time, Angel."

She was quiet, save the shivering sounds she made.

Karl had cranked up the heat, but it wasn't enough to thaw either of us.

We arrived at my house in short order, and Karl sprinted to the door. He had a key for when he had to get things for me, and he'd unlocked the door by the time I got there carrying my frozen girl.

"Thanks, Karl. You can lock up and call it a night."

"You sure?"

I nodded. "I got it from here." If I was going to do anything, it was take care of Jennifer.

I heard the deadbolt click behind us as I carried her to the master, dripping all the way.

She still hadn't said anything beyond mumbling a few times that she was cold.

I set the shower to lukewarm, carried her in, and set her on her feet.

We were both in the spray, still clothed with water running off us.

I pulled one of her hands to the wall to brace her. "Can you stand?"

Her dress hung open, revealing her tits. She nodded.

I knelt to pull off her remaining high heel.

Once it was off, she was more stable.

I raised the temperature and turned her slowly in the spray.

The water running off of her began to warm as she thawed.

~

JENNIFER

I KEPT MY EYES CLOSED AND MY ARMS WRAPPED TIGHTLY AROUND ME, LETTING the water run over my body. The shivers slowed. I knew the water was only warm, but at first it had felt scalding hot against my cold skin and was only now bearable.

Dennis kept me rotating in the spray, and the water running down to my feet was no longer icy cold. He adjusted the temperature up again.

I opened my eyes to the marble wall of the shower and turned to face him. The water had made the white shirt of his tux sheer and plastered it to his chest. The chiseled physique hidden behind his daily suit was finally on display. The ridges and valleys of his muscled form warmed me as much as the water. I glanced up to see the smile he wore, having caught me checking him out.

"You're ruining your tux," I said.

Without a doubt the expensively tailored tux he'd worn tonight was dry clean only.

He laughed. "It'll match your dress."

I looked down. The dress was ruined all right, and my boob was hanging out. The tape was no match for the water.

I covered up and wrapped my arms around him. "Why did she do that?"

He turned us so the water ran down my back. "There's no accounting for crazy."

"What did she mean, she'll ruin you?"

"She said *us*."

I waited for an answer.

"I don't care. She's not worth the effort of thinking about. Getting caught up in her mind game is a losing proposition."

Having experienced her rage up close, I wasn't so sure ignoring her was a wise idea.

I'd accomplished my original goal of getting her mad at him, but I hadn't anticipated that her anger would be directed so squarely at *me*. A scowl, a mean comment or two I had been prepared for, but not being attacked like this. She was crazy in a dangerous, unpredictable way.

He rubbed my back, and the brain fog started up again.

"Thawing out?" he asked.

I nodded against his chest—his rock-hard, muscled-like-Apollo chest. "Uh-huh, thank you." It was the most intelligible thing I could manage as I hugged him. I looked up. "We didn't get our last dance."

He started to sway me side to side, without turning as we would have on the dance floor. "This will have to do."

The muffled sound of a phone ringing began. It was coming from his pants pocket. Apparently, he could afford a waterproof phone—mine would have been history in this shower.

One arm let me go as he fished for it.

I didn't want the moment to end. "Let it go," I urged him.

He brought the phone up to eye level. "I can't. It's family." He answered the call. "What?… Slow down. I can't understand a thing you're saying. He turned and opened the door to the shower, leaving me alone under the warm water.

I adjusted the temperature up a bit more.

His voice was agitated. "Where again?… I'm on my way." He put the phone on the counter and rejoined me, lifting my head with a hand to my chin. "I have to go. There's been an accident."

The words chilled me, as if the water had turned cold once more. "Who?"

"My brother. Now listen. You stay here. You can sleep in the room across the hall. Don't you dare leave. I'll talk to you in the morning."

"I can come with you." I knew it was a stupid suggestion as soon as I said it, but I didn't want to be alone.

"No way," he growled. "You're safe here. Don't you dare leave, Angel. Now promise me you'll stay."

I nodded. His calling me *Angel* sealed it.

The next minute he was gone, and I was alone. Ending the evening at his place wasn't supposed to be like this.

Eventually I got out, dried off, and located clothes in the room across the hall—women's clothes. When I found my clutch and phone, I sent a text to Ramona.

ME: Staying out will call tomorrow

It only took her a minute to respond.

RAMONA: Good for you I'm envious

Wait until I told her how tonight had gone.

DENNIS

I PULLED ON DRY CLOTHES AND SHOES AND WAS OUT THE DOOR AND IN MY Jaguar in record time. The cat's engine growled as I sped down the street and almost didn't make the turn at the end. I chastised myself out loud in the empty car.

"Slow the fuck down. One accident tonight is more than enough."

Serena had called, and all I could understand between her sobs was that Josh had gotten into an accident and had been taken to UCLA Medical Center.

The decision to tell Jennifer to stay had been an easy one. After Melissa's meltdown, I wasn't taking any chances. Jennifer would stay under my protection until I understood why my ex had become so unhinged and literally dangerous. It also could have been an act, a small part in some elaborate play of hers that was beyond me to understand. With Melissa, there was no telling. Logic was not her strong suit.

I slowed for the red light, and gunned the car through the intersection when I didn't see any cross traffic. In daytime traffic, it would have taken at least a half hour, but this time of night it would be quicker. The next red light was not so forgiving, with steady traffic from the right.

Following the signs to the hospital's emergency entrance, I parked, grabbed my phone, and ran for the door.

"Where are you?" I asked when my sister picked up.

"Fourth floor ICU, four-four-three-one."

"I'll be up in a sec."

At the elevator bank, it took forever for a car to arrive. But it did, and the door finally opened on the fourth floor. I only got held up at the nurses' station for a minute, pulling my license out of my soaked wallet.

When I found the room, I stopped.

"What happened?" I asked as I entered.

Josh was in the bed with a bandage on his head, attached to IVs and wires galore.

Serena and a nurse were on one side, with Dad and Bill Covington closest to me on the other.

My father urged me into the hallway and away from the door before speaking. "He got pretty banged up in the roll-over. The doctors are reviewing the MRI now and deciding if he'll need surgery."

The word *surgery* when we were talking about a head wound was alarming. "What happened? I told him he shouldn't be driving that pickup of his."

Pickups, especially raised 4X4s like his, were notoriously easy to roll.

Dad shook his head. "He was driving the Jaguar."

"The Jag? That doesn't make sense." Josh's Jaguar was an F-type, same as mine, even the same year. The car had a seriously low center of gravity and was nearly impossible to roll.

"Nevertheless, that's the information we have now. I called young William in to get a little leverage with the hospital."

With three buildings on campus named after Bill's grandfather, the Covingtons had more pull here than the governor.

"He has their neurosurgeon on the way in now, just in case," my father added.

"When can we talk to him?"

"That's for the doctors to decide. He's sedated right now."

I still wanted something to do. "So what's the plan?"

"Nothing much for us to do but wait."

Dad went back into the room, and Serena came out, with a question on her lips.

"That was quite the spectacle Melissa put on."

"No shit. I don't know what got into her."

"Of course you do."

"Do not."

"Do too." She argued as if we were still little kids.

"Then tell me."

"She saw the same thing the rest of us did. I could see it in your eyes. You never once looked at Melissa with the eyes you have for Jennifer."

I couldn't believe I was hearing this. "Huh?"

"Don't *huh* me. I saw you two dancing. It was pretty erotic for two people with their clothes still on."

Dancing with Jennifer had been hot as hell, but I wasn't admitting that to my sister. "She's a good dancer."

"Where is she, by the way?"

I hadn't expected that question. "Back at my place."

"See?"

"It was closer than her apartment, and I needed to get her warmed up before she froze to death. And then you called."

"Uh-huh." She poked a finger in my chest. "I like her, so go slow and don't screw this up is all I have to say."

That was a lie. There was no way she wouldn't bring this up again.

"I like her too."

"Duh." She turned and reopened the door to Josh's room.

I followed her inside. I hated waiting, but there was nothing else to do at this point.

How the hell did he roll the Jag?

CHAPTER 22

JENNIFER

I PRIED MY EYES OPEN ON SUNDAY MORNING, AND THE FIRST THING I COULD MAKE out was the empty wine glass on the nightstand. It brought last night back to me.

The room Dennis had pointed me to across the hall from his was a second master with its own huge bathroom. I'd located a T-shirt and sweats in the dresser and, with a towel wrapped around my wet hair, quickly toured a few of the rooms in the house. I'd steered clear of his bedroom after leaving the shower he'd thawed me in.

Everything about this house was on a scale I'd only seen in pictures, and the kitchen was immense. I had a thing for checking out kitchens in the magazines, wondering what it would be like to have one as nice. His had many of those beat.

I'd waited up for Dennis and located a bottle of wine in the fridge. It had become my companion for the evening when he didn't return. I'd tried to wash away the memory of the evening's shitty conclusion with at least a glass or two too many.

Eventually, the soft bed had beckoned, and I gave up the vigil, hoping his brother was all right, but knowing in my bones that Dennis's absence meant things were the opposite of good. The wine and soft, million-thread-count sheets had brought slumber quickly.

Padding to the bathroom, my tongue now felt fur-coated from the wine. Dennis had a nice setup for guests here, including a fresh, plastic-wrapped toothbrush, toothpaste, and mouthwash.

Wearing the Dodgers T-shirt I'd slept in, I looked like death warmed over in the mirror. Sleeping on slightly damp hair would do that.

A metallic clank sounded down the hall, and I stilled myself to listen. Nothing.

I ventured to the door, and when I cracked it open, the faint aroma of coffee tickled my nostrils.

Somebody was here.

Quickly, I retrieved the fluffy bathrobe from the bathroom before venturing out. He'd probably hired a cook to make him breakfast, and the poor lady didn't know he wasn't here.

When I rounded the corner to the kitchen, I found him with his back to me, working at the stove.

Dennis turned. "Sleep okay?" He didn't have a cook after all.

I nodded and walked his way. "Uh-huh. How's your brother?"

He pointed to the breakfast bar attached to the island. "Coffee's on the counter. Cocoa powder is on the end, if you want."

I wrapped my fingers around the hot cup of java. "Thank you. How's your brother?"

"Josh gave us quite a scare last night, but according to the experts, he'll be okay in the long run. He has a tube in his skull to monitor the inter-cranial pressure."

I shivered at his description. It sounded pretty damned serious to me. "But he'll be okay?"

"Nothing broken. A nasty bump to the head, but he's already driving the nurses crazy. Good thing he has the thick Benson skull."

I spooned some of the cocoa he offered into my coffee and stirred. "What happened?"

He turned off the stove and brought the two frypans over to the counter. "He was driving home and had an accident is all we know. I'll find out more later."

"That smells wonderful." It looked it as well.

"Omelets." He slid them one at a time onto plates.

"When did you get back?"

"About four."

"You should have woken me."

"After last night, you deserved the rest." He lifted the empty wine bottle I'd left on the counter. "And after emptying this, I probably couldn't have woken you if I'd tried."

I broke eye contact. "I didn't drink the whole thing."

"Did you pour the rest down the sink?"

I shrugged, unwilling to lie.

He picked up the plates and walked toward the table in the nook.

I followed with my coffee mug.

The news was playing softly on a TV mounted on the wall.

He set the plates down and held out a chair for me before taking a seat himself. "I want to apologize for the way Melissa acted last night."

"It's not your fault."

"Sure it is. It wouldn't have happened if I hadn't invited you."

"You forget, I sort of invited myself."

"It's still on me."

"I had a wonderful time, up until—"

"The eruption," he offered.

"Yeah. How did you ever..." I stopped before making a complete ass of myself.

He knew exactly where I'd been going. "Marry her?"

I nodded.

"She was an actress before we married, and she was obviously good enough to fool me. It's my fault, really."

"How so?"

"I was in a hurry. Dad was pressuring me, and I gave in."

"That doesn't seem like you."

"I know better now, but at the time, let's just say I wanted to get him off my back. We've patched things up now, but it was what made me leave the family company."

I digested that for a while as we ate. "Did you love her?"

He stared into his coffee cup before answering. "That's a hard one."

"I'm sorry. It's none of my business."

"No." He reached to put his hand over mine. "It's one of the things I like about you. You're frank, and you push me out of my comfort zone."

"I didn't mean to pry." That was the polite thing to say, but I remained curious about how a guy who seemed so level headed and was rich and good looking enough to have his pick of women would end up with such a wicked one.

He pulled his hand back, and I missed the feel of his touch.

"Yes, you did," he said.

The news flashed to the story of the death of Randy Bethman, with a picture of his young wife, Virginia—very young, very pretty Virginia. Black Widow of the Palisades, they'd nicknamed her.

I pointed my fork at the screen. "I hope they fry her ass."

He looked up and followed the commentary for a moment. "Why would you say that?"

"Just look at her. Forty years younger—of course the trophy wife did it."

"You always jump to conclusions like that?"

"It's pretty obvious." The news had published enough details for anybody to see it. "He was poisoned, and she inherits a fortune. She did it for sure. She got tired of waiting for him to croak and hurried things along. I'd bet on it."

"If I ever go to trial, I'd hate to have someone like you on the jury."

"What does that mean?"

"You're ready to convict the woman based on a few things you heard, without having all the facts. You don't know she did it. Neither you nor I can possibly know that."

"You think she didn't?"

"I'm saying jumping to conclusions about someone's character without knowing all the facts is wrong. Why does she deserve less benefit of the doubt than you or me?"

"I..." I was at a loss for what to say after he put it like that.

"Wouldn't you want the benefit of the doubt? I know I sure would."

"I guess you're right." Clearly I wouldn't want to be judged as hastily as I'd judged her.

As I ate the rest of the breakfast Dennis had generously cooked me, I couldn't get past the question he'd just raised without knowing it. *Had I possibly judged him too hastily as well?*

The last memo I'd seen hadn't been conclusive. Instead it had opened another question—one I didn't have the answer to. I definitely didn't have all the facts.

Mom had convinced me years ago that Dennis was responsible, and I'd been working under that assumption ever since, looking for the information that would prove it.

Would I want someone judging me and later only looking for evidence to back up the accusation?

As I looked up from my plate, I realized the man in front of me hadn't exhibited any of the traits I'd suspected him of. The opposite was more true.

Mom had always said he was responsible like it was a fact, but was it? Since I'd started working for Dennis, nothing I'd seen or heard had corroborated what my mother and I had been certain he was guilty of.

He wanted the benefit of the doubt, he said. I'd been denying him that by judging him without compelling evidence—without any evidence, it turns out.

What if I was wrong? The thought chilled me.

I'd passed on information that clearly hurt Dennis, and would continue to. What if he wasn't guilty of killing my stepfather after all?

What kind of person did that make me? Was I the one who should be punished?

He caught me staring at him. "Hey, I shouldn't have jumped on you like that. I'm sorry."

"No, you were right." I smiled up at him. "I don't know all the facts."

He couldn't know that I was talking about more than the TV news story. I was convinced now that those other memos held the key.

"What's bothering you, Angel?"

It unnerved me to hear him call me that again. I liked it, but whereas I'd thought he might change his opinion once he learned I was an avenging angel, now I worried I might be a malevolent demon in an angel's disguise.

I decided he deserved an honest answer. "Pondering my future."

He laughed. "Angel, you have a very bright future ahead of you, starting with another date after this last one didn't end so well."

I was tempted. "I really have some thinking to do." A lot of thinking was more like it.

The file I'd retrieved for Hydra gnawed at me. If I passed it on as I had the others, wasn't I passing judgment before the evidence was in? Or was this another hormone vs. neuron battle? This had been so much easier before all this gray invaded my black-and-white view of this man.

He wasn't giving up so easily. "I know just the place. It's where I go when I have to sort things out."

"But—"

"No arguing. You're coming with me."

"I don't have anything to wear."

"There's plenty to choose from upstairs."

"I don't want to wear any of your ex's clothes, thank you very much."

"None of it is Melissa's."

"Then not any of your ex-girlfriends' stuff either."

"It's all my sister's."

"Oh." Once again I'd jumped to a conclusion without any facts.

"Kelly stays with me when she comes out. You two are about the same height."

He didn't seem to realize more than height went into fitting into another woman's clothes.

I stood and picked up my plate.

"Leave it," he said. "I'll clean up while you get dressed."

I put the plate down and retreated toward the bedroom.

"Shorts," he called after me.

Once the door closed behind me, I sent another text to Ramona.

ME: Out with Dennis don't know when I'll be back

She'd want all the details, and I didn't have time for the half hour Ramona would hold me on the phone if I called. I was picking out a top when my phone chirped with her reply.

RAMONA: I warned you about having too much fun

I couldn't decide on the right response to that, so I didn't respond at all.

CHAPTER 23

Jennifer

I slid into the seat of his sleek car. "Where are we going?"

He gave the same answer as the last four times I'd asked. "A place I like to go to decompress. I think you'll like it."

The Jaguar had the smell and look of luxury with supple leather on the seats, and even the dash. The sound when we started out was not obnoxiously loud, but had the throaty exhaust melody of a powerful motor.

I gazed out the window, watching LA go by as we made good progress in the light weekend traffic.

Eventually he turned west on Venice Boulevard, and our destination became clearer. In three miles on this course, we would run out of roadway and be facing the Pacific Ocean.

I'd been wondering, but he hadn't offered any more information about his brother, so I asked. "What happened with Josh last night?"

"All we were told is that he had a single-car accident and rolled the vehicle."

"Was he drunk, you think?"

"Dad asked the same thing. Point zero two—not even close to the limit.

It's all strange. He's not the type to drive too fast and lose control. We'll know more later when we get the accident report."

"But you said he'll be okay, right?"

"I called this morning, and the news is better. He'll be plenty sore, and he's under observation because of the head wound and the fact that he lost consciousness, but I think so. They just have a protocol to follow."

He turned left onto Speedway, the last road paralleling the beach, and in a few blocks, he stopped. A push of the opener button, and a garage door rolled up.

The houses in this area were narrow. We climbed the stairs to the main living area above.

The home was very open, with a parquet wood floor and a full-width window on the beach end of the house.

He ushered me through a sliding glass door to the patio, which boasted a marvelous view of the wide sand of Venice Beach.

"What would you like to drink?" he asked.

"Soda is fine, or just water."

"In life you have to make choices, so which is it?"

"Water, then."

While he fetched the glasses, I sat on the comfortable couch and surveyed the scene: people walking just below us on the Ocean Front Walk, couples on the sand, a guard tower that looked straight out of *Baywatch* to the right toward the Muscle Beach outdoor gym, and the fishing pier off to my left.

He'd said we had to make choices in life, and he was absolutely right. I had to choose the woman I would be—the cocksure one of a few weeks ago that knew in her bones how evil he was, or the woman he challenged me to be, the one who would demand evidence to evaluate before pronouncing judgment on him. Life had been simpler before his challenge, and I didn't know if I could do it, even if I wanted to. Mom had been so sure. For years, I'd believed my duty was to be the avenging angel.

He appeared from behind and handed me a glass of ice water. "Deep in thought, I see. Anything I can help with?"

"No, just enjoying the view."

"Close your eyes."

"Why?"

"Stop asking silly questions for once. Just close your eyes."

I relented and did as he asked.

"What do you hear?"

Kids had been bicycling by a second ago. "Kids."

"And?"

The muffled voices of people walking by caught my attention. "People talking."

"Behind that."

The noise of the teenagers slowly receded. I smiled as I realized the answer. "The waves."

"Very good. Now focus on that and relax."

I lay back and focused to bring the ocean sounds forward out of the background. The soothing, rhythmic sound became easier to pick out as I stayed still.

"Now synchronize your breathing with the waves."

I had trouble with that because the waves were slower than I wanted to take breaths. "I can't. It's too slow."

"Take deeper breaths. You can do it."

I opened my eyes to confront him, but his were closed. I sat back again. "If it's so easy, you do it."

"I do it every time I come out here. I think you're scared to try, scared to learn."

I wasn't scared of anything. "Shut up. Give me a minute." I took in a deep breath and concentrated on listening. Deep breath in, deep breath out, deep breath in, deep breath out. Eventually, I got the hang of it.

"Now," he said. "Ask your question."

"What question? I don't have a question."

"Sure you do."

I didn't argue further, and instead did as he asked. Deep breath in, deep breath out. *Which woman am I?* Deep breath in, deep breath out. *Which woman do I want to be?* Deep breath in, deep breath out.

It didn't take long for the answer to become clear. Deep breath in, deep breath out. I never shied away from a challenge, and I couldn't live with myself if I settled for less than I could accomplish.

He would get what he wanted. I would accept the challenge he hadn't realized he'd set for me and give him the benefit of the doubt. I'd demand evidence.

"I heard that," he said.

I still had my eyes closed, but I could envision him pointing an accusatory finger at me. "You heard what?"

"You got the answer. It works every time."

"But I didn't even have a question."

"Yes, you did. Now what was it?"

I fumbled for a way out of this. "Okay, I was deciding if I should let you kiss me again."

He laughed. "That's not a real question."

"How can you say that?"

"Because you already knew the answer was yes."

"If you don't like my question, what was yours?"

"I can't say. Mine is X-rated." His words sent heat to my core.

I sat up, opened my eyes, and threw the aptly named throw pillow at him. "I am wearing underwear, if that was your question."

We had gone from some yoga-style relaxation technique to talk that brought me back to all the things I'd like to explore with him if he wasn't really the devil in a suit.

He laughed again. "No, that was last night's question. And what was the answer, by the way?"

"I'm hungry."

"Now who's deflecting?"

"Do you have anything to eat here, or do we have to go out?"

He stood and grabbed my hand. "Stand up and close your eyes."

I gave in and stood. "Not again."

His arms encircled me. "Keep your eyes closed."

He pulled me close and my chest pillowed against his, bringing back vivid memories of last night on the dance floor, last night before the fountain.

His breath was hot against my ear. "Now tell me honestly. Do you want to kiss me again?"

The heat of his body against mine would allow only one answer. I nodded.

He released me without the kiss I'd requested. "See? I was right."

I huffed. "And you're a tease."

"I wasn't the one wearing the waist-high slit last night."

"Thigh high," I corrected him.

He pulled me back into the house. "We're going for a walk. Trust me. Later, I won't be teasing you."

The naughty implications melted my panties on the spot. "Those are dangerous words, mister."

"Better be careful. You have no idea how dangerous I can make things. Now, let's get going."

"What if I like dangerous?" The statement escaped my mouth before I realized how un-Jennifer I'd suddenly become.

The smirk he wore grew to a smile. "I'm going to remember you said that. Let's get a move on, Angel."

There it was again. *Angel.* The word that sent a tingle through me every time.

～

DENNIS

I TOOK HER HAND AND LED HER OUTSIDE.

The woman was an enigma—smart, talented, a little sassy, and a lot sexier than she gave herself credit for.

We walked the path along the edge of the beach toward my favorite taco stand in this part of town. Her head was on a swivel, taking in the sights, all with an excited smile pasted on her face.

I squeezed her hand. "Ever been down here before?"

"No." She looked away. "I've only been to the beach at Santa Monica once."

"Only once? If you live in LA, you have to come to the beach more often than that. Here you get away from the endless city. Half the horizon has no people and no buildings."

She shrugged. "It is nice."

Perhaps I was happier to be with her than she was with me. That was a disturbing thought.

Something had bothered her this morning that she wouldn't talk about, but true to form, the beach-breathing technique I'd long practiced had helped her deal with whatever it was. I'd seen it in her face as she'd silently matched her breaths to the ocean waves. It had given her a moment of calm.

In time, I hoped she'd trust me enough to open up. "Have you lived with your sister's family long?"

Her smile dimmed. "Since Mom died. It's just the three of us now: me, my sister, and Billy."

"What happened to Billy's father?"

"He didn't stick around long. Ramona's raising Billy herself."

My heart went out to them. "That must be hard." With what my father meant to me, I couldn't imagine a boy growing up without one. It would leave a huge hole, and the workload for Jennifer's sister had to be tough without the father around to help.

We kept walking.

Jennifer didn't elaborate, and I didn't pry.

Taco Bandito was just opening up when we arrived.

I knew how she liked her coffee from Starbucks, but I had no idea what food she preferred. "I forgot to ask if Mexican is okay."

"Sure." She perused the menu for a second. "Are the chicken tacos any good?"

"Everything is good. Just take it easy on the salsa."

While I ordered for us, she took the drinks to a table under an umbrella.

I joined her with the chips and salsa.

She absentmindedly twisted the silver ring on her finger.

I pointed to her hand. "You do that a lot."

She pulled her hand away. "Sorry."

"It's special to you, isn't it?"

She looked down at the ring with a smile. "It was the first ring my stepdad gave my mother."

"That is special."

She tilted her head and nodded. "It's so I don't forget them." Her eyes misted over with the memory.

The sentiment was one I understood.

I grabbed a chip. "Freshest chips on the beach."

She was ready to dip a chip in the red salsa when I warned her. "You'll want to stick to the green."

"Really?"

"You won't be able to handle the red."

"Is that so?"

"I can see it in your eyes. You're scared."

She heaped the red on her chip and took the whole thing in her mouth.

I stuck to the green and waited for the fireworks. I'd just learned something interesting about her—she couldn't resist a dare.

In less than a minute, beads of sweat had formed on her forehead, and she sucked down half her Coke.

I waved my next chip at her. "I warned you."

"It's not that bad." She switched to the green after that. Three chips later she said, "It is hard for her."

I was glad she'd decided to open up about her sister and nephew. "How old is he?"

"Seven, and he's a good kid. I help out, and with the two of us, we make it work."

Our order was up, and I went to retrieve the plates.

She took a small sip of her almost-depleted Coke. "I wanted to thank you for the raise."

"You already did."

"We've been wanting to move into a larger place for a while. Billy's getting a little old to sleep in his mother's room."

In my quick visit, I hadn't guessed that her apartment was that small. "Have you found a place yet?"

"Not yet. Ramona's doing the scouting. I'm pretty flexible. The most important thing is for her to be happy with it."

I asked, and she continued to tell me about her sister and nephew. I soaked it all up. Her dedication to her family struck a chord with me.

None of her sentences began with *I*. Everything was *we*, and sometimes *they*. Her attachment to them seemed almost maternal. She'd stepped up to replace her mother in providing for her sister and nephew.

She asked about my family, which took longer, running through my two brothers, two sisters, and their whereabouts.

I pushed my empty plate to the side. "You mentioned your mother passed a little while back. What about your father? Is he able to help at all?"

Her expression told me instantly I'd stepped in it. "My stepdad died just before she did. An industrial accident."

"I'm sorry to hear that."

I didn't have anything better to say to comfort her. My friend Bill Covington had lost both his parents, his mother long ago and his father recently. It had taken a toll on him.

She lifted a chip from the basket, scooped up a large helping of the red salsa, and offered it to me. "You made me eat one."

There it was again, her change of subject. This was another taboo topic.

I wasn't going to push the conversation. Her expression when I'd brought up her stepfather had been more anger than remorse. He'd obviously wronged her somehow.

There was a story hidden there, and I wasn't trusted enough yet to share it. Perhaps someday I would be. She wasn't one to grant trust quickly, it seemed, but I could be patient.

I wouldn't back down from a challenge either, and I had enough of my Coke left, so I accepted the chip and put on a brave face while it scorched my mouth.

CHAPTER 24

JENNIFER

DENNIS DIDN'T HESITATE. "ANYTHING FOR YOU."

He took the chip and shoved it into his mouth, chewing loudly. He swallowed and opened his mouth, taking a deep breath and blowing out before finishing his Coke and chugging half his water glass.

I loaded up another chip and held it up to him.

He didn't flinch and ate the second just as quickly, washing it down with more water. The sweat on his brow showed he wasn't immune to the heat.

"Did I pass the test?" he asked.

I nodded with a giggle. Mom had told me one of the indicators of a guy's interest was how much of your bad cooking he'd put up with. I got goosebumps realizing Dennis's interest in me matched mine in him.

"Can we go back now?" I asked.

He took his tray to the trash, and I followed with mine.

A seagull cawed loudly as it flew by, looking right at me with accusatory eyes.

I cringed.

"You cold, Angel?"

"I'm fine," I lied.

I wasn't fine, and even the bird knew it.

Now I'd lied to Dennis.

I hadn't meant to, but when he asked if I'd been here before I couldn't share that Dad and I had once ridden bikes on the beach path near here all the way to Marina Del Ray. That had been the last weekend I'd shared with Dad before the accident.

We'd laughed, raced a bit, stopped for food, laughed some more, and had a great afternoon. It was the way I wanted to remember him: carefree, happy, and alive. Then he was gone.

Instead of walking back south, Dennis pulled me along to the north.

"Hey, that's the wrong way."

The gull cawed again and swooped toward us.

Dennis was stronger than me, and the tug-of-war was no contest. He stopped, and I was instantly in his arms, shielded from the angry bird.

I didn't fight him. Instead I relished the contact, the safety of his embrace.

I knew he hadn't meant to hurt me by asking about Dad, but that didn't make the questions any easier. They were normal questions about family, siblings, parents, and history, but it was a history I couldn't share with him.

He still had a full complement of family members. He couldn't understand the anguish of losing one, much less two.

It was hard to talk about, like the loose sand was harder to walk on than the cement of the path we'd taken here.

He rubbed my back. "I'm not done with you yet, Angel."

"But I thought—"

"No. You didn't think. You assumed. You know what they say about the word *assume*?"

"Yeah, it makes an ass out of you and me."

Today seemed to be one big lesson in not drawing premature conclusions.

"I told you I was taking you somewhere to relax so you would forget what's bothering you."

"And we did. On your patio. Remember? Your silly wave listening."

"On a scale of one to ten, how relaxed are you?"

I didn't have an answer for that, so I chose the safe middle ground. "Five."

"That won't do." He started off again and pulled me along.

It was getting more crowded along the boardwalk. The little shops had rolled up their doors and were hawking their sunglasses, T-shirts, hats, and all manner of things.

He stopped at a skate and bike rental booth. "Can you skate?"

"It's been a long time."

He pulled me up to the counter. "Then it's time again."

They handed me roller blades and pads.

When he took off his shoes, I noticed something.

"Who was the lucky girl?" I pointed to the name tattooed on his ankle: DEB. I laughed. "Do you have Melissa hidden somewhere else?"

He didn't join my laugh, and for a second I feared I'd overstepped a hidden boundary.

"I'm sorry. I didn't mean to pry." Another lie of sorts, but a white one.

"Deborah Ellen Benson, my cousin. She was kidnapped as a child. And... well, the kidnapper died in a shootout with the cops. We didn't get her back, and we never even found her body... We all got these a few years ago."

"I'm sorry."

"We don't talk about her. It's too painful." He smoothed a finger over the letters and blinked back the hint of a tear. "But she's not forgotten."

The sentiment was one of the sweetest things I'd heard a man say in a long time.

"I'm sorry," I repeated. Delving into the particulars seemed over the line, so I didn't ask any of my morbid questions. I placed a hand on his knee, and for a few moments, his pain and mine were linked. We'd both suffered tragedy and loss.

"Thank you. " He patted my hand and sniffed in a breath. "Enough of that. Today is for new memories, not reliving old ones."

We laced up and strapped on our pads in awkward silence.

He'd given me a peek behind his shell, and I'd learned another thing about Dennis I hadn't suspected.

He slapped on a smile. "Ready to go?"

He had me start out ahead of him, presumably so he could pick up the pieces and administer first aid when I fell.

After a few hundred yards, it all started coming back to me, and I didn't feel like such a klutz anymore.

We zoomed up north past the Santa Monica Pier and kept going.

It was a beautiful southern California day with a light, cool breeze off the water—nothing but sunshine and the smell of the ocean.

"How much farther?" I asked.

He pulled ahead of me, turned, and started skating backwards. "To the end."

"Where is that?"

He smiled. "You'll see."

I pointed ahead. "Bicycles."

He flipped to skating forward in time to dodge the two-wheeled menaces. Some of the kids either didn't appreciate the rules of the road, or merely didn't have good control, but we routinely had to dodge them.

We were almost to Malibu when the path ended at a parking lot up against the hills of the Pacific Palisades.

As we returned, we passed numerous bikini babes of the kind you saw all over TV—girls skating the path in barely there swimsuits. Yet every time I checked, Dennis's eyes were either on me or looking out for the next hazard on the path. This was the kind of attention I could get used to.

We made a pit stop at the Santa Monica Pier, and I almost asked if we could go on one of the rides, but I chickened out. Dennis was calling the shots, and I was along for the ride.

He bought us waters and handed me one.

After several good slugs, I put the cap back on my bottle. "Why did we have to go so far?"

"I'll tell you when we get back to the house." He had me lead and insisted on skating behind me.

I preferred it when he chose whether to dodge left or right, meeting others on the pathway. "Why can't you go first?"

"I could, but I like the view from back here better."

I laughed. I knew he didn't mean the ocean or the beach.

We skated on, and two more attempts to get him to answer my question were for naught.

Back at the rental shop, we returned the roller blades and retrieved our shoes.

I sidled up next to him as we walked back. "Are you going to tell me now?"

"I said when we get back to the house. You have to learn patience, girl."

Today everything was a lesson. "Denny, you're being annoying."

"I'm being consistent, Angel."

I didn't have a comeback to that, so I put my arm around him. This had been fun, and not something I would have thought of.

His arm came over my shoulder, pulled me tight, and he adjusted his stride to match mine.

I glanced toward him.

He smiled back.

All I saw beyond him was the expanse of the ocean—no buildings, no people, just the two of us, sunshine, and warm sand. Being with him had lightened my mood to match the brightness and warmth of the day.

DENNIS

BACK AT THE HOUSE, I FOLLOWED HER UP THE STAIRS TO THE MAIN LEVEL. THE way her ass looked in those shorts from down here almost had me drooling.

Once upstairs, she turned and asked again "Why did we have to go so far?"

I put down my water bottle. "Did you finally stop thinking about what it was that bothered you this morning?"

She lolled her head back. "Yeah."

"That's why. I wanted your full attention."

Her eyes narrowed. "For what?"

I cupped her head in my hands. "For this." I brought her in for the kiss I'd promised earlier—the kiss we should have gotten to last night. The kiss I'd waited patiently for.

She didn't waste any time meeting me. Her lips tasted salty from the exercise. At work she dressed demurely, but as soon as I had her in my arms, the passion beneath her cool exterior came out. Her hands clawed at me, pulling her soft form closer.

My cock went hard in an instant. She wasn't holding back, and we were going to take this where it could have gone, where it *should* have gone last night—just without the sexy red dress.

Our tongues sought connection and began the sensual dance of learning one another.

She was hot against me as I searched to feel the hardness of a nipple under my thumb.

She squeezed my butt, and I gave her back the same as she ground herself against my erection, making it difficult to hold back from ripping her clothes off.

I pulled back and broke the kiss. "I need an honest answer."

She looked up at me and blinked. "Yeah?"

I needed her to commit now or back away before we started. "I'm not a nice guy."

"So you say."

"No. I'm dangerous. We need to stop now if you're not ready for that."

She pulled away.

I'd misjudged her.

CHAPTER 25

JENNIFER

YESTERDAY I WOULD HAVE BACKED AWAY FROM DANGEROUS. YESTERDAY I WOULD have run.

I pushed back out of his hug.

His face fell.

Today I probably should as well. But the rebel in me had another idea. I pulled my shirt over my head.

"Bring it on." I launched myself into his arms and back into the kiss. I speared my fingers into his hair. As his hands found my ass and lifted me, I wrapped my legs around him.

He might be the devil, he might be dangerous—and I'd been warned—but this afternoon I didn't care. I'd tried safe before and ended up with boring too many times.

Our tongues dueled as he kissed me with a fervor equal to mine. He smelled of spice, manliness. We traded breath and desire like wild animals. He lifted me up and down, rubbing against his hardness as he carried me into the kitchen. Guys had kissed me before, but never like this. This was a real kiss, even better than the one in his office. A kiss with a man, not a boy.

I'd had no idea a kiss could convey such passion. His mouth branded me, with intensity and pure, panty-melting lust.

I had never done anything remotely like this. I'd never even gotten beyond second base with a guy on the first date, and here I was shucking off my shirt and attacking him. A week ago—hell, two days ago—I would have stopped and run, but today I was going to taste the wild side of life.

In an instant he'd unhooked my bra with a practiced, single-handed motion and pulled it away as I untangled my arms.

The feel of my breasts against his muscled chest was heavenly, and the heat in my core built to an intolerable level.

He set me down and pulled off his shirt. Then he undid my shorts, pulling them to the floor. With one hand on my shoulder, he slid the other down through my curls.

"Last chance to change your mind."

I gasped as a finger traced my drenched slit and entered my slick heat. It was decision time, but I wasn't going back to boring.

"More," I told him. I was ready to mingle sweat. I reached for his belt.

"No," he told me sternly. He removed his finger and stepped back. "Lose the panties and the shoes."

I pulled them down and removed my shoes, while he took his off as well, though he kept his pants on.

"Stand still," he said.

If anything, the bulge behind his zipper had grown. His hands cradled the weight of my breasts.

Hot tingles shot through me as his thumbs traced lazy circles around my nipples. I remained frozen in place as he pulled his hands away and stood back to look me over.

"Now turn around."

I did. Guessing what would come next, I spread my legs and leaned over, placing my hands on the counter.

"All the way around."

I'd guessed wrong. I turned further until I faced him again.

He looked me up and down with unmistakable heat in his eyes. "Again."

Instead I moved toward him

He pushed me back. "Again." His voice was firm, commanding, and building a naughty heat within me. My pussy sizzled with anticipation. This was unlike anything I had experienced before. The raw power of his voice and the animal look in his eyes demanded obedience.

I'd been told who was in charge here. I turned a slow circle for him, like the gazelle turning for the lion.

His eyes left my body to lock with my eyes. "Angel."

I trembled, waiting for the next words. My nipples were hard with excitement, and my thighs slick with anticipation. All my nerves tingled with impatience for his touch.

"You're beautiful." He pulled me to him, and his mouth devoured mine again.

I laced my fingers through his hair and pulled myself up.

His hands roamed my body, leaving trails of hot sparks everywhere they went.

I rubbed myself against the bulge in his jeans, trying to coax him to show me. Another try at his belt ended up with the same admonition. I wasn't in charge here.

He lifted me suddenly and sat me up on the edge of the counter. A wicked smile came to his face as he took in the sight of my spread pussy.

I was completely open to him. The lights were on, and I wasn't prepared for this. Modesty pulled my legs closed, but he pushed them apart.

He went to a knee.

I gasped as his face approached my crotch. I'd never asked for it, and only one guy had gone down on me before. That had lasted a half a minute before he asked how he'd done. Maybe honesty hadn't been the best policy that day.

Dennis put his mouth to my pussy, and his tongue traced the length of my folds, parting my soaked lips, teasing my entrance. His stubble scraped my thighs as he moved in. His tongue circled my clit several times before he sucked on my little bud.

As his hands went to my breasts, all I could do was run my fingers through his hair as his tongue worked my clit. My legs opened to him as his magic mouth sent sensations crashing over me, in crescendo after crescendo.

I'd had no idea what I was missing. Every stroke of his tongue, every little suck took me by surprise. My nerve endings lit on fire in a way I hadn't experienced before.

His tongue alternately circled my opening and moved up to my clit, stabbing, stroking, and sucking in a delicious torture.

I widened my thighs and pulled at his hair. I needed him closer, harder—just more. Waves of pleasure rolled over me in ever-increasing strength. I had never been this high off the ground as my blood boiled and my eyelids clamped shut.

Every fiber in my body tensed as he drove me closer to the cliff and finally over into the spasms of my climax. My back arched, and my legs shook. I pulled at his hair, threatening to suffocate him against my throbbing pussy. Instead he pulled back, and a thumb pressed hard against my clit, intensifying the final throes of my release.

I had fingered myself to climax plenty of times, but he had shown me the better kind of orgasm. Catching my breath, I opened my eyes to find his belt unbuckled and him shoving down his jeans.

His cock sprang loose and rose against his stomach. He stepped out of his jeans. Dennis was a tall guy, and I should have expected big, but his long, thick, beautiful rod was more than I'd guessed at. I was about to be tested.

I grasped it and pulled.

He groaned a wonderful sound of pleasure. Pulling away, he grabbed the jeans, took a condom from his pocket, and handed it to me.

When I had trouble opening the packet, he tore it with his teeth and handed the little disk back.

He took a finger and wiped the bead of pre-cum off his tip. He put the finger to my lips.

My eyes went wide as I sucked—salty, naughty, forbidden, dangerous.

After he pulled the finger away, I fumbled with the latex.

He put a gentle hand on mine. "This side."

Duh. I didn't have any experience with this. Other guys had never wasted any time and had always rolled the rubbers down themselves. The sounds Dennis made as I rolled it down his length were well worth the wait.

He moved between my legs and began to enter me, stretching my walls, as it had been a while—too long a while.

I bit my lip as he pushed in.

His eyes locked with mine. "Hurt?" He pulled back.

"No," I lied. I didn't want to stop now.

He obviously didn't believe me as he pushed in slowly and slid out again, a little farther each time.

I took in a breath. "Keep going. I want you. Don't stop."

I needed to give him back what he'd just given me, and I knew I could do this. I wanted this. I wanted him. Wrapping my heels behind him, I pulled him to me and let the pressure build.

With a final push he filled me to the limit.

The small flash of pain was quickly overtaken by layers of pleasure as he began to thrust.

I kept my legs behind him, pulling him in with each push and rocking into him.

He groaned. "You are so fucking good, so fucking tight, baby."

My words surprised me. "Then fuck me."

And he did, bouncing against me at a furious pace. The animal in him took hold. There was no holding back now.

Clawing at his shoulders, I pulled him in to kiss me and rocked my hips with his rhythm.

He held my hips, pounded into me and bit my neck. The animal in his eyes matched his actions. Dennis showed me sex on a different, more primal level—rough, urgent, intense.

I gave him back rough as I clawed at him.

Without warning, his thumb went between us and pressed my clit with each thrust.

I lost my battle trying to control the sensations, to drag it out longer. My nerves were on fire as the tension grew and the spasm of ecstasy overtook me again.

He rubbed harder. "That's it, baby. Let yourself go."

My walls clenched around him, and in a few more thrusts I felt him tense up as his orgasm followed mine. I used my legs to clamp him deep within me.

He stayed deep, his cock throbbing, as his mouth met mine for another breathless kiss.

We were both panting too raggedly to maintain the kiss, and he wrapped his arms around me, pulling my breasts to him. His fingers softly rubbed my back as I came down off my high.

I nestled my head on his shoulder, relishing the last throbs of his cock deep inside me. If this was the dangerous life, I was signing up. The post-climax pressure between my legs didn't trail off quickly as it always had before.

He pulled out and lifted me down off the counter, urging me toward the bathroom. "Shower time."

I followed him on wobbly legs, enjoying the view. The red streaks of my scratches on his back contrasted with the white below the tan line of his tight ass.

After disposing of the condom, he turned on the water and pulled me into the shower with him. What followed was the opposite of the sex. His hands soaped me slowly, softly, caressing all my skin from head to toe. Dangerous had morphed into gentle, even soothing.

I did the same for him, enjoying the response I got as I washed his balls and cock. He cuddled with me, rocking me in the water in a motion that recalled our dancing before his awful ex had shown up.

"You okay, Angel?"

I nodded into his shoulder. "More than okay." I hugged him tighter.

He laid his chin on top of my head. "Good."

My pussy still throbbed, reminding me that sex with Dennis was like the potato chip commercial. Even if I'd wanted to, it would be impossible to stop at just once. I'd denied myself too long, but no longer.

The girls at Starbucks who hid behind their lattes and secretly drooled over him had no idea how good it felt to be in his arms.

Jennifer wasn't in Kansas anymore, and she liked it.

CHAPTER 26

Dennis

ON MONDAY MORNING, MY DICK STILL TINGLED AS I RODE THE ELEVATOR UP TO the top floor. I smiled recalling my session with Jennifer in the shower this morning. We'd stayed at the beach house until this morning, and the time we'd spent together had recharged my batteries. It had been way too long since I'd felt this good, and it was all because of Jennifer.

I'd dropped her off at her place on my way in, and I knew she'd be in the office before long.

That would present the next problem. How good would I be at keeping my hands off her in the office, and keeping my feelings under wraps?

Melissa had been an excellent actress—seeming to care when she didn't. I needed to pull off the reverse with Jennifer. Studied ambivalence was the goal.

When I opened the door to the executive area, Cindy spoke before I could ask why my door was already open.

"Your father is waiting."

Since when did Dad come over here unannounced? His usual routine was to summon me to his building.

I walked into my office. "Good morning, Dad."

"Not so good, I'm afraid. Please close the door."

His words were ominous. It took a lot to rattle the great Lloyd Benson.

I closed the door and took my seat behind the desk.

He slid a folder across the desk to me. "The report on Josh's crash."

I took the folder and opened it. "What's the conclusion about the accident?"

"It wasn't an accident."

That stopped me cold. I looked up. "What does that mean?"

"It means the crash wasn't Josh's fault. Keep reading."

I read down the page. Most of it was physical descriptions of the location, a diagram, and most importantly Josh's blood alcohol, which thankfully was a quarter of the legal limit. It would have been terrible if this had been caused by his drinking at Dad's fundraiser.

The second page contained the kicker. "Two bullet entry holes were located on the right rear quarter panel of the subject vehicle and one in the passenger side door."

My jaw dropped. "Three bullet holes?"

Dad nodded. "Keep going."

The next paragraph had another surprise. "Subject vehicle's right rear tire was deflated, and additional holes consistent with bullet entry and exit were located on the outer and inner sidewalls of that tire. Two bullets were recovered from the vehicle interior."

The report concluded that the rollover of the car down the embankment was due to the loss of air in the rear tire and subsequent loss of control.

I looked up after finishing. "It was deliberate?"

"Not much doubt about that. You don't fire multiple shots at a car by accident."

"Do they have any leads?"

"Not yet. Josh couldn't be much help. All he knew was he had just passed a black car when it happened."

I ventured a guess. "Road rage?"

"That is possible, but there are other theories."

"Who would want to hurt Josh?"

It didn't make sense. Josh was mild mannered compared to me, and he hadn't been in much of a position to piss anybody off.

"Nobody comes to mind." Dad rubbed at his goatee. The zinger was coming. "He drives the same car as you."

His implication floored me. "You think the bullets were meant for me?"

"You have had a rather nasty public fight with that Cartwright fellow."

I'd called Carson Cartwright a few choice names, but that was all.

I shook my head. "That's a financial spat. Resorting to violence doesn't seem his style. He's a boardroom bully, not a street fighter."

"How can you be certain? The man is a snake."

Dad had expressed his opinion of Cartwright before. The man called himself an activist investor, but he didn't care about any investors beyond himself. *Extortionist* fit better as his title.

I just couldn't be sure. "Is that what you think?"

Dad shrugged. "Do you have a better suspect? I'm here because it makes more sense than Josh being targeted, and I want you to promise me you'll be careful."

"I will."

This was the first time since college I could remember my father asking me to promise anything, and saying yes was a no-brainer. Later I'd have to figure out what being more careful entailed. Carrying a gun seemed extreme.

I closed the folder and slid it his way.

He stood. "You can keep that, and I'm putting the Hanson team on this to see if they can come up with anything more. As far as the police are concerned, I'm afraid that folder is all that we're likely to get."

Cartwright targeting me still struck me as absurd, but I didn't have anything better to offer.

He stopped at the door. "Can I tell your mother you'll be careful?" He had to be very worried to pull that trick out.

"Absolutely."

After he left, I turned to face the window. Somewhere out there was Josh's attacker. I quickly discarded the idea of verifying Cartwright's where-abouts Saturday night after I realized Dad could be on the right track. I hadn't met Cartwright, but I doubted he was personally brave enough to carry out what had happened to Josh. But I couldn't rule out his hiring somebody. That scenario upped the odds that Dad was right.

∾

JENNIFER

. . .

Dennis had dropped me off at home early this morning.

Ramona was herding her son toward the door when I came in.

Billy rushed to hug my legs. "I missed you."

I hugged him back. "And I missed you too."

Ramona arched a brow. "You look tired. You'll have to tell me all about it later."

I shot her my best evil eye. "Later."

She opened the door. "Come on, we gotta get you to school."

Billy let go of me, and in a moment I was alone.

The apartment looked different, a little more drab, like my life before this weekend—plain vanilla, safe and drab instead of dangerous and interesting. Brushing aside the useless thoughts, I hurried to get ready for work—the work where I'd be back with Dennis, but with everybody else around we be required to abstain from any public displays of affection.

I hadn't talked to him about avoiding PDA—a pretty big oversight. But I decided our weekend would be my little secret until we talked, although *little* didn't describe it very well. Spending the weekend with the CEO sounded wrong. Had it been merely a hookup, or time with my new boyfriend?

I started changing and smiled as the word rolled around in my head. *Boyfriend* sounded good. We hadn't discussed anything. Was I getting ahead of myself by assuming we'd get together again? I mean it had only been a weekend.

By the time I was ready to leave, I'd talked myself out of *boyfriend*, but still didn't like *hookup*.

Why was I overanalyzing this? It was what it was—fun, interesting, exciting, and soothing at the same time. It wouldn't be right to categorize it yet. It had been something completely outside my previous experience—not just the sex, but the way he talked to me, and the way he looked at me.

Out of habit I checked my email. I smiled when I didn't find anything from Hydra.

I closed and locked the door and started counting.

One hundred and three, when I reached my parking space. I had a habit of counting the steps to my car in the morning as a way of clearing my mind for the day ahead. It was always one hundred and nine or ten.

It had only been a day, and already things were different.

Jennifer has gone from Kansas to Oz.

∾

I MIGHT HAVE TAKEN FEWER STEPS TO MY CAR, BUT THE ELEVATOR WAS JUST AS slow and just as hot this morning on its trip to the top floor.

Once inside my office, I busied myself. Ignoring the temptation to wander down to Dennis's office was like staring at a piece of chocolate cake just out of reach after a long fast. The strain interfered with my concentration, and I ended up having to reread sections of the report I was studying. My legs were covering more ground this morning, but my eyes weren't.

After an hour I'd reached my limit with the endless Stoner documents and turned to face the expansive window. The coastline lay in the distance.

Closing my eyes, I recalled Dennis's technique and took a deep breath in followed by a slow deep breath out. How would I handle this work situation? Deep breath in, deep breath out. *How do I handle it?* Deep breath in, deep breath out.

When it came to me, I opened my eyes and stood, refreshed and relaxed —another Dennis Benson benefit. The coffee machine beckoned, and that was an urge I didn't need to put off.

When I turned the corner to the coffee room, there he was. We were on the same wavelength coffee-wise.

"Good morning, Mr. Benson."

He turned with a creased brow. "What did I do to go back to Mr. Benson?" The hint of a grin escaped to tell me he was messing with me.

"Sorry, boss. Good morning, Dennis." The room was empty save us, but that could change at a moment's notice, so I didn't add anything about the weekend.

His grin increased as his eyes traveled over me.

I couldn't hold back my return smile at his appreciation of what he saw. "We should talk."

His smile disappeared. His words came out curt and business-like. "I can't fit you in until the end of the day."

I nodded. I'd meant now, but I'd been put in my place, and coldly, officially. This was work, and here he was king.

As he passed, I turned to find Larry behind me. I hadn't heard him approach. I moved to the machine, and it started concocting my java as soon as I punched it in.

Larry came up to the counter and rinsed out his cup. "Exciting night at the museum, huh?"

I watched the coffee pour. "I could have done without the swim."

He sucked in a breath. "She's a real piece of work."

I was tempted to correct him to *piece of shit*, but this was the office. "That's one way of putting it. What is her deal, anyway? I didn't do anything to deserve that."

Larry might know some of the history that Dennis hadn't been willing to share.

"You know that saying *hell hath no fury*? It was written with her in mind."

"But how dare she? We only met once."

"Who knows? I'd be careful around her. She's capable of pretty much anything."

He made her sound like a complete psycho.

I pulled my steaming cup from under the spout. "What happened between them?"

He put his empty where mine had been. "Dennis married her in sort of a hurry. I warned him, but his father was pressuring him. This was while he was at his dad's company, and his father had the idea that Dennis wouldn't be mature enough to follow in his footsteps until he was a family man, so to speak." He put air quotes around that last part. "Dennis has never been good at reading women, and he fell for Melissa's act." Larry punched in his coffee preference.

I waited for more.

"She's a social climber, wanted Dennis's name and money, and when he put his foot down on the spending side, she threatened divorce. I guess she didn't expect him to take her up on it. You notice she didn't go back to her maiden name, Melissa Kaltehande."

I joined him in a chuckle at the name, which sounded like German for cold hands. Cold heart was more like it.

"If they dislike each other so much, why is she still on the board?"

I'd chickened out on asking Dennis this directly. Letting her stay on the board only gave her another way to cause trouble for him.

"Part of the divorce. It was a trade-off for him to retain more shares, and she doesn't have enough support on the board to cause any serious problems. I wouldn't have done it, but it was his call."

I sipped from my cup and waited, hoping for the next juicy detail.

"She's been hassling him ever since with the courts, demanding a redo on the divorce settlement. She'll never be satisfied, if you ask me."

I liked this version of Larry better than gala-night Larry. Perhaps all it took was Dennis setting him straight, or for him to be sober.

"Wasn't she an actress before?"

He pulled his finished cup from the machine. "She was on a series for three years, but she only got that job because Daddy was the show runner. Daddy's retired from the business now, and I heard she developed such a reputation as a diva that she's not likely to get another gig as good as that one."

"Dennis called her crazy."

"No. She's crazy like a fox. She'll act crazy or nice, depending on what it is she wants. She's a manipulator, and with someone as logical as Dennis, crazy works for her because it gets under his skin."

I sipped again from my cup. "I'll go with total bitch."

A nod was his only response. "You and Dennis looked pretty cozy out there on the dance floor."

I had to nip this in the bud. "Dennis's idea. He wanted to act that way to piss her off."

"It worked." Larry's expression indicated he bought my line.

"Yeah, more than I expected." This topic wasn't a good one to linger on. "How's the dog?"

He added sugar to his cup. "We'll see about tonight, but yesterday no mistakes, thanks to your advice about the mats. I owe you one. He was driving me crazy."

"I'll keep my fingers crossed for you and Binky." I stirred my cup and walked toward the door with a much better feeling about Larry this morning, especially his devotion to Dennis. Once again there was a chance I'd jumped to a premature conclusion.

I turned around before I reached the door. "Hey, I know this is going to sound sort of stupid…"

He chuckled. "Go ahead. I majored in stupid."

"I need to find some files for the Stoner deal, but the filing system is so confusing here with all the numbers. How do I navigate it to find something specific?"

He nodded. "I know what you mean. Each of us has an index for our department, but if you need something broader, talk to Cindy. She can set you up with a company-wide index."

That company-wide index must be what Hydra had.

"Thanks. I'll do that."

Back in my office, I tried to stay awake while taking notes on the endless Stoner documents. The ringing of my cell provided a break. The screen had a name from long ago—Suzanne from college, a person I hadn't heard from since graduation.

I answered hesitantly. "Hello?"

"Jennifer. It's Suzanne Murtog from Pepperdine."

"Hi, Suzanne. I remember. How have you been?"

"Good. I'm new—well, not new in town, really *back* in town, and I wanted to see if we could get together at lunch to catch up."

The request seemed a bit odd in that we hadn't been very close at school.

"Sure." I needed a break from the monotony of my reading, and all my work friends had relocated to the Pasadena Hydrocom building.

"You're at Vipersoft, right? I've got an interview in a building near there tomorrow. How about eleven thirty tomorrow at the Panera Bread near you?"

I agreed, and we ended the call. Lunch out would be a welcome change, and with my raise, I could finally afford it without feeling guilty. Plus, I deserved it.

CHAPTER 27

DENNIS

IN THE COFFEE ROOM, JENNIFER HAD ASKED TO TALK, AND I'D ALMOST LET something slip before I noticed Larry.

I'd put her off until later, but now I had second thoughts.

After a half hour, she passed by.

I left my office to follow. When she reached a spot outside the small conference room, I called to her.

"Jennifer, got a sec?" I nodded toward the conference room door.

Her initially flustered look quickly relaxed. "Sure."

I opened the door. The room's vertical blinds were partially drawn.

She followed me in and closed the door.

I pulled the blinds the rest of the way.

She turned. "What can I do for you?"

I approached without a word.

She backed away, stopping at the door.

I put a hand on the wood at either side of her. I kept my voice low. "You said you wanted to talk." I was mere inches from her and could feel her body heat.

The color of a blush rose in her cheeks. "I had a good time this weekend."

"That was the idea. I did too." I didn't add that it had been the best time in what seemed like forever.

Her breath was halting. "We need to...to talk about how we're going to handle it."

I cocked an eyebrow. "It's pretty simple. I'll pull down my zipper, and you can handle it any way you want." Her peachy scent invaded my nostrils, and it took all my will power to not move closer.

She giggled. "This is serious. How are we going to handle the situation here at work?"

"I'll lock my office door before I take you over my desk. Is that good enough?"

She pushed against my chest. "Cut it out. This is serious."

"I was being serious. You drive me crazy, and you are definitely getting introduced to my desk."

"People will talk. Larry's already suspicious."

"Let them." My cock was getting all kinds of ideas, just talking about this, and I inched closer, anxious to feel her body against mine.

She stomped her foot. "You might not care, but I do. People will think I got the job because I was...you know..."

Her mood was a sweet angry that made her even more irresistible.

"What? Banging the boss?"

"Yeah. If you were a gentleman, you would understand."

That hurt because I was a gentleman, at least I liked to think so. "I understand. Hush, hush, nobody knows. I can be very discreet."

"And no special favors. You can't act too nice to me, or they'll get ideas."

"Right, mean boss it is. I can be mean."

"Be serious."

"I am," I lied.

Being mean to her was the furthest thing from my mind. She was going to get the best version of me, not the worst. I couldn't resist any longer and closed the distance until I could feel her tits against my chest, with just the fabric between us.

She looked up. "You're making this hard."

My lips were an inch from hers. "I've been hard ever since the door closed."

She took a long, slow breath. "We can't be alone in the office. You can't be making eyes at me, and I have to stay at my place during the week."

"Those are harsh rules."

"You have to agree. This is important."

"I will on one condition."

She closed her eyes. "What?"

I brushed her lips with mine. "You remember you have a date with my desk at some point." I backed away.

Her chest was heaving as I put my hands in my pockets to conceal what she'd done to me.

I left the room first, and she followed, turning the other direction.

I knew two things. First, it was going to be hard in more ways than one to be near her at work and not be able to touch her. And second, I was absolutely having her over my desk at some point. That would be my reward for behaving myself for the time being.

Larry came around the corner in my direction. "Dennis," he called.

I raised a hand and ducked into the men's room and then into a stall. It would take the effects of my dirty talk with Jennifer a few minutes to wear off, and I wasn't jabbering with Larry in the hallway in my current condition.

The bathroom door opened.

"Dennis, Jay and I need a word with you." Larry had followed me in here.

"I'm busy. Can't it wait a minute?"

"Sure thing. We'll be in your office."

The door closed, and I willed my dick to deflate by visualizing the ocean waves. Unfortunately, my imagination drifted to seeing Jennifer sitting beside me, with her eyes closed, listening to the waves, and me staring at her erect nipples. Blood flowed back to where I didn't want it, and it took another few minutes till I got myself under control. Maybe mean boss wouldn't have this problem. If I stayed horny boss, I would have to sit behind my desk most of the day.

When I returned, the duo had taken up residence in my office, as Larry had warned.

Jay was the first to speak as I sat. "There's been a development."

I nodded and waited. Development in Jay-speak could mean anything.

Larry let the cat out of the bag. "Cartwright filed a 13D this morning."

That wasn't good news. They'd only have to file that with the SEC if they'd accumulated a sizable position in the company stock.

"How much?" I asked Jay.

Jay opened his folder. "Nine percent, actually a little over. About half of it on the down day of the news story last week."

I didn't correct him. It hadn't been a news story, more like a hit piece. "They were already at five before that and we didn't know?"

Larry jumped in. "Not quite."

Jay adjusted his glasses. "They're not required to file until they hit five percent, and it looks like they stayed just under that until last week."

"When did they start buying?" I asked.

Jay turned the page. "About a month before that. Almost all on the day of the prior article from our good friend Sigurd."

I slammed my hand on the desk. "Are they coordinating with that asshole?"

Larry cocked his head. "Wouldn't surprise me."

Jay was more cautious. "We don't know that. Cartwright has a reputation for buying on dips. It could be coincidence because those were the weak days for the stock."

Weak didn't begin to describe it. They were blood-letting days, painful days.

Larry faced Jay. "And what are the odds that they buy on the absolute lowest days of the year?"

Jay's eyes narrowed. "I didn't say it proves anything either way. Until we know who Sigurd is, we don't know anything for sure."

It was a true enough statement, but it ignored the odds.

Larry wasn't giving in. "I say Sigurd works for Cartwright."

"Fine," Jay agreed. "Now all you have to do is prove it."

I had another worry. "What does it say about intentions?"

The SEC required filers to be frank about their intentions for holding a major stock position.

Jay turned another page. "I'll read it for you. Due to the incompetent marketing efforts of the company recently, the filer will be…"

Larry's eyes bulged.

Jay continued. "Working with management to locate better talent—"

Larry lunged for Jay's folder. "It doesn't say that."

Jay held the papers out of Larry's reach and continued. "Better talent with which to staff the marketing function of the company."

I laughed.

"That's not funny," Larry complained.

Jay joined my laugh. "Sure it is."

I pointed a finger at Jay. "Enough of that. What does it really say?"

Jay had trouble controlling his laughter. "It…it says the position is for financial gain while they engage in discussions with the company's management and evaluate the company's status."

Larry shook his head. "That doesn't mean squat."

"Exactly," Jay concurred. "It's a place holder that they can and will change later to say they want changes from us and they're going to challenge the board, or whatever their tactic becomes."

I raised a finger. "It says one more thing. We can expect a visit from them."

"Should we prepare anything?" Larry asked. "Or call them?"

I shook my head. "No way. We give them nothing. We shouldn't make any assumptions about what they want, and certainly none about what we're going to give them, if anything. And, if fucking Cartwright wants to talk, it'll be on my schedule, not his."

Jay tilted his head. "I don't know. I wouldn't antagonize him, if I were you."

I shot back. "Bullshit. Being nice to him wouldn't change a thing. He's a thug and a bully. What he deserves is a swift kick in the nuts."

They departed, and after a few minutes, I pulled out the very first communication I'd gotten from Carson Cartwright, by certified mail no less. It had seemed innocuous enough on the surface. He'd offered his services as a *consultant* to help me maximize shareholder value and went on to list his many accomplishments.

It went back in the drawer, and I cursed myself for not taking steps earlier to fend him off. The letter was his first step in eventually making a case to the shareholders that he was their savior. In failing to avail myself of his advice, I was ignoring the shareholders' interests, yada yada yada.

He'd followed it up with multiple public comments about us, and me in particular. He'd even managed to get quoted in more than one of Gumpert's commentaries. The shtick was an old and well-worn one, and it sometimes played well if the stock suffered setbacks, as we had with the damned Sigurd articles.

He had to be tied into it somehow. There had to be a link.

I wasn't going to leave this to Dad any longer. I strode to the door and opened it. "Cin, get Baird up here pronto."

She lifted her phone and nodded.

A few minutes later Ed Baird, our head of security, was in my office, notepad in hand. "What do you need?"

"You know we've had leaks from the company that ended up in the paper."

He nodded. "I'm still looking for any links to that Sigurd character or the paper."

I raised a finger. "There's been a new development."

He leaned forward.

"I think this is all tied into the Cartwright group, Carson Cartwright in particular."

"You think he wrote the articles? The hedge fund guy? You think he's behind all this?"

I sucked in a breath. "It's possible, but it's more likely he got the info from someone here and paid somebody to write them. So I want you to change tacks and stop trying to find links to the paper. Instead look for anybody here with a connection to Carson Cartwright or his firm."

He wrote on his pad. "You still think it's somebody inside."

"That's what I want to find out."

He rose. "We'll get started right away."

"And Ed, overtime's no issue on this. Whatever resources you need."

"You got it." He closed the door behind him.

Fucking Carson Cartwright. The more I thought about it, the more sense Dad's analysis made. Cartwright's demands had started as a distraction, become an annoyance, then an irritant, and lately a threat. Last month, Jay had pointed out the possibility of a proxy fight materializing. His contacts in the financial community had mentioned rumors of just such potential. Still, a physical attack seemed out of bounds for corporate-raider types. The attack on Josh didn't fit.

AFTER LUNCH, I WAS IN MY DOORWAY TALKING SCHEDULING ITEMS WITH CINDY when Jennifer walked up.

"Do you have time to go over some things?" she asked.

"No," I barked.

She blinked, and the drop in her countenance was immediate. "How about later?"

I gave her another firm answer. "No."

Jennifer spun and slunk back toward her office.

I caught sight of Cindy's questioning expression. "What?"

She pointed at her calendar. "You have time after three."

I put a hand in my pocket. "I need that time to think."

She picked up her pen. "Let me write that down. Three o'clock: time to think about how to be more considerate. Now, how long do you think that will take?"

I turned back into my office and closed the door firmly.

Mean boss wasn't as easy as it sounded.

CHAPTER 28

JENNIFER
(Three Days Later)

IT HAD BEEN THREE DAYS SINCE OUR CONFERENCE ROOM CONFRONTATION—THREE difficult days.

The week had been hectic, with Dennis calling meetings on the Cartwright group left and right.

I'd been assigned to look over everything we had assembled on them. The stack was enormous, given all the SEC reports they'd filed.

Meanwhile, I'd received the master index from Cindy to find the memos I'd been waiting all this time to uncover about Dad's accident, but I hadn't gotten the courage to retrieve them yet. Now that the truth was within my grasp, it frightened me. Dad's death had led to a month of nightmare-filled nights I dreaded reliving.

I also hadn't sent Hydra the information he'd been after. The no-man's land of limbo was where I was stuck. If the memos exonerated Dennis, I'd betrayed him and the company. If the memos proved him guilty, I'd slept with Dad's killer. The situation was lose-lose for me, and procrastination had taken over. If I didn't know the truth yet, I couldn't convict myself of either sin.

Last weekend had shown Dennis Benson to be the opposite of what my picture of him had been based on Mom's accusations.

I exited my office for lunch, but retreated behind my door when I saw Dennis come out of Larry's office. The flush in my cheeks would've been too obvious. Lunch could wait.

WHEN I WAS READY TO CALL AN END TO THE DAY, DENNIS WAS STILL STUCK IN his office with Jay Fisher. I hadn't managed any alone time at all with him since the Monday Cartwright emergence broke.

My rule about avoiding each other at work had resulted in us both being horny and sharing a few late-night phone calls and text messages.

Dennis's demeanor at work had been the mean boss I'd suggested times about ten, and it bothered me more each day—a lot more.

It might be the hell I'd condemned myself to, but that didn't make me feel any better about it.

To brighten my mood, I pulled up last night's texts on my phone.

ME: How about Saturday breakfast on the beach?
    DENNIS: I know what I'm having
    ME: What?
    DENNIS: U
    ME: And what do I get?
    DENNIS: Do you like popsicles?
    ME: Depends
    DENNIS: On what?
    ME: Warm or cold
    DENNIS: Getting warmer right now
    ME: Will it be big enough to be filling?
    DENNIS: You can count on it
    ME: Can't wait
    DENNIS: Have to

The wait for the weekend was killing me. Since it looked like I wasn't getting any time with him today to go over work, I packed up to leave and locked my door behind me.

Cindy collected her purse as I approached and joined me in the elevator.

She punched the button for the garage. "Long day, huh?"

"I'm used to it." What I wasn't used to was the feeling of helplessness at the situation I'd created between Dennis and me.

"I'm worried that Dennis is going to burn out if he doesn't take a little time to relax."

I couldn't tell her how relaxing last weekend had been, and how I planned to relax him this weekend. "I'm sure he'll find the time sooner or later." The thought of the coming weekend sent a tingle up my spine.

"It better be sooner. I've had all the Mr. Grumpy I can take. He's wound so tight, he's going to snap."

The doors opened to the garage level.

She stepped out, but I made a different decision. "I just remembered I forgot a file I need for tonight."

I was responsible for Dennis's mood, and I planned to address it.

"Okay. See you tomorrow."

I waved as the elevator doors closed.

Back upstairs at Dennis's door, I listened for a few seconds.

Hearing no sounds of conversation, I let myself in and closed the door behind me.

He looked up from his papers. "I have to finish this response." He smiled, but then looked back to his desk and the smile faded.

I pulled the pins from my hair as I approached. "I'll let you work."

He flipped a page. "You shouldn't be in here."

Shaking out my hair, I walked around his desk, and put my purse on the corner. "It's my rule, so I'll break it if I want to."

He didn't look up. "Capricious, a little?"

"You keep working while I do what I came for."

I rolled his chair back, and he looked up at me, surprised.

When I knelt and reached for his zipper, surprise became delight.

His eyes went wide. "We can't be caught like this."

I quickly loosened the belt and zipper to pull out my prize. "Then you'll have to be quiet, won't you?"

He spread his legs and pulled the lever to lower his chair. "Did you know I've fantasized about this?"

I licked the tip of his cock. "I guessed." After undoing two buttons on my top, I took the quickly hardening rod in my mouth. I started the popsicle treatment I'd planned for the weekend just a little early.

He quickly grew under my hand, tongue, and lips. His light groans told me what he liked. He leaned forward to pinch the back of my bra strap through my top and undid the hooks.

I used both hands to stroke him and pull him to my lips. Circling my tongue around the tip and licking the underside pulled the best sounds out of him.

He stretched forward to put a hand down my shirt and knead my breast.

A knock sounded at the door.

My heart stopped.

Shit.

He pulled his hand away.

I scooted back under the desk, and he rolled his chair toward me as the door opened. He lowered my purse to the floor.

"We should go over this press release one more time."

It was Larry. His door had been closed, and I'd been wrong to assume he'd gone for the day.

"How about tomorrow?" Dennis asked.

I went back to work on him. The excitement of almost getting caught made me instantly wet.

"This needs to be on the wire at six in the morning. It has to be tonight."

Dennis's breath hitched as I circled his tip again and tickled the underside of his gorgeous cock.

"I trust you to handle it."

Larry didn't give up. "I really need your input to get this right."

I heard the shuffle of papers above me as I scraped my teeth lightly over him.

Larry tapped the desk. "You okay?"

"Sure. The timing just sucks."

I gave Dennis an extra hard pull and suck after he said that. I was rewarded by a tremor in his legs.

Dennis tried once more to get rid of him. "I'll look at it later and leave you my notes before I leave. How's that?"

"I can wait," Larry replied.

He wasn't going anywhere quickly.

This was going to be a contest. I held back a laugh. Could I get Dennis to come before he got rid of Larry? I went about the task of pulling, licking, and sucking, careful to stay quiet as they talked through the two paragraphs Larry wanted to go over.

Larry didn't say anything more about Dennis's obviously halting speech.

I was going to get lockjaw if this went on too long. I used my hands more, and the tenseness in Dennis's legs told me I almost had him at the end of his rope.

"Thanks. That helps," Larry said.

I heard him scoot his chair back.

"Next time find me earlier," Dennis said. "And lock the door on your way out. I have to finish something here, and I can't be interrupted."

Larry chuckled. "Sure." I heard the click as he turned the lock on the knob and closed the door.

Dennis pushed back and away from me. In an instant he had me out of my hiding place and on my feet.

"That was dangerous," he said softly.

"You promised me dangerous."

I looked down at his cock poking up at me and grabbed it to finish him.

He quickly undid the remaining buttons of my top. It and my bra ended up on the floor. His eyes turned feral as he palmed my breasts. "I promised you something else as well."

I yelped as he turned me around.

"Quiet."

My heart raced as he lifted my skirt, pulled down my panties, and pushed me over against the desk.

"I told you you'd get this."

I braced myself against the cold wood as I heard him rip open the packet. I lifted a shoe to free my ankle from the panties and looked back to see him struggling to roll the latex down his length. "Want me to help?"

"You be quiet."

I spread my legs for him and braced my hips against the desk. The wood was cool against the heat of my breasts. I'd lit the fuse, and he was about to explode.

His tip found my soaked entrance, and he didn't go slow this time.

I yelped again as he pushed in forcefully, seating himself fully in two thrusts, his hips flush to my ass.

He started to pump and grabbed my hair. "Is this what you want, dirty girl?"

"Yes, boss."

It's what I hadn't been able to admit, even to myself. I'd wanted this since the moment he mentioned it—naughty with a side of danger.

He let go of my hair, and one hand went to my breast as the other held my hip. He pounded into me like the king of the jungle he was.

I was done being the good girl. I wanted the dangerous he'd threatened, the dangerous he'd promised.

The slapping sounds of flesh on flesh grew louder as the feral animal in him took over.

Bigger and bigger waves of pleasure broke over me as he took it to the next level.

"Fuck me harder, boss. Harder."

My words added fuel to his fire, and his grunts became louder as he banged against me. Without notice, he pulled my hips back a few inches and his hand circled me to find my clit. "You want harder?"

The sudden pressure on my little nub took me higher, and I braced against the desk to match his thrusts and rock back into him.

He filled me fully, and his rubbing of my clit sent me over the edge as fire filled my veins and the spasms shook me.

I moaned. Only the clamp of his hand over my mouth kept me from screaming out his name.

My legs shook as all the cells in my body tensed.

With a final groan, his hand left my mouth and he pulled my hips back into him as he found his release deep inside me.

I locked my knees to stay standing. I was a boneless, sweaty heap leaning over the desk.

He leaned forward. His weight pressed me against the desk. "That's what you get for being naughty."

"I'm leaving," Larry yelled from beyond the door. "Don't stay too late."

Dennis didn't answer him, instead he kissed my neck. "It's been hard."

"Hard is good."

He slapped my butt lightly. "I don't want to be the mean boss anymore."

Those were the words I needed to hear—the words I'd hoped for.

"I missed you too."

Insisting on the mean boss had been my mistake.

CHAPTER 29

DENNIS

I ROLLED OVER SATURDAY MORNING TO FIND JENNIFER STARING AT ME. "HAVE you been awake long?"

She stroked a few hairs behind my ear, her sweet smile filling her face. "No. Just enjoying it here and listening to the waves."

The window was cracked open, and the sound of the ocean beyond the beach was soft, but distinct.

I pulled her toward me. "Figure anything out?" I placed a kiss on her forehead.

She nodded, and her hand came behind my head. "Yeah. I don't like your mean boss impression anymore."

It was tough to carry off, but I'd tried hard. "I thought I was doing it perfectly."

"Maybe you were, but it's not you, and I shouldn't have asked for it."

"So what, then?"

Her fingers stroked my cheek. "Can't we just be like normal employees? Hide our feelings? Can you ignore me without being mean?"

"That might make it easier for people to figure out. Are you okay with that?"

"I guess?"

I kissed her again. "You need to be sure, Angel, because it's not something we can undo."

"I think I am."

"*Think* doesn't cut it. You are, or you aren't."

She took in a deep breath, as if she were preparing to step off a high cliff. "I am."

No doubt the statement was like jumping off into the unknown for her.

"That's good, because I wasn't sure how much longer I could keep up 'mean boss' without Cindy killing me."

Jennifer rolled over to go to the bathroom.

I watched her and realized I wasn't only fixated on the bob of her tits or the sway of her ass, but the whole woman. When she returned, I couldn't help but smile. It wasn't that I didn't enjoy the bounce of her tits as she approached, but she was more than the sum of her physical assets—more than her smile or her wit. In an impossibly short time, I'd come to appreciate so much about her. How had that happened?

She stopped. "What?"

"Just thinking."

"Don't wear yourself out." She picked up her panties from last night and pulled them on. "I have to go."

I swung out of bed. "What's the hurry?" I quickly enveloped her. I wasn't about to give up the heavenly feel of her warmth against my skin.

We rocked in each other's arms for a minute, and it calmed me.

She, apparently, wasn't eager to go either. "Ramona has a study group all day, and I have to watch Billy."

"Great. I'll watch him with you."

She snorted. "And hang out at my apartment?"

I pushed her back to look into her face and held her shoulders. "No way. Let's bring him here for a beach day."

Her brows furrowed. "You know he's only seven, right?"

I pulled her back into a hug. "I'm great with kids. I was one once."

I wandered into the bathroom to get ready.

She was fully dressed by the time I'd finished brushing my teeth.

"I don't think today is a good day," she said.

Her face wasn't the happy one she'd started the morning with.

I spit and rinsed the toothbrush. "What's wrong?"

She swayed a bit. "We haven't talked about…"

I waited for the clue. We had talked about a lot of things, but I didn't know what we'd missed. I passed her to get dressed for the drive.

"Ramona doesn't want…"

That didn't tell me enough to guess yet either. I pulled on a pair of shorts, waiting for the bomb to drop, whatever it was.

"She doesn't think it's good for a lot of men to go in and out of Billy's life."

That was the bomb. The unasked question—what was our future?

This had always been the beginning of the end of a relationship for me. When a girl got to asking about the future, I cut bait and found another, less-clingy one, and then another.

I turned, and the fear in her eyes petrified me. "Come here." I held my arms out and waited.

A second later, she plastered herself against me.

"I'm not asking for anything." Her words were muffled by my shoulder.

I stroked her back. This was make or break time, and for once I didn't feel like running. "I'm not going anywhere." I smoothed over her hair and kissed the top of her head. "Trust me."

"It's just that—"

"I know. Trust me, I know. Angel, you make me very happy, and I'm here for you."

Her voice was tinged with fear, but it was only half as scared as I felt.

In a typical snap judgment, I'd committed myself to uncharted territory, but I trusted my gut. She was different in ways I couldn't describe. She felt right in my arms, right by my side in bed, and right across the table at work. Somehow she was what I hadn't realized I needed.

I let go of her and located a shirt in the dresser.

She wiped her eyes. "Sure you don't mind?"

"It'll be fun."

That was one thing I could count on. Nephew or no nephew, I would enjoy the day with my girl.

My girl had a nice ring to it, I decided.

I laced up my Adidas and headed for the door. "Come along, woman. We don't want to be late."

Downstairs, she went around to the passenger side of her car, expecting me to drive that shit bucket of hers.

Instead, I opened the door to the Jag.

She looked confused. "There's three of us. We have to take my car."

"Trust me, he'd rather ride with me. You can follow."

She shook her head. "That's a waste."

I opened the garage door. I wasn't giving her a choice. It was no contest that a boy would rather ride in the Jag any day of the week over her car.

She opened the rear door of her car. "He needs his booster seat then."

A minute later the booster seat was strapped in. I revved the engine, the cat roared, and we were off.

~

JENNIFER

THE DRIVE TO MY PLACE HADN'T TAKEN LONG IN SATURDAY TRAFFIC.

Ramona cocked her head when I told her what we had in mind. "The beach?"

Her words were polite, but her scowl wasn't.

Billy jumped off the couch. "I wanna go to the beach."

Dennis stood with his hands in his pockets. "We won't let the sharks get him."

Ramona's huff said that wasn't the right approach. "I don't know."

Dennis looked up. "Or we could stay here and see if we can get marshmallows to stick to the ceiling."

"Do they really stick?" Billy asked.

Dennis tousled Billy's hair. "If you throw them hard enough."

Ramona finally got Dennis's sense of humor and smiled. "Maybe the beach would be better."

Billy had another idea. "Can we do both?"

Dennis tousled his hair. "We don't have time for both. Let's get your swim trunks."

They left us for a moment.

Ramona leaned close. "Is he always like that?"

"Only when he's nervous."

"You'll be careful, right?"

"Aren't I always?"

The boys returned before Ramona could answer, and we were off.

Dennis had been right. Billy's eyes lit up at the sight of the Jaguar, and the choice of riding with his aunt or the stranger with the hot sports car was no choice at all.

I lost sight of them twice as Dennis did his James Bond imitation and roared away from the stop lights.

When we arrived, Billy was wide eyed as he described the car to me. "It goes fast, and it roars like a lion, and it can go two hundred miles an hour, and…"

I didn't catch the rest as he ran up the stairs after Dennis. I was clearly the third wheel here. That feeling was rectified as soon as Dennis's arm came around my waist upstairs.

While Dennis took Billy out on the patio, I poured orange juice for the two adults and milk for Billy.

I carried the glasses outside.

Dennis put his finger to his lips. "Listen carefully. It's there," he said to Billy.

Billy had his eyes closed, getting Dennis's brand of meditation instructions.

"I don't want to listen." He opened his eyes.

Dennis took his glass from the tray I offered. "That's okay. You're probably not old enough yet."

Billy couldn't resist the challenge. "I am too."

"Then close your eyes and listen." Dennis didn't tell him to breathe to the tempo the way he'd done with me.

After about a minute, Billy's eyes popped open. "I heard it."

I held out his milk. "Good for you."

"I don't want milk."

Dennis fixed him with a glare. "A man doesn't talk to his aunt that way."

Billy slumped back. "But I don't want milk."

"Before we talk about that, a man would apologize."

Billy's nose turned up, but he got the message. "I'm sorry."

"Apology accepted."

Dennis wasn't done yet. "Now you can decide about the milk. Do you want to grow up to be big and strong or weak?"

Billy didn't bite on the question. "Joey says only sissies drink milk."

Dennis chuckled. "Joey is an idiot then. Do I look like a sissy to you? Do I?"

Billy shook his head.

Dennis held up his arm and flexed his impressive bicep. "I drank milk when I was your age, and all through high school too. It's important to do what's right instead of worrying about what other people think."

Billy reached for the glass and started to drink his milk so fast I thought he'd choke. Ramona's little guy was under Dennis's spell.

I took back Billy's glass. "What do you want for breakfast?"

Billy leaned back with a shrug.

"I'd like Cocoa Puffs," Dennis answered.

"Me too," Billy shouted.

I took the milk glass back inside and located the cereal for them. I wouldn't have guessed Dennis for a guy that ate kids' cereal, but there was a lot I didn't know about him. Granola would have suited me better, but I poured myself a bowl of the dark little balls as well.

The three of us ate on the patio while Dennis quizzed Billy about his school.

Dennis ate slowly and was the last to finish. "Should we start by skating, or swimming with the sharks?"

Neither of us answered right away.

I shot Dennis a disapproving glance. Hanging out was a better idea.

Dennis stood and grabbed his empty bowl. "Skating it is, then."

Billy followed Dennis's lead and brought his own bowl to the sink— another first. "But I don't know how."

"Today's a good day to learn." Dennis grabbed a hat.

Billy went first down the stairs, and I followed Dennis.

"Cocoa Puffs?" I asked.

"Chocolate is the food of the gods."

The man surprised me at every turn.

At the rental shop, I got outfitted with roller blades, and Dennis chose easier-to-balance roller skates for himself and Billy.

Billy also got the full pads, gloves, and helmet treatment.

Our shoes went into a backpack Dennis had brought along.

Dennis held Billy up between his legs for the first half mile or so, working with him on balancing and understanding the basics of pushing off one foot onto the other.

At an open stretch, Dennis let him go. "Turn right. Lean right."

It was no use. The little guy went left, off the cement, and face planted in the sand. But he got up laughing.

After several more tries, my nephew got to where he could turn the right way and stay on the path if Dennis kept giving him a boost to keep going.

Dennis kept at it patiently, and by the time we got to Santa Monica, Billy didn't look elegant, but he stayed upright and was nothing but smiles and laughter. The pads had done their job, and he was still in one piece.

"Here's where we stop," Dennis announced.

Billy scowled. "But I'm not done yet."

The disapproving glare Dennis sent his way changed that instantly.

"Can we please do some more?" Billy asked.

Dennis had already chided him twice about talking back.

"Sure," Dennis answered. "Later. First we have some rides to check out."

Dennis sat on a bench to undo his skates, and we followed. The shoes came out of the backpack, and the skates went into a locker.

From there it was a series of rides and games, with Dennis challenging Billy every step of the way until we got to the rollercoaster. The cars only sat two across, so Dennis took Billy with him, and I slid into the seats behind them.

Starting at the first plunge, Billy screamed the whole time, but he kept his hands up in the air, mimicking Dennis.

When we got off, I was the weak-kneed one Dennis had to help.

"I want to go again," Billy announced.

He modified that as soon as he noticed Dennis's stern glance. "Can I please go again?"

Dennis checked his watch. "Maybe after lunch."

He offered me his hand, and with interlaced fingers, I strode to lunch linked to my man, Billy's new idol.

Billy turned up his nose at the suggestion of the Bubba Gump Shrimp Company, and we settled on Pier Burger. Leave it to Billy to insist on lunch at a burger joint and then order a hot dog, but that was his prerogative.

I went for the chicken sandwich, and Dennis was the only one of us to order their signature Pier Burger.

"How old are you, Billy?" Dennis asked.

Billy sipped his Coke. "I'll be eight in October."

"October, huh. Let me see…" Dennis rubbed his chin for a moment. "I guess that makes you old enough then."

"Old enough for what?"

"For a grown-up name."

"What's a grown-up name?"

Dennis poked the straw in his shake. "Let me guess. Your full name is William?"

Billy nodded and sucked on his drink.

"Billy is a kid's name. I think you're ready to be called Bill, unless you like William better."

Billy looked at his cup and turned it. "Mommy calls me William when she's mad."

"Then it should be Bill, unless you like Will better. That's another choice."

Our number was announced, and Dennis got up to retrieve the tray with our food. He returned and set the tray in the middle of the table.

"Have you decided?"

Billy shrugged.

"A man needs to know how to make decisions. Maybe you're not ready for this yet."

"I am too."

"Then which will it be?"

Billy straightened up. "Bill."

Dennis offered his hand across the table. "Pleasure to meet you, Bill. My name's Dennis."

Billy shook his hand with the widest smile I'd seen on him in a long time.

"What was your kid's name?" he asked.

"Growing up my name was Denny. I made them stop when I was about your age. I've been Dennis ever since."

Billy thought for a second before taking a bite of his hot dog.

I finished chewing the fry I'd snagged. "People used to call me Jenny."

Billy finished chewing and ignored my comment to ask Dennis, "And nobody calls you Denny anymore?"

"I only let one person call me that."

I choked on my drink, realizing who that was.

Dennis patted my back. "Are you okay, Angel?"

"Yeah." I coughed. "The fizz just tickled my throat."

"Just one person?" Billy asked.

"Just one."

Billy attacked his hot dog again before asking. "Why?"

"She's very special."

The room suddenly seemed ten degrees warmer.

~

AT THE END OF THE DAY, WHEN IT WAS TIME TO DRIVE BILLY BACK HOME, IT FELT silly to be taking two cars, but I didn't have the heart to deny Billy another ride in the Jaguar. And in the back of my mind, I doubted I would have won the argument with Dennis anyway.

With my nephew around, I'd had to be on my best behavior with Dennis all day. We'd held hands, walked the pier with his arm around me, laughed together, and even snuck a kiss when Billy was in the bathroom. But that was all. Being close to Dennis all day, yet having to keep my distance had made Jennifer an anxious girl—anxious to be alone with her man after the enforced separateness I'd insisted on at work, and now in front of my nephew.

The drive also gave me time to reflect on what I'd learned. In a few short hours I'd seen Billy develop more than I'd expected. Dennis had a way with my nephew that neither Ramona nor I could replicate, and it was more than Dennis's imposing physical stature. Billy had instantly looked to him for guidance and accepted it.

Dennis hadn't needed to offer Billy anything more than a play outlet or babysitting today, but he'd gone out of his way to fill the male-role-model void in my nephew's life. We'd even had lessons on manners that went better than I'd expected.

~

RAMONA TURNED AS WE WALKED IN. "DID YOU HAVE A GOOD TIME, BILLY?"

My nephew didn't waste any time. "I want to be Bill."

"What does that mean?"

"My name is Bill."

"Of course, but you'll always be my little Billy."

"No, I'm Bill." He caught Dennis's disapproving glare and quickly corrected himself. "Please."

Ramona took in a breath. "Well then, Bill, want a soda?"

207

"Can I have milk?"

Ramona's mouth dropped. "Milk?"

"Yes." A second later he added. "Please."

Ramona's eyes popped as she looked to me for confirmation.

I tilted my head. "He grew up today, what can I say?"

She opened the fridge. "Are you guys available to watch him next weekend?"

I couldn't tell if my sister was being serious or not before Dennis answered in the affirmative, and we were locked in to another Saturday with our mini chaperone.

Dennis pressed a key into my hand. "I'm going to stop by the store for some steaks. I'll see you back at the beach house."

"Thanks again," Ramona added as Dennis headed for the door. "What do you say, Bill?"

Billy stopped playing with the TV remote. "Thank you."

"See you next weekend," Dennis said on his way out.

Ramona sidled up to me. "If he can get Billy to drink his milk, I like him."

"Bill," my nephew yelled from the couch.

"It's probably time," I told her.

She shrugged. "It's just that he's growing up so fast."

"I need to get some clothes and get going."

"Do I need to plan on taking him to school every day now?"

I placed a hand on my sister's shoulder. "It's just the weekends. I'll be here during the week."

I meant it, but her expression said she didn't believe it would stay that way.

CHAPTER 30

DENNIS

MONDAY MORNING I SQUINTED INTO THE BRIGHT SUNLIGHT AS I DROVE EAST toward the office. The lack of coastal overcast this early in the morning pointed to a warmer than usual day today. But even that couldn't match the heat Jennifer and I had created between the sheets this weekend.

It had started out slowly, but enjoyably, with Jennifer's nephew keeping us from devouring each other, and quickly progressed to red hot that night and all day yesterday.

The woman was a balm to my soul. In her arms, I could let go of my Cartwright obsession and unwind the tension that had built all week long.

Since I was in early, I made coffee for Cindy and put it on her desk. Back in my office, while the computer booted up, I watched the city come alive out my window.

Cartwright was out there somewhere, but it wouldn't be long before he showed himself and appeared on my doorstep for "the talk." It would start out innocently enough, but progress to the veiled threats he was so good at.

I'd read up on him, and last week I'd gotten the chance to debrief two of his previous victims. With a basic understanding of his modus operandi, I now figured he had a plant or two in the company feeding him information, and would soon be ready to make his next move.

"Do I have you to thank for the coffee?" It was Cindy from the doorway.

I spun my chair around. "The least I could do."

"Thank you. Did you have a good weekend?"

I couldn't hide the wide smile that came to my face. "Yes, thank you. What about you?"

"We survived a dinner with my mother-in-law."

"One of those dinners, huh?"

"I swear my husband must have been adopted. George isn't much of a complainer, but his mother… My yard needed sprucing up, the house wasn't properly decorated, the vegetables had too much salt, and… Well, it just went on and on."

"But you avoided bloodshed, I hope."

"Barely."

I hazarded a suggestion. "Next time she comes to town, meet her at a restaurant and give her something different to complain about."

Cindy's face perked up. "I like that idea. And maybe halfway through, you could call me with a work emergency."

I chuckled. "Happy to."

"I'm going to remember that." She backed away. "Glad to see you're in a better mood."

I turned back to the window to think. Better mood was right—much better mood. When I looked back over last week, I realized the weekend with Jennifer and her nephew had re-centered me. He was a great kid, and she was quite a woman.

Jennifer

Monday morning, after Ramona and Billy left, I was alone to put my hair up and trade my weekend shorts for my work attire. I also had to prepare myself for another five days of avoiding non-essential interaction with Dennis—not looking his direction, not smiling as soon as I saw him, and not calling him Denny.

We'd had another wonderful weekend together at the beach. Once again we'd taken Billy off Ramona's hands Saturday, and enjoyed Sunday with just the two of us.

Walking the beach path south instead of north yesterday, Dennis had surprised me when we got to Marina Del Rey. He'd rented us kayaks.

I knew squat about paddling a kayak, and I had trouble keeping up with him for a while. That made splashing him all the more fun when he finally slowed down enough for me to catch him.

He'd introduced me to another thing I'd never experienced, and made our day nonstop fun. The fresh air, sunshine, and ocean water had invigorated me, and also worn me out by the end of the day. As expected, trading back rubs had led to more hands on skin in more places, which led to another night in his arms that I didn't want to ever forget.

My life had become two days of delight followed by five days of frustration before the next round of delight. It was the personal trial I'd have to endure for a while. Three months should do it, I figured. Then we could pretend we'd just started dating. Although that seemed like an awfully long time to keep this up.

I checked my computer before leaving, and found the message I'd dreaded.

> To:Nemesis666
> From: HYDRA157
> Still waiting. What is taking so long?

I sent a quick reply.

> To:HYDRA157
> From: Nemesis666
> Have not had the right opportunity.

Time was running out. Being around Dennis had melted my resolve, but I couldn't put it off any longer. Today I was going to have to read the memos and discover which sin I was guilty of. Then I'd know whether to drop off the file for Hydra.

∼

ONCE IN THE OFFICE, I PULLED UP THE COMPUTERIZED INDEX AND PERFORMED THE search I'd done last week regarding Dad's accident. The results came back with the same file number I'd memorized last week.

I stopped by Cindy's desk. "I need something out of File Storage B."

She opened a drawer and handed me the key. "Knock yourself out."

I accepted the key to my unknown future. "Thanks."

This retrieval was much simpler since it didn't involve a headlamp and my pick set. Back in my office, I opened the folder I'd pulled and found three memos in it. As I read down the first one, my feelings tangled in an unimaginable jumble.

I re-read it twice.

As a corporation, it is imperative that we accept full responsibility for the fire, not withstanding the accident report. Our position is clear. Allied Insurance is instructed to not dispute the company's liability in any proceeding, in any jurisdiction. Our official position is that the accident is due to management's failure to ensure a safe working environment—in particular the CEO's waiver of rules meant to forestall accidents of this nature and prevent outcomes such as these.

It was what I'd hoped to find months ago, but it was a gut punch today. Dennis and his company were responsible, and I had the evidence I'd promised Mom I would find.

I'd been sleeping with the enemy. Regardless of his intentions, Dennis was directly responsible, and I'd slept with the man. My stomach rioted.

My dash to the bathroom was almost not quick enough. I retched my breakfast into the sink. The woman already in the room practically ran out as I did. The waves came again and again.

After several dry heaves, they finally stopped. Looking up into the mirror, all I saw was a girl with *traitor* stamped on her forehead. Rinsing the disgusting taste of my own bile from my mouth didn't improve the picture in the mirror. I'd betrayed Mom and Dad. I was a failure for allowing attraction to cloud my judgment.

Cindy entered, probably alerted by the fleeing woman that I was ruining the place. "Are you okay?"

I managed a half-smile. "I shouldn't have had leftovers for breakfast."

"Can I get you anything?"

"No. Just give me a minute."

She departed, and I was alone again with my guilt.

After washing my face, I made it back to my office and closed the door. There were two more documents to finish reading to complete my promise to Mom. The whole truth regarding my stepfather is what I'd committed to.

The next document had an odd passage.

We are committed to the welfare of our employees and their families. I allowed our employee to work afterhours on a personal project. The accident report notwithstanding, I take full responsibility for the incident, and that is our final position.

The note was intended for the insurance company again and signed by Dennis. Another nail in his coffin.

The third document, the accident report Mom had said they'd refused to provide her, wasn't as legible, so I struggled reading it.

I stopped to reread the most important section.

The fire was triggered by Mr. Davis's failure to follow well-known safety protocols. Namely, the video clearly shows Mr. Davis cleaning the bicycle frame with acetone, placing the open acetone can on the welding table, and starting to weld the bicycle frame in close proximity to the open can of solvent in clear violation of prohibitions against any flammable liquids being outside their respective fireproof cabinets while welding is performed.

I swallowed hard and continued.

It is therefore the conclusion of this committee that the accident was caused by Mr. Davis's failure to follow safety protocols well known to him. A contributing factor was management's waiver allowing Mr. Davis to weld without a second employee in the room. This waiver, although it did not contribute to the fatality, allowed the fire to cause more damage to the facility than would otherwise have been the case.

Closing the documents, I dumped the folder in my drawer. I sat back and closed my eyes. This changed everything all over again. Dad had been at fault, not Dennis. Mom had been wrong. *"The fire was triggered by Mr. Davis's failure to follow well-known safety protocols."* The words stung.

After gathering my purse, I locked my office. I needed time alone to think.

"Going home?" Cindy asked as I passed her desk.

"Yeah."

"That's a good idea."

She had no idea why I felt so terrible.

Mom had been dead wrong about Dad's accident. If she'd known the truth, would she have drunk less and be alive today? There was no way to know, but the possibility haunted me.

As I punched the button for the garage level, I almost upchucked again, thinking of the damage I'd caused Dennis and the company.

Dennis's call came an hour after I got home.

"Cindy said you weren't feeling well. Anything I can do?"

There was no right answer to that question.

"No. I just shouldn't have had the leftover shrimp," I lied.

What was one more lie on top of what I'd already done to hurt him?

I heard the sound of a door closing.

"I could come over tonight, if you feel like breaking our rules."

"That's sweet, but I'll be okay by tomorrow."

Another lie. I'd have to find a way to tell him, and that couldn't happen without a face to face—and without me owning up to what I'd done.

The worst part of all this kept gnawing at me.

Dad had been trying to fix my bike when it had happened.

CHAPTER 31

DENNIS

(Four Days Later)

FINALLY IT WAS FRIDAY. THE WEEK WAS ALMOST OVER, AND TONIGHT I COULD relax across the dinner table from my girl.

Mid-morning, Ed Baird was at my door.

"Do you have a sec?" he asked. "I have something on that matter you asked me to look into."

I waved him in.

He closed the door behind him and brought a folder to my desk. "I think I found the conduit to Cartwright." He took a seat.

I leaned forward. This could turn out to be a much better week if we had a lead on Cartwright. "Go ahead."

"We spent a lot of time and effort on this last week."

"I'm sure you did. Now what did you find?" I'd save the back patting for later.

He pulled out a photo and laid it on my desk. The photo wasn't very good quality—actually it was pretty crappy.

I looked up from the picture. "What am I looking at?"

He pointed to the window of the restaurant. "These two women having lunch. One is a girl who works here, and she's meeting with a person from Cartwright's firm."

"Who?"

"The lady's name is Suzanne Murtog." He pulled out another picture. This one was clearer, of a woman going into a building.

"But I don't see her face."

"It's the same woman from the restaurant, I guarantee it. And Cartwright has an office on the fourteenth floor of that building."

"I meant who did she meet with?"

"Jennifer Hanley."

I quickly schooled my expression to hide the horror I felt. "Jennifer Hanley?"

"That's right. I followed her myself from our building to the restaurant."

I went back to the first picture. "I can't make her out through this window."

"Trust me. It's her on the left."

A few seconds later, I decided it could be her, but it wasn't a good enough picture or from the right angle to be sure. "You're sure?"

"Absolutely."

I sat back. It didn't make any sense. Jennifer didn't have a reason to meet with the Cartwright people. "There has to be some mistake."

He produced two printouts from the folder. "Here's a list of top employees at First Century, which is a Cartwright subsidiary."

Suzanne Murtog was highlighted on the page.

Another sheet landed on my desk. "And this is from their website." It had her name again and a head shot. "I can interrogate Hanley this afternoon."

I shook my head. "Not so fast."

"If you prefer, I'll loop Mr. Fisher in, and he could talk with her instead."

I wasn't going that route either. "No, thanks. Let me figure out what to do next. I'll be in touch."

Disappointment crossed his face. He surely had planned on some high-pressure interrogation to round out his investigation. Probably something straight out of a TV show—bright lights and lots of yelling.

He placed the folder on my desk. "I'll leave these with you." He stood. "Good work, Ed. Thanks."

"It's what you pay me for. I'll keep digging on this."

A minute later I was alone with a pit in my stomach and questions that needed answers.

~

Jennifer

When I'd passed Dennis in the hallway just before lunch, I'd gotten the mean boss treatment again. He'd scowled and looked away as he went into his office—worse even than ignoring me.

After fuming over it for a few minutes, I sent him a text.

ME: Can we talk?

I also texted Cindy to tell her I wanted to talk to Dennis.

Ten minutes later, I called her. "Did you tell him I needed a few minutes?"

"He knows, but I'll tell him again when he comes out."

That meant he was alone in his office, so ignoring me had been deliberate. I went back to my office and closed the door.

Over lunch down the street, I thought back to what I could have done. Staring out the window didn't make the answer appear. Neither did running my fingers up and down the condensation on my drink cup.

I almost puked as a dirty, sweaty construction guy passed by on the way to a booth behind me. His BO was terrible, but in my current emotional state, it didn't take much. I was a mess, and looking at my half-eaten sandwich only made it worse.

After lunch, I was specifically excluded from the meeting on the Cartwright response.

I couldn't have been imagining this. I was sure we'd agreed that there wasn't a need for the mean boss treatment anymore, so what had I missed?

If I'd said something, or done something, I couldn't put a finger on it. It wasn't like I'd forgotten his birthday. I didn't even know when it was. A brisk walk twice around the block didn't help.

By the end of the day, I'd had enough.

"Is he in there?" I asked Cindy.

"Yes, and I hope he stays there. Today started off so well, and then he nearly bit my head off at lunch time."

"Mean boss."

"Pardon?"

I grasped the door handle. "Oh, nothing." I opened the door, stepped inside, and closed it behind me.

He glanced at me only briefly before turning back to his computer. "Whatever it is, I don't have time."

Refusing to be intimidated, I walked up and took a seat across from him. "We agreed that mean boss was over."

There, I'd said it, and that should have been enough to jog his memory. It had only been last week.

"I don't have time," he repeated.

"And I don't deserve this." I sat and waited.

He typed on his keyboard, ignoring me.

"Why are you being like this again? You agreed to stop it."

He looked up with cold, piercing eyes. "That was when I thought I could trust you."

The comment froze me. "You...you can. You know that."

I'd thought he knew that. He should have known that.

He turned back to his monitor. "Is that so?"

The words dripped with disdain, another thing I didn't deserve.

Wracking my brain, I couldn't come up with anything that could have prompted this turnaround. "What did I do?"

"How about meeting with Cartwright?"

I cocked my head. I'd never heard anything so outrageous. "I've never even met the man."

"Not him. One of his henchmen, or should I say henchwomen?"

I straightened up. "I have no idea what the hell you're talking about."

Before I got to know him, I would have considered doing something like that, but now? No way.

"Yeah, right."

He surprised me by opening a manila folder on his desk and sliding a picture my direction. "And I suppose this isn't you?"

It was a blurry picture of the outside of Panera Bread.

I couldn't see myself in the picture anywhere. "And just which smudge is me?"

"Did you go there Tuesday afternoon?"

It took a few seconds to register. It seemed so long ago, but I put it together. "Yes," I admitted. "I was meeting a friend."

"And this is her, right?" He slid over another picture. This one was of a woman whose face you couldn't see. It could have been Suzanne. She was entering a nondescript building. "It could be, but what does that have to do with Cartwright?"

He slid another piece of paper in my direction. "Cartwright has offices in that building, and she works for him."

My mouth went dry.

The last piece of paper was a picture of Suzanne, labeled senior analyst, on a page of First Century employees.

"It says First Century."

"That's a Cartwright subsidiary."

I swallowed hard. "I had no idea. I went to undergrad with her. She just called up asking to meet for lunch. She said she was back in town and wanted to get reacquainted. She wanted me to pass her resume around."

"Security followed you to the meeting, so you can drop the innocent act."

The realization of what had transpired was like a gut punch.

Ed was fucking with me, and big time.

"If you got this from Ed Baird, you can't believe a word of it. He's just trying to screw with me...with us."

"Is that so?"

"You wanted to know who my ex-boyfriend, EB, was? EB is Ed Baird, head of security here."

That stopped him with his mouth agape.

I could see the wheels turning inside his head.

"Your ex-boyfriend?"

"That's right, and he's trying to jam me up and mess with us. She asked me to pass along her resume. I printed it out and took it down to HR, and I sent it over to Pasadena. Call them if you don't believe me."

He pondered silently. His eyes were no longer the fierce cold they'd been a minute ago, but we clearly weren't back to Denny and Angel either.

"I swear I had no idea she worked for Cartwright, and that was the only time I've seen her since college. She, Ed, and I all went to Pepperdine."

I hadn't seen the possible setup until I'd spoken the words.

Ed and I hadn't hooked up until after school, and I'd never considered him having a connection to Suzanne. But he could definitely be that sneaky. Had he set me up?

"Your ex-boyfriend?" he repeated.

I nodded. "Don't you see what's going on here? He's pulling a Melissa." I gave him a few seconds to process it all. "Who was it that said we should gather all the evidence before passing judgment?"

He rose, and in a few strides had circled the desk and pulled me to standing. "You're right. I'm sorry I was so easily taken in by it."

I looked into his eyes, which had warmed. "We're even, I guess. I used to think you were a jerk."

"I did sort of set you up with the Talbot meeting."

"Don't remind me or I might change my mind. Can we please drop the mean boss act now?"

His kiss was my answer. Things were going back to normal—whatever that was. We needed more time to get settled, established. Based on his reaction to this news, this weekend would be too early to tell him what I actually had done. I needed him to trust me more before I could apologize for how I'd hurt him. I needed to be sure he'd believe how truly sorry I was.

Leaving his office with a flush in my cheeks from the kiss, I realized I'd just been on the receiving end of a rush to judgment, and it sure sucked. I'd have to admit I'd done the same to him, and that wasn't going to be easy.

Leaving him behind was my other alternative, but he was too good to walk away from, and after what we'd shared, the guilt would eat at me anyway. I needed his forgiveness, and I had to find the right words to ask for it.

DENNIS

THE DOOR CLOSED BEHIND HER. I COULD STILL FEEL HER ON MY LIPS, BUT THE taste in my mouth was one of regret.

She'd called me on my shit this time, just as she had before. There was no doubt this woman was different in several ways, the most important of which was her honesty in dealing with me. She was a refreshing change.

I'd wronged her, and I intended to rectify that by showing her how I felt this weekend. The first step, however, was one I had to take at the office. I opened my door.

"Please ask Ed to come up," I told Cindy.

He arrived a few minutes later. "What can I do for you?" he asked as he closed the door behind him.

I asked him to take a seat, which he did.

"Is there anything else you want to tell me about Jennifer Hanley? Anything else I should know in relation to the report you gave me about her meeting with somebody from Cartwright?"

His eyes flashed fear. "I don't know what you mean."

I spoke slowly so there would be no misunderstanding. "Did you date her?"

He swallowed and nodded. "For a while."

"And you didn't think that was relevant?"

He sat up straighter. "No. What I gave you was factual. Did she say she didn't meet with the Murtog lady?"

I took in a breath. "No, but that's not the point. Have you been texting her since you...since you stopped seeing each other?"

He nodded. "Yes, but that has nothing to do—"

"Even though she asked you to stop?"

He didn't respond to that, but I knew the answer. It had everything to do with his accusation against Jennifer.

I pointed the door. "Next time you bring me something having to do with her, I want to be certain it doesn't have even a hint of your personal feelings attached to it. Are we clear?"

He stood. "Perfectly."

"Ed, I still want you putting a full-court press on this Cartwright thing. Just don't bring me anything half-baked."

He nodded. "Got it." He left without another word.

CHAPTER 32

JENNIFER
(Three Weeks Later)

DENNIS AND I WALKED BACK ALONG THE BEACH PATH AFTER A LATE DINNER
Sunday night. This was our fifth weekend together, and it seemed like so
long ago that I'd been surprised by the kiss in his office meant to piss off
Melissa.

All had been quiet on the Melissa front since the fountain incident, and
Dennis thought perhaps that night had used up a month or two of her anger.
He'd also confided in me that our relationship would likely cost him in his
upcoming court battle with her.

That conversation had brought up conflicting emotions. I felt bad about
hurting him in front of the judge, but nothing could have made me happier
than knowing he felt I was worth it.

It had been an unreal journey from that day to here. I would have
laughed at it as impossible if I'd read it in a magazine, but here I was, arm in
arm with the master of all he surveyed. The king of the jungle had chosen
me, claimed me, and showed me what happiness could be like.

The dreariness of my past life paled in comparison to my future. Weeks
ago I would have laughed at the thought of a future that included Dennis,

but now I couldn't imagine life without him. The only cloud on my horizon was the conversation I knew we needed to have about my past actions. So far, each weekend had been better than the last. That string would be broken when I came clean, as I knew I had to.

Monday we would be back at work, ignoring each other. And it would be another five days before we could express our feelings again on Friday night. Wednesday and Thursday had become the hardest days for me. Every time someone at work mentioned hump day, I had to control my urge to march into Dennis's office and hump him again. My one introduction to office sex over his desk had been beyond naughty and exciting.

I shivered, remembering the danger of it.

He tightened his arm around me. "What's up?"

"Nothing."

"Cold?"

"No, I just don't want this to end."

He stopped and turned me toward him. "This isn't ending. We're just beginning." His eyes held mine.

Even in the dim light, I could see the sincerity on his face. "I meant the weekend."

"Oh… Me, too. You know, we could take this to the next level and tell people."

I'd originally told myself three months of hiding our relationship would probably be enough, but after a month of this, I wasn't sure I could keep it up for another two.

He kissed my forehead. "You're not ready yet, are you?"

"No. Not quite." I did like the sound of the next level, though.

"I can wait. You know I'll do anything for you, Angel."

The name warmed me every time. "I know you think it's stupid. Can you forgive me for not being ready yet?"

"It's not stupid. It's how you feel, and I'd forgive you anything. You know that."

I smiled. I'd need that forgiving attitude when I got up the nerve to tell him what I'd done. And if I didn't get it, I wasn't sure what I'd do.

For now, we resumed our walk to the beach house.

Two more months of office secrecy loomed like an eternity.

~

DENNIS

MY PHONE RANG, AND WHEN I PULLED IT OUT, SERENA'S FACE GRACED THE screen. I showed it to Jennifer before answering.

"Hi, Nina." She hated me reminding her of her childhood nickname.

"Can I come over? I need to talk."

The fact that my greeting hadn't gotten a response was not a good sign.

"I'm tied up right now. How about lunch tomorrow?"

"She's there, isn't she?"

I ignored her question. "What's the problem?"

"Yeah, tomorrow works. We need to talk about Cartwright."

"What about Cartwright?"

"Lunch then. Bye, and my regards to your girl."

"Bye." I ignored the comment about Jennifer—denying it wouldn't have helped. I put the phone away.

Jennifer looked up. "You can go talk to her if you need to. I'll be fine."

I pulled her along the path. " You're my priority tonight. She can wait till tomorrow."

"Want to talk about it?"

I shook my head. The mention of Cartwright had ruined my mood, and I needed a dose of my Angel.

JENNIFER

WE AMBLED DOWN THE PATH IN SILENCE.

"It's nothing," Dennis finally said. "Serena wants to talk about Cartwright, and nothing having to do with that family ever ends up being good news."

Cartwright had been a thorn in his side, and now it was affecting his sister somehow.

"Are you worried about the meeting?"

Cartwright had requested a meeting with Dennis, and so far he'd put them off.

"*Worried* isn't the right word."

"Nervous?"

"Yeah, that works. I have to fend him off, or a lot of people will pay the price."

As usual, Dennis was focused on the effect others would feel, not what it would cost him.

When we got back to the house, I went to get some wine. "White or red?"

He picked up the remote. "White."

"Sweet or dry?" That was as far as my wine knowledge went, although Dennis was teaching me a little more every week.

"Not sweet."

I pulled out a bottle of pinot grigio he'd promised wasn't sweet and unwrapped the foil top.

Dennis scrolled through movie choices. "What do you feel like?"

I put the lip of the bottle up to the wine opener and squeezed the grips to hold it. "Something light and funny."

We'd watched one of the Fast and Furious movies last night, and a change would be good. I pulled the handle forward, and in a quick move, the opener threaded the corkscrew in and pulled the cork out.

"How's *Miss Congeniality*?"

"Works for me." I poured the glasses and brought them over.

As I snuggled in next to my man, the movie started to play.

I clinked my glass to his. "To CC."

"Huh?"

"Conquering Cartwright."

He smiled, and we both drank heartily.

The movie started heavy on the comedy, but then added a little suspense, since nobody knew who the bad guy was.

Dennis laughed when Sandra screamed at the bikini wax scene.

I cringed. I'd been there and knew how painful it could be.

In the end, Sandra caught the bad guy and rescued the pageant. Every time I'd watched this before, I'd wished to be her, the heroine who saved the day.

"What is it?" Dennis asked.

"What?"

"You're off somewhere else. What's up?"

"Just thinking how wonderful you are."

He chuckled. "I'm not buying it, but the flattery is appreciated."

I brought my lips a mere inch from his. "I want to give you something, but there's a condition."

He rubbed his nose against mine in the way I loved. "What's the condition?"

I ran my hand up his inner thigh. "You have to do whatever I say." The agreement wouldn't come easily—giving up control was his biggest hang-up.

He swallowed hard. "Okay."

I pushed away. "Get undressed."

Glee wrote itself across his face.

I went to the kitchen and found the little chocolate pudding containers near the back of the fridge. Two and a spoon would do.

His clothes were in a pile at his feet when I returned. His member was hard and upright with anticipation.

My wetness matched his hardness. We were both ready. I pointed to the bedroom. "On the bed."

His cock bobbed as he walked, and I admired his tight, white ass all the way to the bedroom. He climbed onto the bed and sat up.

I put the pudding down and slowly pulled my shirt off.

His eyes glued to my chest as I reached behind me and undid the hooks of my bra. He scanned me, as if willing me to go faster.

I slowed down. Clamping my arms to my sides to hold the bra in place, I pulled the shoulder straps off one by one, then held it a few seconds before allowing the garment to fall away.

His eyes popped, as they always did.

My boobs were my secret weapon. The right jiggle—especially braless in the morning with my nipples showing through a T-shirt—never failed to command his attention.

I moved one of the puddings to the nightstand. "Lay back and interlace your fingers behind your head."

He hesitated before he did as I asked.

I brought a small spoonful of the pudding to his lips.

He sucked the spoon dry.

Setting it down, I slipped off my shorts. In just panties, I picked up the pudding and straddled his thighs.

The lion emerged in his eyes as my breasts bobbed in front of him.

He moved to cradle them when I waggled my shoulders.

I whacked his hand hard with the spoon.

"Ow."

"Behind your head. Denny needs to behave, or he won't get his treat."

His hands went back where they needed to be, but his eyes stayed glued to my breasts.

I dabbed a bit of the chocolate on one nipple and leaned forward to offer it to him.

He licked, and sucked, and licked.

It was heavenly, and I didn't know which of us was enjoying it more. It didn't matter. I scooted my pussy forward, over his hard length, with a single layer of soaked fabric between us.

I put some pudding on the other nipple and was treated to the same delicious sucking. We went back and forth until the first container was emptied.

Each time he strained up to reach a nipple, I pulled away until he behaved and let me offer myself to him at my own pace.

I climbed down and pulled my panties off before grabbing the second container. I dabbed a bit on his shaft. It sprang as I did.

"Hold still."

"I can't. It's cold."

"Don't be a baby." I moved to lick the pudding off.

His groans were like music to my ears as I added a little here and a little there, followed by slow licks of his throbbing cock.

"You're killing me, Angel."

"Baby." I applied the last spoonful and ever so slowly licked him clean. Putting aside the pudding container and spoon, I straddled him and leaned forward to rub my breasts over his chest.

He strained upward to meet me.

I pushed him down again.

I sat up and ran my slick slit the length of his cock. A wonderful jolt of pleasure ran through me as my clit slid over his tip.

The hitch in his breath showed he felt it too.

I ran myself up and down his length, coating him with my wetness, and pressing down firmly every time I reached the tip. Electricity shot through both of us.

The lust in his eyes and the smile that ate his face told me all I needed to know—this was nearly unbearable for him.

He was nearing the edge, yet still behaving.

I loved that I could drive him crazy like this, the same way he did me with his tongue.

I continued to work him, stopping and starting again, using his moans and breathing as my gauge of how much he could take. I leaned forward to offer him a nipple.

He rewarded me with a hard suck.

I offered the other breast. "You said you want to take it to the next level."

He nodded.

"I want to go bare."

His eyes widened at the prospect. "I'm clean, if that's what you're asking."

"Me too, and I'm on the pill."

In an instant, he'd rolled us over and was on top.

I'd unleashed the animal, and I was no longer in charge. The change suited me fine as he entered me, skin on skin. The primal beasts in each of us took over, and there was no controlling this, no slowing it down. That time had passed.

We quickly found our rhythm, and I couldn't hold off as I ground against him to get the clit pressure I sought. He speared me deeply. Each thrust sent shocks all the way to my toes.

"You feel so fucking good," he groaned, breaking his silence.

He worked me quickly to the edge.

The shocks of pleasure overloaded all my nerves. My blood sang, and I came with a vengeance, clamping around him.

He went stiff and followed me over the cliff with a loud groan.

The pulsing of his naked cock inside me without the latex was a special closeness. It soothed me as all my muscles went limp.

He collapsed on top of me, but quickly moved to the side, sparing me his full weight.

I rubbed his back and scratched his scalp as we slowly got back our breath. We fit together, and things couldn't have been better.

He stroked my hair. "That was terrific."

I stretched to kiss him. "Get me a washcloth, and we can do it again."

He slipped out and off me, and returned with a warm, wet washcloth for me.

"Give me a little while to recover."

I cleaned myself and set the cloth aside. "What? No stamina?"

He lay down beside me. "Very funny."

I snuggled up to my man.

BEFORE I DRIFTED OFF TO SLEEP AFTER OUR SECOND ROUND, I THOUGHT BACK TO tonight's movie.

Tonight I no longer wanted to be her.

Even though I couldn't save the day the way Sandra had, I realized I had something more important. I was here with a man who'd told me we were only at the beginning, a man who wanted to take things to the next level.

I had something that had eluded Sandra in the movie. She'd succeeded on the job, but I'd succeeded in a more important area.

Soon, Dennis's soft, rhythmic breathing indicated he'd passed into sleepy-land.

I definitely had something that had eluded Sandra. I had Dennis. He was a real man, and most importantly, he was my man, and he knew I was his.

Life couldn't get any better.

I still had to find a way to talk to Dennis about what I'd done, but that seemed so long ago now, and it could wait. Maybe next month I'd find the right words.

In a flash, I realized I might be able to have both. I couldn't defeat Cartwright for Dennis the way Sandra had saved the day, but I might be able to do something nobody else could. I might be able to unmask Hydra. That would make the talk easier, wouldn't it?

CHAPTER 33

JENNIFER

MONDAY MORNING I TRUDGED UP THE STAIRS IN OUR APARTMENT BUILDING.
Going latex free had meant even more *exercise* and less sleep than before.

Sleeping at my place during the week meant I could catch up. The weekdays were for helping Ramona with Billy, but starting Friday night, Dennis and I could escape again to his beach house.

So far nobody at work had figured it out, that I could tell.

We'd fallen into a routine the last three weeks. No PDA, no lunches or dinners together—except for the occasional lunch meeting in a conference room with others present—and absolutely no mean boss.

He'd offered to have me join him at Saint Helena's again last week, but Cindy had invited me to lunch that day, so I declined.

It had been three weeks since Ed had tried to torpedo me with the accusation about the Suzanne meeting, or maybe he'd even set it up. Luckily he hadn't tried anything since, and I probably had Dennis to thank for that.

The one time I'd asked Dennis about it, I'd gotten nothing but a grunt.

Dennis had crazy Melissa, and I had vindictive Ed. But, now that Ed's texting had stopped, we might be down to only one ex who was a problem.

Larry had said he thought crazy Melissa was an act, but if so, she'd perfected it. I couldn't help but think about what she might be capable of, even though she hadn't shown her face in weeks.

Every time I'd thought I was ready to broach the subject of what I'd done with Dennis, I chickened out. I convinced myself I didn't have the right words, or the setting was wrong, or we didn't have enough time, or a million other reasons to put off the inevitable.

Procrastination, thy name is Jennifer.

My latest excuse was that I would track down Hydra first, and I had a plan for that, but I needed Ramona's help.

After briefly fumbling for my keys in the hallway, I opened the door.

Billy and Ramona were eating breakfast.

Ramona looked up, with excitement on her face. "Come take a look."

I put my heavy purse down. "What is it?"

She waved me over. "We got accepted for that place on Annapurna Drive."

Billy held up Ramona's phone. "And I get my own room." Billy swiped to a picture of a bedroom when I made it to the table. "This one is mine."

The pictures were nice. The unit was clearly larger than this place.

"Which one is mine?" I asked.

Billy looked to his mother, who answered my question. "Your choice, of course."

"I think she should get the big one," Billy suggested.

His mother had a better idea. "Maybe she should get the smaller one, if she's going to be gone all the time."

I didn't have the energy for this right now. "Maybe so." In the end I knew Ramona would insist that I take the bigger one. She always had. "Well, I'm sure it's great."

"Wanna see the pool?" Billy asked.

I tousled his hair. "I have to get ready for work. You can show me tonight." I left the table for my room. "Can you help me with my hair?" I asked my sister.

"Sure." She followed me with a confused look.

I closed the door after her. "I need your help."

"Okay. What?"

"I want to tell Dennis about the...you know."

"Your sick, evil plan? You should have come clean weeks ago."

I didn't want to have the argument again. "I need your help catching Hydra."

"Your sick email buddy? I have no idea how to trace somebody on the internet."

I'd been thinking about this over the weekend. "No. I owe him a file. If I drop it off, can you watch the location on Saturday and get pictures of him for me when he picks it up?"

She sighed. "Okay. I'll see if we can move the study group to Sunday."

"Mommy, we have to go," Billy called from the other room.

I gave Ramona a hug. "Thanks a million."

She opened the door. "You know, none of this would have been necessary if you'd listened to me in the first place."

I nodded. She had a point, but arguing about my promise to Mom wouldn't get us anywhere.

"We have to put down a deposit today," she added, leaving my room.

"Write down the details for me, and I'll send the money."

That needed to be job one today—making sure that apartment didn't get away from us.

While I was still getting ready, Ramona called from the door that they were leaving. "The deposit information is on the table."

I yelled back, "Have a great day."

Now, with a bigger apartment in sight and a plan for Hydra, things were really coming together.

After a final mirror check, I took the payment information Ramona had left and tucked it into my purse.

My laptop taunted me. I opened it and logged in to check my mail.

Hydra's message was dated Saturday.

> To: Nemesis666
> From: HYDRA157
> Stop stalling. Get me the file or you will regret it. Would you
>   like me to publicize where I get my information?

Time had run out. I couldn't wait until the weekend, and I couldn't turn over the file I already had without Ramona in place. That would only be compounding my errors. I had to find a way to tell Dennis the truth.

~

DENNIS

SERENA FINISHED CHEWING. "I JUST HAVE TO SAY, SOMETIMES YOUR COOKING IS better than Mom's."

Lunch had been called off in favor of dinner tonight at my house. She wanted to chat about Dad, Josh, and Cartwright, and it had turned into a long discussion.

"It's just spaghetti and meatballs, for God's sake."

She raised her fork. "But you get the spices just right."

"You can't be in a hurry. You have to let the sauce marinate for a long time."

I'd seen Serena's attempts at anything with marinara sauce. They started with opening a bottle of sauce and ended with a microwave.

"Well, it's delicious, and thank you for listening to all my whining."

I put my wine glass down. "What else are big brothers for?"

Dad was still convinced that the Cartwright family had something to do with Josh's accident, and Serena worried it was turning into an unhealthy obsession.

I could understand her concern, but I didn't share it.

"I need your help," she said.

"Name it." She was family, and I'd do anything for family.

"I want you to teach me to cook chicken parmigiana."

I couldn't help but laugh.

"What's so funny?"

"Since when are you interested in cooking?" Of all my brothers and sisters, she was by far the worst cook. A tuna fish sandwich was a challenge for her.

"I need to make a special dinner."

I lifted an eyebrow. "For a special someone?"

She grimaced. "Are you gonna help me or not?"

It seemed we both had a special someone we were hiding.

"Sure. How about Thursday? Will that be soon enough?"

"Thursday would be great." She leaned her elbows on the table. "I have to say, you've been in an unusually good mood the last few weeks."

"What can I say? Things are going well at work." I didn't intend to explain that there was one person in particular responsible for that.

"What's her name?"

She often tried to catch me with a surprise question.

"Like I said—"

"Right. Things are good at work."

Last week she'd asked about Jennifer from the gala, and I'd explained our dancing close had been a dig at Melissa. Tonight I wasn't sure she was buying it anymore.

Serena pushed back and put her napkin on the table. "Thank you for this. I've got to get going."

Sometimes I had to hold her here for a while until she was safe to drive, but tonight she'd barely touched her wine.

"Stop in anytime."

"You know I'm going to find out."

I shrugged and walked her to the door. "By the way, who are you seeing right now? I want to let Dad know who to start a background check on."

Her scowl told me my question had hit the mark. She could dish it out, but she couldn't take it.

"Don't try that on me. You're just deflecting."

"So you are seeing somebody. I picked up a week-long trip for two to Hawaii at the fundraiser. It's yours if you tell me his name."

"We were talking about you." She turned to leave.

My question had gotten to her, and we both knew it. Tonight we would call it a draw.

I walked her to her car, held open the door, and got a quick hug.

She stood back and held my hand. "All joking aside, I'm here when you need an ear."

I tried to keep my expression neutral. "Thanks, but there's nothing to talk about."

Her smile and the tilt of her head told me I hadn't gotten neutral quite right. "When you're ready." She settled in to the seat. "I'll see you Thursday at six."

I nodded. "Six works." I closed the car door for her.

After seeing her off, I went back in to tend to the dishes.

"When you're ready," she'd said. I didn't know when that would be.

∽

JENNIFER

AFTER THE MESSAGE THIS MORNING, IT WAS CLEAR I HAD TO CONFESS WHAT I'D done to Dennis, and it couldn't wait until Friday.

I'd gotten Subway for lunch and driven to the parking lot at Target to practice my speech. All afternoon I was a wreck, and I clearly couldn't put this off any longer.

After Dennis had been gone from the office for an hour, I finally got up the courage. Leaving the garage, I turned my car toward his house—the one he called the "big house." There was no turning back now.

When I reached Dennis's street, there was another car in his driveway, a pricey one. Someone else was visiting. I drove to the end of the cul-de-sac, turned around, and stopped two houses short of his across the street.

My legs shook as I turned off the motor. "I need to tell you something," I said out loud in the empty car. "I'm the mole."

My throat clenched. I'd thought this would be easier. I'd put it off, convincing myself that the more he got to know me, the less important it would seem. The shaking of my legs said otherwise.

His door opened, and he came out, walking a woman to the strange car.

She faced away from me. I couldn't recognize her from this distance. It was just someone visiting him. What was the big deal?

He held the door for her the way he did for me. He hugged her the way he did me. The instant pang of jealousy stabbed me in the heart, though I urged myself to calm down, get all the facts.

I rolled down my window but couldn't make out their words from this distance. The warm smile on his face, though, was one I knew well, and I'd thought it was reserved for me. Perhaps I was less special than I'd thought.

She backed out in her expensive car.

I hadn't expected this to be an easy conversation, but now I definitely wasn't ready. Seeing this other woman had scrambled my brain.

After her taillights disappeared around the corner, I started my shit bucket to leave. I was making comparisons? How pathetic. I pulled forward, and when I reached his house, I thought about turning in to his driveway, but chickened out. Barely able to breathe, I pulled over down the street.

I couldn't leave. I had to do this, but I couldn't do it. I was a complete mess.

My head came down on the steering wheel. I didn't know the right words anymore.

A crow cawed at me from a tree branch. I couldn't understand the bird any more than Dennis would understand me right now.

CHAPTER 34

JENNIFER

He opened the door. "Jennifer. It's a weekday."

"Am I intruding?"

"Not at all. Come in." He held the door open. "Good thing you weren't ten minutes earlier. Serena just left."

His words were a relief as I entered. That I'd so misjudged the situation made me feel even worse. Why did I always jump so quickly toward the wrong conclusion?

"We have to talk," I told him.

"Sure." As soon as he closed the door, he took me into a hug, one I couldn't fully return.

With my face buried in his shoulder, I managed a few words. "I'm so sorry."

That only made him hug me tighter. He smoothed my hair with his hand. "Talk to me, Angel."

I wasn't so sure he'd be ready to hear what I had to say, because he didn't know the weighty baggage I brought with me. Baggage I'd tried to ignore for weeks now. I shivered at the realization that time might not have made this easier. As the tears came, I clung to him tighter.

I concentrated on what he'd just said. It might be the last time I heard him call me Angel, and I desperately wanted to hang on to that memory.

He pushed back far enough to lift up my chin. His eyes gazed into mine with warmth and caring. "Want to sit down?"

I nodded.

He tried to lead me to the couch, but I pulled him to the small breakfast table instead. He held my hands across the table as we sat.

I had no idea how to start. None of the words I'd practiced made sense to me now.

His kind eyes hadn't changed yet, because he didn't know my sins. "I told you, whatever it is, we can fix it. I meant that."

"I've been bad." I sounded like a child saying it that way, but I was feeling my way into this.

"That's nothing special. We've all done something bad at one time or another. But let's quantify bad. Did you kill a dozen people?"

That bit of nonsense coaxed a half-smile out of me. "No. It's not that bad."

"Then we can get past it, Angel."

I still doubted he'd want to call me that after I got this off my chest.

The warmth of his hands holding mine gave me the courage to go on. "You know the articles in the paper about the company?"

"Yeah, the ones in the *Times*?"

"They're my fault."

His grip on my hands tightened as he chuckled. "Don't be ridiculous. They're not anybody's fault. It's just some sicko who wants to torment me and everybody who works at the company."

"No, you don't understand. He got the information from me."

There. I'd said it.

His grip on me faltered as his mouth dropped open. "You what?"

The words spilled out in rapid fire. "I'm sorry. At the time, I didn't know you weren't responsible."

He let go of my hands. His words came out slowly and deliberately. "Slow down. You're not making any sense. Are you saying you provided the leaks to that Sigurd asshole?"

I nodded. "I'm sorry. I didn't know."

He sat back, and his eyes went wide with disbelief. "Why?"

"I didn't know," I repeated.

The room was suddenly cold.

The kindness in his eyes skipped through disbelief on their way to anger. "Didn't know he would write what he did? Didn't know it would hurt the company? Didn't know it would hurt me, and all the people you work with?"

The accusation that I'd wronged not just him but everybody at the company hung over me like a guillotine.

"I thought you killed my dad."

That set him back even farther in his chair as he cocked his head. "I don't go around killing people," he spat. "I don't even know your father. You're the only Hanley I've ever met."

"It's complicated. This was all before I knew you."

"And you thought it was okay to attack me because you didn't know me? That's a stupid-ass thing to believe. Do you have any idea how many people's lives you've hurt?"

I felt even worse. "Do you remember Robert Davis?" I shivered, having to say Dad's name out loud.

His eyes narrowed for a second as he tried to recall. "Yes. But what does that have to do with you?"

"He was my stepfather."

He nodded as the memory registered. "He died in an accidental fire at the company. How could you possibly think I killed him?"

It sounded stupid now, but I had no choice. "My mother was sure it was your fault. You wouldn't let us see the accident report. I promised her I'd get to the bottom of it."

"And because you thought the company was responsible, you thought you'd take it out on all of us? That's stupid, and frankly, mean."

I deserved the criticism. "I'm here to apologize."

"Do you want to know what really happened? Or do you and your mother not care about the truth?" The words were tinged with anger.

"I know the truth now."

"I'm not sure you do. I spared your mother the knowledge that your stepfather caused his own death. And do you want to know why?"

He continued when I didn't say anything.

"I did that to maximize the insurance settlement she got. If it had been ruled his fault, your mother would have gotten almost nothing."

"We didn't know that."

He rubbed it in. "I didn't do it because I had to. I insisted on it because it was the decent thing to do for her." He shook his head. "How could you?"

I didn't have an answer. There was no way for me to repent for the sin I'd committed. "I judged you without the evidence, and that was wrong. I was wrong. I'm so sorry."

He stood. "I think you should leave."

I got up, pulled my employee badge from my pocket, and put it on the table. "I really am sorry."

"You think you can come in here say you're sorry for ruining my life and just walk away?"

I didn't understand the question. "I can't stay after what I've done."

"You can't leave the company until I say so."

"What?"

"I don't know what to think, other than I'm angry and you're stupid. I need time to process this. You stay at the company, and every time you pass someone in the hallway, think about what you've done to them, what you've cost them."

I backed away from the table.

"Take the badge with you," he ordered.

I picked it up and slunk to the door. "I didn't mean for this to happen. I'm sorry."

He shook his head, but didn't say anything.

I opened the door and closed it behind me as I walked away from the one good thing that had happened to me in years. Outside I was alone and cold. My legs were wobbly as I made my way to my car.

I hadn't known what to expect, and my stomach was about to turn itself inside out as I climbed into the driver's seat.

If this had been a movie, he would have come running out the door to tell me it would be all right. A quick glance at his door confirmed this was no movie, and a happily ever after wasn't in the cards for me.

I'd made a terrible mistake, and with that came consequences. Being told I still had to work among the people I'd wronged was a penance I hadn't seen coming. But then maybe Ramona had been right all along. My path here had been wrongheaded from the beginning, and I deserved whatever I got at this point.

My phone chirped. As I pulled it from my purse, I expected the text to be from Ramona, but it wasn't.

EB: We need to talk

Another problem I didn't need.

CHAPTER 35

DENNIS

I HADN'T SLEPT HARDLY AT ALL LAST NIGHT, UNABLE TO GET MY MIND AROUND how Jennifer could have betrayed us all like that.

Tuesday at work was a blur. I couldn't concentrate, and by the end of the day I was glad to leave for my brother Zack's barbecue to meet his fiancée.

I arrived fashionably late.

Zack put a beer in my hand and introduced me to his lovely Brittney. She had been around when we were kids, and now that she'd come back to town, it hadn't taken long for things to heat up between the two.

I didn't expect to see either Kelly or Vincent, as they were both back east, Mom was still in Paris, but Dad and Serena were here, and Josh had made it too.

He'd been released from the hospital four days after the accident. Luckily, the brain swelling they'd worried about hadn't occurred, and he'd passed all his concussion protocols. His bruises had healed, and you couldn't even tell now that he'd been in that horrific accident.

Serena walked my way. "Where's your girl?"

"What girl?" I wasn't sure it would work with her, but I needed to keep the denial going. It was better than admitting I'd been taken in by a person trying to destroy me.

She cocked her head. "I know that look. You're trying to hide something, but it won't work."

"Yeah. You got me. I'm planning on penis-reduction surgery later in the week, but you have to keep that to yourself."

She laughed. "And disappoint half the women in LA?"

"It's so I won't hurt them."

"Very funny. You know I'm going to find out."

Bill Covington and his wife, Lauren, joined us, putting an end to Serena's interrogation.

I'd had only a short chance to catch up with the Covingtons when Dad corralled me to join him.

He re-introduced me to Doug, Brittney's brother, who had been one of Zack's friends from way back. Doug had joined the Marines and was on a short leave from Okinawa. Having been a Marine himself, Dad was enthralled with Doug's stories of his current life in the Corps.

Dad set his beer down. "Excuse me, I'm going to have another go at Zachary." He took his cane and strode toward my brother.

"What's that about?" Doug asked after Dad was out of earshot.

I lifted my bottle. "Zack hasn't escaped the family company yet, and Dad is trying to convince him to go to London for more training."

"I bet Zack can hold his own."

"We'll see. Dad can be a pretty irresistible force, if he wants to."

"I hear you got out of the family business, though."

"Yeah. It wasn't easy, but I like being my own boss."

"No orders from above, huh?"

"No direct orders, but I do work for the board, and the Wall Street bozos who take every opportunity to tell me what they think I'm doing wrong. It sucks."

Doug nodded.

"Not a one of them has run so much as a successful hot dog cart."

Doug swigged more beer.

I listened from a distance, and luckily for Zack, Dad didn't seem to be putting on the hard sell.

After a moment, Phil Patterson, another regular at our Habitat for Humanity weekends, came up and rescued Zack from Dad's clutches.

Not one to give up easily, Dad followed them into the house.

A few minutes later, Phil jogged up to us. "Dennis, you gotta fucking come to the front right now. There's news about Debbie."

I put my beer down and sprinted to the front door. Debbie was a name I hadn't heard in a very long time. We never spoke of her abduction and death.

When I reached the door, Zack and Dad were talking with a woman and a man in FBI windbreakers. Closer to the street were two sheriff's deputies.

"Phil said it's news about Debbie?" I asked breathlessly.

Phil arrived right behind me.

The short woman spoke. "We have evidence that she's alive."

"And may be involved in a bank robbery," the other agent added, which earned him a stern look from the woman.

Dad grabbed my shoulder. "Dennis, you're the oldest. You need to go out east and learn everything you can. Get back to me when you have something solid to report."

I had a better suggestion. "Vincent's already in Boston. Why don't we call him?"

Dad's jaw ticked. "You're the oldest. It's your job."

Clearly this was not up for debate. I was the oldest, and with that came responsibilities.

He turned to Zack and Phil. "In the meantime, we have a party to get back to. Not a word of this to any of the others until we know more."

Zack started to object. "But—"

Dad cut him off. "Not a word to anyone—not a single, solitary word. Understood? That means you too, Phillip."

We all nodded. Dad's tone said he was serious, and there would be no changing his mind. The decision had been made, a task had been assigned, and the rules stated—end of discussion.

In a blink, everything I'd known about Debbie's disappearance had changed. The kidnapper had died in a shootout with the authorities, and since his communications had said Debbie had less than a week of air, we'd all assumed the worst when she couldn't be located.

Dad and Uncle Seth had paid privately for a search after the FBI stopped looking, but nothing ever came of it.

We'd never known of an accomplice in Debbie's kidnapping. But if she was still alive, there had to have been one.

"We should leave Dennis to it," Dad announced as he herded the others back inside. "And I'm serious about keeping this under wraps."

I closed the door after them and spoke to the FBI agents. "I'm Dennis Benson. Debbie's my cousin. So tell me what we know."

"Special Agent Liz Parsons," the woman said, introducing herself. "And my partner, Special Agent Paul Newsom."

She offered her card.

Evidently the FBI didn't shake hands.

I accepted both agents' cards and stashed them in my pocket.

The man was obviously the junior partner here, as Parsons did the talking.

"When Deborah was abducted, her DNA was entered into the National Missing Persons Database. A search was initiated on a sample obtained in Maryland that generated a hit on Deborah's record today. The original agents on her case have retired, so we're now lead on her disappearance."

I noticed she'd switched from *abduction* to *disappearance*. "How sure are we it's her?"

"It was a total match. The sample is definitely hers."

I breathed a long sigh. After a lack of closure, this was welcome news. "You said something about a bank robbery. Was she injured?"

The agents looked at each other before Parsons continued. "She's a suspect."

"That's not possible."

Parsons held up her hand. "I understand it's a shock. But all we know at the moment is that DNA evidence collected at the scene of the robbery matches Deborah Benson."

"A shock? I told you, it's not possible she'd be involved in something like that," I argued. She was a Benson, and I knew she wouldn't have, couldn't have changed that much.

"Sir, don't get belligerent."

"Belligerent? First you guys shoot the kidnapper so we can't get her back, and now you want to accuse a helpless girl of bank robbery?"

I must have given off a dangerous vibe, because Agent Newsom braced, as if expecting me to lunge at him.

Parsons advanced on me instead. "Dennis, you need to calm down."

The switch from *sir* to *Dennis* surprised me.

"I worked with your sister-in-law Ashley in Boston, and I've met your brother Vince. I asked to be assigned to this case because I'm on your side here. This is a notification visit only. You know as much as we do at this point."

That changed my perception of the pint-sized agent, and put an item on my to-do list. I was calling Boston first thing to get the lowdown on this woman.

"The local field office in DC is working the robbery case, and that's all they've shared with us so far," Parsons said.

I took a breath and backed up, which got Newsom to relax.

"Okay, so who do I get in touch with out there?" I asked.

"We're handling the original kidnapping angle, so we'll visit DC and make a determination as soon as we can."

Shifting back to calling it a kidnapping was a step in the right direction.

"We'll see that you get introduced to the team out there, and you can discuss the bank case with them. Will that be acceptable?"

I was grateful for the Vince connection, because the federal government was now asking me if their plan was acceptable.

I nodded. "Of course.

"How soon can you get to DC?" she asked.

"Probably quicker than you can, with the company jet. I can provide transportation, if you like."

Parsons backed up. "Thanks, but we can't. Text your contact info to my number on the card, so we can connect with you in DC. We'll meet at the field office on Fourth Street Northwest."

Newsom's look said he wished they could have accepted the flight.

"Thank you." I waved as the duo departed toward their SUV and immediately texted my phone number to Parsons. I sent a second text to Newsom for good measure.

The deputies that had been at the curb then got into their vehicles as well. Apparently their time babysitting the agents was over.

Five minutes later, I made an excuse that I had to leave and wished Brittney and Zack the best. Dad had called his flight department, and his jet would be fueled and ready for the trip to DC by the time I got to the airport.

Serena caught me on the way out. "Still not going to admit it?"

"Shhh. Surgery's not till Friday."

Outside, I composed a text to Cindy.

ME: Not in the rest of the week - No calls - Jay is in charge until I return

That should allow me to concentrate on the only thing that mattered—Debbie. The next few days were not for multi-tasking.

Once in my car, I dialed Vince in Boston.

He picked up after a few rings. "Hey, big brother, what has you calling this late?"

"I need the skinny on an FBI agent who just visited us out here by the name of Liz Parsons, says she knows you and Ashley."

"Sure, I remember her. She worked with Ash before transferring to California."

"Can I trust her, and what kind of cooperation can I expect from her?"

"Hey, Ash," he yelled away from the phone. "Dennis wants to know if he can trust Liz Parsons, and will she cooperate with him?"

I heard the *"Hell yes"* part of Ashley's answer, but I didn't catch the rest.

Vince spoke into the phone again. "She'll call Liz tomorrow and make sure you get full cooperation. What's the case?"

"I can't say."

"Give me a break. You're not keeping it from me. Ash can find out in ten seconds."

"You have to promise to keep this to yourself. Just you and Ashley, nobody else—Dad's orders."

"Okay."

"I'm coming to check out evidence that Debbie is still alive."

He was silent for a second. "Deb?"

"Yeah. I can't say any more. I'll let you know when I have something solid."

"Holy shit. You can count on Ash to make sure the Bureau is cooperative."

"Please ask Ashley not to call. The whole thing is sensitive at this point. For the family's sake, this needs to stay under wraps."

"Okay, if that's the way you want to play it. Look, Liz owes us big time, and if you need anything from her and you want a little leverage, ask her if she remembers Kirk Willey."

"What about him?"

"Just mention the name. Like I said, she owes us. That should be enough to get you any help she can arrange, and she can be pretty damned resourceful."

"Thanks. I won't use it unless I have to."

We hung up after I refused again to tell him any more, and he assured me he'd keep Ashley under control.

My mind returned to the person I'd misjudged: Jennifer. My feelings were a jumbled mess, and I doubted tonight would be any better in terms of restful sleep.

Everything had gone to shit in the last month. Josh shot at, Melissa attacking, Cartwright after me, and now Jennifer undermining me. What had I done to deserve this hell?

Maybe finding Debbie would turn my luck around.

I noticed the text as I was boarding Dad's jet. It had come earlier, but I hadn't heard it at the party.

CINDY: Jay says the Cartwright Group wants to meet tomorrow afternoon.

One more thing I didn't need right now. I typed my response.

ME: No fucking way

I didn't hit the send arrow. Instead I retyped it.

ME: No meetings - No calls

The first version more clearly matched my mood, but I didn't need to take this out on Cindy.

Aboard Dad's jet, the seats were comfortable leather, and the glass of wine I helped myself to was perfectly chilled. But nothing about this trip felt right.

I was leaving town right when I needed to talk to Jennifer. I needed to sort this out. How could it work between us if I couldn't trust her?

After another sip of wine, I decided to focus on tomorrow instead of yesterday.

Finding evidence that Debbie was still alive after all these years created a slew of uncomfortable questions. Where had she been all this time?

If the kidnapping had been about ransom, why hadn't there been another demand after the first foiled attempt? The fact that there'd been a shootout with the FBI might have answered that, but these days kidnappers could demand untraceable Bitcoin payments and not risk being followed from a money drop. With our family's resources, they could have demanded a king's ransom, but they hadn't.

If this wasn't about money, had the original ransom been a diversion, or merely an added bonus to their goal of child abduction? That thought sent a chill down my spine.

What had Debbie had to endure all these years? Jaycee Dugard was the only long-term child kidnapping survivor that came to mind. Her ordeal had lasted 18 years. Elizabeth Smart had escaped after eighteen months, Jamye Closs had escaped after three months. But by far, the majority of child abductions that lasted over a month didn't end well.

Deb had only been five when they took her. Would she even recognize her own name at this point?

Then the specter of Patty Hearst raised its ugly head. Could Debbie have joined her kidnappers?

CHAPTER 36

DENNIS

THE FLIGHT HAD BEEN MOSTLY TURBULENCE-FREE, AND THE RIDE INTO TOWN WAS a quick one in the darkness.

Yet when sunlight began filtering around the edges of the blackout curtains Wednesday morning, I'd only managed a bit of fitful sleep.

After showering, I went downstairs for an early breakfast. I needed something to keep me busy. My thoughts had bounced from what Jennifer had confessed Monday night to the Patty Hearst scenario as it related to Debbie, and back again. As the cycle repeated, I only felt worse.

Hearst had been raped and threatened with death. And yet she'd still gotten jail time for participating in a bank robbery with her captors. That didn't bode well for Debbie.

The text from Liz Parsons arrived while I was eating.

PARSONS: Noon meet at 601 4th St. NW ask for Boxer

I tapped out my response.

ME: I'll be there

If I had to wait till lunchtime to get started, I could hit the gym and burn off a little nervous energy while muddling through my feelings about Jennifer and what she'd done. When it rained it certainly poured.

I took a minute to call my sister Kelly.

"Hey, Dennis," she answered. "I hear from Serena you've got a new girl." Just what I didn't need.

I ignored the jab. "I flew in last night for a customer meeting. Want to do dinner?"

Her hesitation was palpable. "Dinner?"

"Yeah, you know, food, wine, family."

"Sure." Her voice betrayed her.

"Is everything all right?"

"Sure. I've just got stuff going on."

Whatever stuff she had going on, I needed to hear about it.

"It's your town—you pick a place, and I'll call you later."

I gave her a brief Josh update, and we ended the call.

AFTER MY WORKOUT, I LEFT THE HOTEL FOR MY WALK TO THE FBI FIELD OFFICE, which wasn't far. A few blocks down Massachusetts Avenue and a right turn on 4th Street brought me to the building. Just like every other government building in town, it was built with granite, not the steel and glass that would've been common in California. They loved their granite here in DC. Even the curbs of the streets were granite blocks instead of the simple formed concrete we used on the west coast.

I took the right-hand doorway marked visitors, which led to the expected security check—much like going through the airport, except these guys all packed weapons.

Telling them I was here to see Boxer got me a reprimand for not calling him Special Agent. Apparently everybody in the FBI was a Special Agent.

I was escorted to a conference room on the fourth floor, where Parsons and Newsom were eating sandwiches.

Parsons looked up. She noticed me looking at their roller bags in the corner. "We didn't get a meal on the flight."

"I told you I'd beat you here."

She took the final bite of her sandwich and didn't respond.

Newsom pointed to a chair. "The DC team should be here in a moment."

I chose the seat next to Parsons.

A few minutes later, two more suits joined us.

The first one offered his card. "Special Agent Neil Boxer."

I accepted it and gave him mine. "Dennis Benson."

I recognized the second agent before he said a thing.

He offered his card. "Special Agent Adam Cartwright."

The same Adam Cartwright who had fought me many years ago—and the son of my current corporate enemy. My luck sucked.

We exchanged cards, and I pasted on a smile. "It's been a long time." I hadn't known or cared what had become of him after high school.

Adam nodded with cold eyes that said he hadn't forgotten. "It has."

The glance I got from Parsons indicated she'd noticed the frostiness. "Neil, why don't you run us through what you have?"

"Adam's lead on this," Boxer told her.

She shrugged.

Adam smugly opened up a laptop and with a few keystrokes, the monitor at the end of the table came alive. "Let's start with the outdoor feed."

The image wasn't as clear as they looked on TV shows, but we could see the street, people, and traffic.

Adam began to narrate. "Here's where they pull up."

He stopped the feed when a dark, older-model Chevy pulled to the curb. He ran it forward.

"Two suspects get out, and the driver remains." The two moved across the frame to the area of the door. "One vehicle, three robbers this time. Two go inside, and one drives. Next we go to the inside feeds."

The screen split into four viewing angles, and in the upper-right frame, the two from the car entered through the glass doors.

"Here we have a man and a woman. The woman is your vic," Adam continued. He moved the video forward a bit. "Here they pull out guns and start issuing commands."

In the next several frames, the customers all panicked and started getting down on the ground. There was no audio, but the video was clear. They were ordered to the floor.

"He fires one shot into the ceiling for effect, and the woman goes to the tellers to collect the cash."

On the video, the male robber waved his gun at the woman, motioning her to the line of tellers, and then trained it back on the customers.

"Hold it," Newsom said.

Adam halted the video.

Newsom pointed. "Why is the man masked and the woman not?"

Adam shrugged. "She's not smart enough, is my guess."

Parsons put a hand on my arm as a warning before I could protest.

Adam started the video again. "These three are amateurs, dangerous amateurs. The driver and the man have pulled off two other jobs nearby, but this is the first one where they bring her along." He pointed at Debbie on the screen. "She's our best lead so far to get this group. Let's go on and see the rest."

The video continued as the woman put the gun in her coat pocket, then stopped, probably surprised, and looked straight at the camera for a second before going down the line, collecting cash in a duffle bag. Her face was pale, and she reminded me of the way I remembered Debbie... But then she'd been five at the time, and her most notable characteristics had been the tiny birthmark on the back of her neck and the green in her eyes.

The quick video shot wasn't clear enough to determine the presence of either of those things.

The tellers appeared scared as they handed over the money, and some of the customers were squirming a bit on the floor.

He stopped the video again. "This is where it went wrong."

He restarted the video as the woman brought the bag back to the man. Then the man turned to his right and fired a shot. A teller dropped to the floor in a separate frame, and the others dove behind the counters.

He stopped the playback again.

"What's the teller's condition?" Parsons asked.

"Stable," Boxer replied.

"Good thing he was a terrible shot. We've been worried about exactly this, because the guy likes to shoot his gun," Adam added.

I hadn't seen anything to provoke the gunman, and all that ran through my head was the Patty Hearst scenario.

"Why did he shoot?" Newsom asked, echoing my question. "Get anything from the witness statements?"

Parsons leaned over to whisper. "This is not good."

I nodded. No matter how it had started, she had joined in the robbery, and when she was found, she'd be treated as the accomplice, not the victim, especially with a shooting involved. She hadn't pulled the trigger, but that wouldn't matter to the prosecutors. The circumstances were damning.

"Don't know. Maybe she said something, or moved too fast," Adam answered. "So that's the first screwup, and here's the second."

He restarted it and the pair left, the man followed by the woman.

"What did we miss?" Parsons asked.

Adam backed it up and went forward in slow motion. The man turned, and the woman leaned over a bit, then straightened and followed.

"See it?" He backed it up and restarted it.

On the second try, Parsons saw it. "She spit on the floor."

"That's right. Forensics pulled DNA from that spit, and that's when you got the call."

"Why did she do that?" Newsom asked.

Adam shrugged. "Don't know. Like I said, stupid. Once we catch her, we got a sure conviction on the robbery and attempted murder—thanks to DNA, because we got no prints at any of the scenes."

"The car?" Parsons asked.

Boxer shook his head. "Stolen plates, no defining decals, a dent in the right front is all we have to go on so far."

"Video of them casing it ahead of time?" Newsom asked.

Adam stiffened. "As hard as it is for you west coast whiz kids to believe, we do know what we're doing. We checked the old footage, back six weeks. So far nothing, but we're still working it. Like I said, amateurs. This is a new crew. They got a little money out of the heists, so they'll be back and shooting other people if we don't find them first. Sorry you had to make the trip out, but we've got it from here, and we'll let you know when we catch her."

He hadn't used the word *find*. Instead he'd said *catch*.

I couldn't believe he'd just dismissed us like that.

"Kidnapping takes priority," Newsom said.

"That was yesterday. Already ran it up to the AD. Because of the shots fired, the robbery takes priority, and we have the lead."

"Assistant Director," Parsons told me, explaining what AD meant.

"What do you have that can help us find her?" Adam asked.

"Nothing at all," Parsons answered. "Kidnapped at five years old. At the time it was presumed to be a single kidnapper who died after the ransom pickup. When no further communications came, the child was assumed deceased. Until now."

Boxer looked at me. "And no communications with the family since then?"

I shook my head. "Not a one."

Adam shut down the video. "Thank you for your time, then."

I couldn't believe that was it. There had to be more. "I'd like updates as you get more."

He scoffed. "I'll let you know when we catch her."

"She's my cousin, and a victim here," I complained.

He scowled. "She's a suspect. The victim is the lady in the hospital who took a bullet."

Parsons interceded. "She's both. The kidnapping is still open, and she's the victim in that. You can send me the updates, and I'll pass them along."

"Sure." Adam sighed.

"And," I added, "I'd like a hard copy of the frame where we see her face."

Parsons beat Adam to it. "Not a problem. I'm sure the family would like to see what she looks like after all these years."

Boxer frowned—even he thought Adam was being an ass.

Fifteen minutes later, Parsons, Newsom, and I were outside on the sidewalk.

Parsons stopped not far from the door. "Time to go home and wait. At least you got a picture."

"That's all? We don't get more? What about witnesses? They might be able to tell us something."

Newsom answered for her. "He got to the AD and got the lead assigned to him, so that's it. And, I heard he was a…"

Parson's scowl stopped him mid-sentence. "It doesn't matter."

I couldn't live with that. "What do you mean it doesn't matter?"

"Because they have the boots on the ground here. They get the credit if they find her, and the shit if they don't. All of that means…" She stopped while another local agent walked by. "That means they'll work hard on it, which is what we want. Boxer and Cartwright will work the team hard to find her, trace the car, track down sightings. Those are *his* leads right now. If he gets told to report to us, he'll drag his feet, resources will go to other cases, and we won't get anywhere."

She was short on height, but not on savvy. Her analysis was solid.

"Anyway," Newsom said. "You can call your friend Cartwright, and maybe he can give you a little insight."

I shook my head. I wasn't going into particulars. "He's not my friend. If I show up missing, he's the first one you should question."

Parsons chuckled. "Then it's a good thing you're not sticking around to annoy them." She cocked an eyebrow the way my sister did when she had a zinger. "And they missed the most important part."

Newsom asked the question for me. "What?"

She smiled. "When was the last time you spit on a marble floor inside?"

"Never," I answered.

Parsons nodded. "Exactly. She didn't have a mask, she looked straight into the camera, and then she spit on the floor after the guy turned his back. She wanted to be ID'd. Smart girl. This is still a kidnapping investigation."

That put an entirely different spin on today.

∾

JENNIFER

WEDNESDAY, AFTER LEAVING WORK EARLY, I GOT THAT SAME ODD FEELING THAT I was being watched. Looking over my shoulder, I didn't see anyone or anything out of the ordinary. But nothing had felt right since the night I'd tried and failed to explain myself to Dennis. Every person I encountered in the company made me feel the same awkwardness. Did they suspect what I'd done? Were they watching me in order to catch me in the act?

Dennis had left town last night—that was all I could get out of Cindy today. She either didn't want to say any more, or really didn't know. I couldn't tell which.

After shucking my heels, I wandered to the cupboard and located the bottle of Jim Beam Ramona had hidden away. I poured the first glass. It was time to determine how many it took to deaden the guilt I felt.

My phone still held the latest text from Ed, which I'd ignored. He now represented another level of problem for me to deal with—eventually.

EB: I know what you have been doing - we need to talk

I deleted it.

It didn't matter anymore what Ed knew or didn't know. I'd told Dennis the awful truth, and no suspicion of Ed's could be worse than that. It didn't matter if he knew when I'd started seeing Dennis, or how often. That embarrassment didn't matter anymore.

Dennis's command to stay at work had seemed odd at first, but now I understood it. With every person I passed in the hall or saw in a conference room or the cafeteria, I was reminded of his question. *"What have they done to deserve the way you treated them?"* I'd not just failed them, I'd sabotaged them. Though meaning to strike at Dennis, I'd hit the company and all the employees. And, worst of all, their families.

A stinging gulp of the amber liquid took my mind off the problem for a second. But the sting was replaced by warmth in my stomach, and my mind returned to the darkness.

In the cafeteria at lunch, I'd overheard a conversation about how one person's plan to buy a house had to be put on hold. He'd planned to use his stock options for the down payment. There wasn't anything I could do to fix that. None of it was fixable. It had all been avoidable though, if only I'd listened to Ramona months ago when Hydra had first approached me.

Why hadn't I listened?

Why had I put my faith in Mom's anger instead?

It was so obvious, in retrospect. She'd lashed out in fury and despair, and I'd allowed myself to get swept up in it. For what? To accomplish what?

Vengeance that was misplaced, and worse than that, so misdirected that it affected innocent members of the company I worked for, my teammates?

The door opened as I took another gulp.

Ramona closed the door behind her. "You're home early."

Billy ran over to give me a hug.

I set the tumbler down. "How was school, Bill?"

After the hug he grinned. "I got an A on spelling today."

"That's great. Can you spell pizza?"

"T-A-S-T-Y."

"Perfect, and I'll only put half the olives on because you aced your test."

"No olives," he countered.

"Half," Ramona said. She gave me the stink eye for the bottle in front of me.

Billy ran off.

"What's got you down in the dumps?"

I looked over to see that Billy was far enough away. "I fucked up."

I hadn't told her anything last night.

She'd been busy studying for a test, and if I'd started, we would have been up half the night. If that had affected her test, I would have been the cause of another disaster.

She joined me on the couch. "Let's hear it."

"First, how was the test?"

"Hard. Good thing I spent all last night studying. Eloise told me she didn't 'cuz she thought she had it down cold. Bad move."

Hearing that made me extra glad I'd held off.

"So what's got you into the hard stuff?" she asked.

I sniffed. "Dennis. I went to see him."

She waited silently for more.

I stared at the little liquid left in my tumbler. It didn't hold any answers. "I told him what I did."

She gasped and moved closer. "And it didn't go well, huh?"

"He told me to get out of his house."

She sighed. "You sort of knew that would happen."

"I thought it would be easier. I thought as we got closer, what I did before would be less important."

She put her arm around me. "So what happens now? Do you have to leave the company?"

She nicely didn't remind me that she'd warned me I couldn't have it both ways.

I gulped down the last of the bourbon. "He won't let me leave yet. He said I need to be around the people I hurt."

"Huh?"

"The other people that work at the company."

"Oh."

"I hadn't thought about how it would affect them. But at lunch..." I sniffled. "...I overheard someone saying he couldn't buy the house he wanted to because our stock was down. I never thought..." I didn't finish the sentence.

Ramona leaned forward to pour more bourbon into the glass, and then she took a sip. "That sucks."

I couldn't hold the tears back. "I really fucked up."

She handed me the glass.

I gulped some more down. It didn't alleviate the pain. "What do I do?"

"You finish the glass, and another if you want. Then you find a movie to take your mind off it, go to sleep, and in the morning you get back up and deal with life. One foot in front of the other. That's all any of us can do."

I nodded and sipped the drink. "He was the best thing that ever happened to me."

She held me. "Do you love him?"

I nodded. "So much it hurts."

"Then talk to him. Try to work it out."

"He's out of town."

"Talk to him when he gets back, then. He's got to be hurt by what you did. If you get a paper cut, you suck on your finger and go on a few seconds later. If you stub your toe, you curse and jump around on one foot for a minute or two before you can walk again. The time to get over something changes with how big the hurt is. You can't expect him to get over this in a few minutes."

"You think he'll ever forgive me?"

She took a deep breath. "That's something even he probably doesn't know yet."

I nodded.

She got up. "How about if I make the pizza and you find a movie?"

I scrolled through the choices and settled on the same movie I'd seen a while ago: *Two Weeks Notice*. At least in that one things had worked out in the end.

I was about to pour another glass when I decided it could wait until bedtime. I'd need all the help I could get finding sleep tonight.

DENNIS

"I DIDN'T EXPECT YOU BACK SO SOON," DAD SAID.

We sat in the Atlantic Aviation conference room at the airport. I'd left DC quickly after being told twice by Parsons that staying would only make things worse.

"The agents out there weren't going to let me stick around to look over their shoulders, and Kelly called off our dinner."

"I expected them to be more cooperative now that we've got a lead on Debbie. I could get young William's Uncle Garth involved."

I waved him off. "Let's hold off on the big guns until later. The local agents will keep me up to date, but the ones out there aren't worth pissing off—antagonizing right now."

Parsons had said they wouldn't give me the time of day, and pissing them off would only make it harder for her to get any cooperation out of them.

I believed her.

Dad held up the picture I'd brought, which was less than ten hours old. "This is Deborah?"

"No doubt about it. The DNA sample is definitely from her. Agent Parsons thinks she did it on purpose."

"Parsons…I know that name."

I filled in the blanks for him. "In Boston she worked with Ashley."

"Yes, I remember. I met her at Vincent's place. Short girl?"

"Yup."

"Smart cookie, that one." He stroked his goatee. "She thinks it was purposeful?"

I used the same line Parsons had. "When was the last time you spit on the floor inside a building?"

"I see."

"Parsons' thinking is that Debbie wanted to be identified. She spit when the other robber's back was turned."

"Good thing, then. Otherwise, we'd never have known."

"Exactly." I hoped Parsons was right, because I'd drunk the Kool-Aid and bought into her hypothesis. "It implies but doesn't prove she was coerced."

He lifted the picture again.

"You can keep that. I've got another."

"Let's keep this under wraps for now. The last thing we need is a Benson in the news as a bank robber."

"I had to tell Vincent and his wife."

His eyes narrowed. "Unfortunate. I'll have a talk with them. Nobody else, though. We have to keep this from getting out."

"There's one other problem. I bumped into Adam Cartwright. He's one of the agents on the case, so we're not going to get much cooperation."

Dad sucked in a breath. "That's not good. Bad apples popping up everywhere. And his father is circling you like the vulture he is." He stroked his goatee again. "I see why you didn't want to stay out there."

CHAPTER 37

DENNIS

AFTER ANOTHER NIGHT OF FITFUL SLEEP, I WAS IN THE OFFICE EARLY THURSDAY morning.

Cindy was nice enough to bring me a second cup of coffee. "Jay says he needs to talk to you about Cartwright."

"Okay, send him up."

"And there's another thing. You should talk with Jennifer."

I sat back in my chair and steepled my hands. "And why is that?"

She leaned on the desk. "She needs some cheering up."

I crossed my arms. "You can handle that. Buy her a donut or something."

She spun around and went to the door, closed it firmly, and turned toward me. "I think it's something you need to handle."

A week ago somebody mentioning I should handle Jennifer would've brought pleasant thoughts to mind, but not this morning.

"It's not my job to keep everybody around here happy. My job is to make sure we can earn enough that everybody keeps getting paid."

She advanced toward the desk. "I'm not blind, you know. It's an issue you need to address." Her implication was clear.

Jennifer and I thought we'd been coy enough that nobody caught on. But nobody didn't seem to include Cindy.

She sat down in the chair opposite me. "She asked me three times when you'd be back. I can read between the lines. With all she's done for you, for us, since coming upstairs, don't you think you owe it to the company to talk to her?"

I didn't answer.

She crossed her arms. "I can sit here all day until you say yes."

"Yes."

"Yes what?"

She was being a real hard ass today.

"Yes, I'll ask her what's bothering her. But what's bothering me right now is that my assistant won't let me get back to work."

She rose and headed toward the door. "Yes, boss." The sarcasm in her voice wasn't lost on me.

After the door closed behind her, I knew what I wanted to ask Jennifer. The one question that kept coming up: *How could you betray us all like that?* I'd spent hours and hours on the subject. It ate at me day and night. My stomach was so sour thinking about it, I'd been chewing Tums like they were candy.

I didn't get any more time to ponder what else to say to Jennifer.

Jay knocked and let himself in, closing the door behind him. "Cartwright's coming in at ten."

"I thought I left word that we weren't having a meeting yet?"

"He called yesterday afternoon to set it up, said he heard you were going to be back in town this morning."

Fucking Adam must've told him.

Jay leaned against the chair, not bothering to sit. "Who do you want to invite?"

I had an easy answer. "You, me, and Larry should do it."

He cocked his head. "What about Jennifer? She seemed pretty canny at reading Talbot and Zarniger."

"Fine. Her too." I didn't need another person asking me why I was avoiding Jennifer.

After he left, I kept my office door closed. I wasn't dealing with Cindy's suggestion before this meeting. Instead, I spent the time reviewing what we'd previously gotten from Cartwright.

~

CARSON CARTWRIGHT STOOD AS I ENTERED THE CONFERENCE ROOM AND MADE A point of checking his watch. "Glad you could make time to see us on such short notice."

I was my usual intentional five minutes late. "Always a pleasure to meet our shareholders."

It was true in general, but not this time.

The corner of his mouth ticked up. "Adam sends his regards."

Obviously not everybody in the FBI was as tight-lipped as they liked to pretend, but at least we hadn't come to blows again in DC.

Cartwright was shorter than I'd guessed and considerably older looking than the pictures I'd seen. I'd had run-ins with his sons, but never met the father in person. Vanity had him using at least a ten-year-old photo on his website.

I shook hands with him, followed by the two people he'd brought with him, Lester and Swartzman.

I took a seat directly across from Cartwright, with Jay and Jennifer on one side of me and Larry and Syd on the other. "What can we do for you this morning?"

Cartwright sat up in his seat. "I'm here as a courtesy."

That was a crock. He was here to threaten us.

"Today we're filing a revised form 13." He let the implication hang in the air. They were increasing their holding of our stock.

I had his business card on the table in front of me and slowly turned it around, waiting for him to continue.

"We've increased our position to twenty-four percent of the outstanding shares."

The words almost knocked the air out of me. I twisted his business card around one more time, doing my best to appear unfazed. "I'm glad to hear you have such confidence in our future."

Lester held back a laugh, and Swartzman smirked.

Cartwright's expression, though, didn't shift one iota. "Also, we're amending the form to state that we intend to become active in advocating for better management of the company."

I twisted his card around one more time. "We're always open to suggestions."

Cartwright's eyes narrowed. "I'd like Lester, Swartzman, and myself to be invited to join the board."

He'd made his first move on the chessboard.

I sat back and looked to my right. "Syd, do we have any openings on the board currently?"

I'd be damned if I was going to put him on the board—or any of his goons. Letting the likes of him onto your board was akin to bringing a rattlesnake into your bed.

Syd cleared his throat. "No, Dennis, we don't. We're authorized for seven, and we're at the max."

Syd's statement didn't seem to faze Cartwright. "The three of us are quite experienced at corporate turnarounds."

I knew it was more like they were experienced at corporate dismemberments, but I held my tongue in that regard.

"As Syd said, we don't have any vacancies right now," I offered.

His hatchet man, Lester, spoke up. "Things might go more smoothly if we were invited to the board. The alternative could be a messy proxy fight."

I checked my watch. "If that's all, Carson, I have to get to another meeting. Thank you for stopping by, and for showing such faith in our future by putting your money into the stock."

He shook his head. "I think you're making a mistake by not inviting us onto the board."

Bullshit. He just wanted to avoid the expense of a proxy battle, which would cost him as much in legal fees as it would us leading up to the showdown of the shareholder vote.

I stood. "Thank you again for stopping in." I turned for the door.

"One more thing you might want to consider," the old man said.

I turned back to face him.

"We've been recommended by one of your current board members."

I didn't see that coming. "Is that so?"

Quickly cycling through the list of board members in my head, I didn't find anyone stupid enough to want to deal with the likes of him.

A broad smile came over him. "Yes. Your wife, Melissa Benson."

He knew damn well she was my ex-wife

"She never did have good judgment." I turned and left the room before he could say anything else.

~

JENNIFER

Since Monday night, Dennis had made a point of avoiding me.

I was obviously still in my adult timeout. I was supposed to be off in the corner contemplating how I'd been a bad girl. The problem was, it was working.

When Cindy had come down to tell me I was expected in the conference room for a meeting with the Cartwright group at ten, I couldn't have been more surprised.

I'd expected to be frozen out of anything important.

Dennis hadn't spoken to me as he'd entered the meeting, but he hadn't said anything to Larry either, and those two always had some banter going on.

Watching the interaction between him and Carson Cartwright had been a bit like watching two prizefighters circling each other in the ring—taking little jabs, searching out weaknesses.

Dennis had mentioned he'd never met Carson Cartwright, but when his son Adam was mentioned, I'd caught the tick of recognition in Dennis's jaw. Some history I didn't understand lay beneath those words.

The Cartwright Group had delivered one hell of a surprise this morning. Accumulating almost one quarter of the company stock put them in a very strong position to argue for seats on the board—maybe not three, but at least one.

And their zinger at the end about having Melissa on their side had been another blow. That had instantly put another five percent of the company's voting power on their side and made them extremely dangerous.

I'd looked at Dennis multiple times during the meeting, but he hadn't taken his eyes off the Cartwright team, except to ask Syd a question.

When the meeting broke up, I'd headed to my office and turned to see Dennis inviting the other three to his office for discussion of what had just transpired.

The border of trust had been defined, and I was clearly on the outside.

An hour later, the guilt of what I'd done was back to eating me up, and nothing I did kept my thoughts from returning to all the times I'd ignored Ramona's warnings.

The walls of my office were empty and clean, save the few nail holes where the previous occupant had taken down pictures he'd hung. I'd told myself a dozen times that I'd personalize the space and hang some things. But I'd not followed through, perhaps because subconsciously I'd known from the beginning I didn't deserve this office, and my time here would come to an end quickly.

As I looked around, even the drab beige of the walls was cheerier than my mood, and their emptiness reflected the state of my heart.

Spending the weekends with Dennis had transported me to a happy place, but that had been a dream world, not the reality of the future that lay in front of me now. Melissa had shoved me into the cold water of the fountain, but that was nothing compared to the way karma had smacked me upside the head. For a few weekends, I'd tasted what life could be like, but that life was now out of reach.

The futility of staying was obvious. I didn't have a future here. Dennis would let me go from the company after whatever period of punishment he'd planned.

I couldn't live like this, and I couldn't cede control of my emotions to him that way. I was a grown woman, and it was time to take control of my own fucking pathetic future.

My pen hovered over the paper for a moment before I wrote the words. There truly was no alternative.

> I resign, effective immediately.
>> Jennifer Hanley

Cindy's desk was empty as I passed by and placed the note face down on the surface.

∼

DENNIS

. . .

AFTER THE INVADERS LEFT OUR CONFERENCE ROOM, CINDY HAD LOOKED AT ME expectantly as Jennifer walked back to her office.

I didn't follow her down there, because I still didn't know what to say.

I turned to Syd, Larry, and Jay. "Guys, want to join me for a postmortem?"

The three filed into my office, and I closed the door.

"What do you think?" I asked.

Jay was the first to speak. "I'd heard they were buying up shares, but to tell you the truth, that's way more than I would've guessed."

"Twenty-four percent is almost critical mass," Syd added, "for your standard proxy fight."

Larry shook his head. "It's worse than that if he has Melissa behind him."

Their words weren't cheering me up.

"Do you think he really does, or was that just a bluff?" Jay asked.

I shrugged. "Most likely a bluff, because there's nothing in it for her."

Larry looked at me like I was an idiot. "After the way she acted at the museum party, it's pretty obvious she'd sign on if she thought it would hurt you."

"But that's not in her best interest," I argued.

Larry pointed a finger at me. "Don't you get it? An angry woman doesn't need to be a logical woman. And that's one angry woman."

Larry's words bugged me. Melissa had always been crazy, but behind it she'd always had the goal of helping herself. If that had changed, I'd missed it. The legal maneuvering on the divorce had always seemed to be aimed at increasing her share of the pot.

"I'm with Larry," Jay said. "I doubt it was a bluff. If he hasn't approached her, lying about having her support would only make it harder for him to get it in the future if she found out."

Jay's logic seemed sound.

Syd's silent nodding made it three to one that Melissa had thrown in with him, which made the situation that much worse.

"Thanks, guys. I need to figure out what to do next."

Larry and Syd left.

Jay stopped at the door. "You might want to have some group brainstorming about how to proceed. You know, to get a broader perspective."

"Thanks, Jay."

That was one possibility.

When Jay departed, he was quickly replaced by Cindy at my door.

She waved a paper in her hand and wore a scowl that would drop a buffalo at a hundred paces.

I braced for the storm.

"You promised to talk to her," she spat as she approached the desk.

"I didn't get a chance…yet. Send her down."

She threw the paper at me. "It's a little late for that."

The note said Jennifer was quitting, and my stomach clenched. "She can't just leave."

"Day late and a dollar short, I'd say." Cindy turned and left.

I pulled the roll of Tums from my pocket and popped another two in my mouth.

CHAPTER 38

DENNIS

I WAS ON MY SECOND SCOTCH WHEN THE DOORBELL RANG.

Serena waltzed in with a bag in her arms as I opened the door. "Did you forget about our dinner date already?"

I had, but it wasn't a good idea to admit weakness with my sister.

I looked at my watch. "I guess I lost track of the time."

"And started early on the drinking, I see. What's wrong?"

"What do you mean?"

She wandered toward the kitchen, ignoring me for a moment before she turned. "You look like shit. I'd ask you if your dog died, but you don't have a dog."

"Things didn't go well at work today."

She started to unpack the grocery bag she'd brought. "I got all the ingredients they listed on a website. I hope I didn't forget anything. What do we do first?"

I'd completely forgotten that tonight was her cooking lesson. "Preheat the oven to four-fifty to start."

"How?"

"I don't believe—"

She hit my shoulder lightly. "I'm just kidding. You need to loosen up a little."

I lifted my scotch glass. "I am."

She set the upper oven to preheat.

"We need bags to flatten the chicken." I leaned over to get freezer bags from the drawer.

After I'd pulled two bags from their box, I found her pouring my drink down the sink. "Hey, that's expensive stuff."

She put the glass in the sink and turned to me. "Not while we're talking."

"We're not talking, we're cooking. Put a chicken breast in each of the bags and close them up."

She took the chicken out of the store package and loaded it in the bags.

I grabbed a mallet from the drawer and handed it to her. "Now you need to pound on it to flatten them down."

She handed the mallet back to me. "You do this part. You're the one that needs to get your frustrations out."

I glared at her as I pounded the chicken into submission. "We're tenderizing the pieces as well as making them thinner. Grab two of your eggs and mix them in a bowl."

"With what?"

"A fork will do."

I kept hammering the chicken while she did the eggs.

"You'll find flour in the pantry, did you bring breadcrumbs?" I asked her when she'd finished. "And we'll need four plates in a line."

She located the items and placed them on the island. "You want to tell me what's bothering you?"

I shook my head and continued pounding the chicken. "I'm fine."

"Bullshit. This is you screwed up. Drinking before dinner isn't you being fine."

She had that part right.

The chicken breasts had taken a good-enough beating. "Sprinkle some breadcrumbs on the second plate, carefully pour the eggs onto the third one, and put flour on the last one." I watched her a moment. "What's his name?"

She ignored me while she carefully poured the egg mixture. She looked up. "What's her name?"

I ignored her the way she'd ignored me. "Now you're gonna add a little Parmesan to the breadcrumbs and mix it up."

"How's this?"

"Looking good. Now, what are we doing for the sauce? You aren't planning to use that jar of Ragu are you?"

She nodded. "Baby steps."

"It's your dinner." I located a frying pan and put it on the stove. "Okay, take the breasts out of the bags, and you want to press each into the flour. Try to get it coated all over so it's dry to the touch."

She did fine with that step. "It's Jennifer, isn't it?"

I put a pot of water for the pasta on the stove. "Now take the first floured breast and put it into the egg mixture. Turn it over and move it to the bread-crumbs. Press it into the breadcrumbs on both sides so it's well coated and then put it on the empty plate."

She did a good job with the first one. "This gets all over your fingers."

"You can wash them off after you're done with the last piece of chicken."

It took her a few minutes to work both pieces through the process. While she washed up, I added some olive oil to the pan and turned on the stove.

"You can get rid of these extra plates, and there's a dish we can cook this in over there on the bottom shelf of that cupboard."

She cleaned up the plates and located the dish. "Why did she quit?"

The question startled me for a second, coming completely out of left field. "Who?"

"Jennifer, of course."

I sighed. "You've been talking to Cindy."

"You know she tells me everything."

"She obviously tells you too much. Wipe a little bit of olive oil on the bottom of the baking dish."

She grabbed a paper towel and did as I asked. "What happened between you two?"

The frying pan was heating up nicely. "What makes you think there's anything between us?"

"She's not stupid, you know."

I turned the gas down. "Cindy reads too many romance novels. She's imagining things."

Serena put her hand on her hip. "And was I imagining what I saw down by the Santa Monica Pier last weekend? You with her and that cute kid? Is he her son?"

There was no sense in denying it anymore. "Nephew."

"You guys looked like you were enjoying yourselves."

We certainly had been. Every weekend.

I pulled a spatula from the drawer and offered it to her. "Now you want to fry each of the pieces for two minutes on each side and then take them out."

She put the chicken in the pan all at once and stepped back from the spatter of the oil.

"Two minutes?" she asked.

I set the timer for two minutes. "Each side."

She flipped them when the time was up, and I reset the timer for her. The second side finished.

"Okay, now bring the baking pan over and put the pieces in there. You can also take the frying pan off the heat."

She moved the pan with the chicken to the island. "What's next?"

I located my cheese grater. "Pour your marinara sauce over the chicken."

"Like this?"

"Not too much."

She stopped.

"Now I would sprinkle basil over the chicken pieces and then add parmesan cheese. You can grate on some provolone or mozzarella, or both—whatever you feel like."

"I didn't bring any other cheese."

I opened the fridge to check. "I've got provolone you can use."

She slowly added the grated cheeses.

I set the timer for twenty minutes. "Now pop it in the oven, and in fifteen to twenty, dinner is ready."

She loaded the dish into the oven and closed it, beaming at her accomplishment. "That wasn't so hard."

"What pasta are you having with it?"

She pulled fettuccine from the bag. "These."

"Okay, you need to warm some of your sauce, and then the pasta goes in the water when the timer gets down to nine minutes."

"Nine minutes. Got it."

When the time was up, I helped her drain the pasta and serve the chicken parmigiana.

We took the plates to the table, and I opened a bottle of cabernet.

273

She cut into her chicken and forked a piece. "Now you can tell me what happened. And, just so you know, I'm not leaving until you do."

I'd had that threat from her before, and I knew she was serious.

"You know those nasty articles about the company?" I asked.

She nodded while she chewed.

"Jennifer was the source of the leak."

"She wrote those pieces?"

I sipped my wine between bites. "No, but she supplied the memos." Just mentioning it made my heart hurt.

"Why would she do that?"

"She thought I killed her father, actually her stepfather."

Her fork stopped mid-flight to her mouth. "What the fuck? Is she delusional?"

"No. He died in a welding accident at the company, though, and I had us take the blame so the family would get the full settlement."

She took the piece from her fork and chewed thoughtfully for a moment before sipping her wine. "And she didn't believe you?"

"No, that's not the problem. Don't you see? She attacked me personally as well as everybody at the company, and she did it on purpose. It wasn't an accident."

She stirred her pasta around a bit. "So Cindy was right. You're the problem."

I put my fork down. "*I am not.* I didn't do anything to hurt her. It's the other way around." I held her gaze.

She blinked first.

I went back to my dinner.

"And when are you going to get past this?"

"I'm not sure I can, knowing what she did."

She ate another few bites. "She lashed out at you because she thought you killed her stepfather. I can see that."

I heaped some fettuccine on top of my next piece of chicken.

"She did a bad thing, the wrong thing."

"Exactly," I mumbled with my mouth full.

"But she did it for a good reason, the right reason."

I'd had enough of this. "It wasn't a good reason. She was wrong. Her father violated safety rules put in place for his own protection, and that's what cost him his life."

"Don't you see? You said it yourself. She didn't know that. She did the wrong thing, but for the right reason. Tell me you haven't ever been guilty of that."

"I always try to do the right thing, and you know it."

"Right. Like with Adam Cartwright?"

That stopped me cold. "But…"

The vision of that day was a cold slap of reality.

"But nothing. That was you doing the wrong thing, but sure, you had the right reason," she said. "Tell me you don't wish you could take that day back."

I hung my head in shame. "I do."

I had often wished I could take that back, but it wasn't possible now— never had been possible. A torn ACL had ruined Adam's dream of an NFL career. An injury I'd caused had cost him his chance, and it had all been due to a lie I'd believed at the time.

"Don't you see the parallel?"

I wasn't giving her this easy a win. "Okay, it's a little similar."

"Bullshit. It's the same fucking thing."

"Stop it already. I get your point."

She continued anyway. "Doing the wrong thing for what you believe is the right reason—should you be punished your entire life for that?"

I didn't answer. I didn't need to. She knew where I stood on that. Adam had retaliated later, and it had cost me. The whole episode had cost us both.

"Answer me. Should you be punished forever for a mistake like that?"

"Of course not, but it's not the same."

She pushed her chair back. "Man up and do the right thing with Jennifer."

We were done here. I nodded. "Think you can remember how to do this for your dinner with Bill?"

"It's not Bill."

"Then John."

She stood and shook her head. "His name's Troy, but keep that to yourself."

She was giving me one win tonight.

I had a lot to think about.

CHAPTER 39

JENNIFER

FRIDAY MORNING, I CHECKED THE MESSAGE ON MY PHONE AGAIN.

CINDY: Let's meet for coffee - Starbucks at 7:30?

I'd felt like putting all things Benson behind me and getting on with my life, but I'd agreed because Cindy had always been nice to me.

Last night had been the first night I'd gotten three hours of uninterrupted sleep all week. The decision to move on had been hard, but empowering in a way.

Ramona emerged from her room and closed the door behind her. "I say you're being a chicken."

"Good morning to you, too."

"You shouldn't give up so easily."

That was easy for her to say. She didn't have to look at the people at work and know the problems I'd created for all of them.

"You just don't want to lose your Saturday babysitter," I shot back.

She and Billy had definitely both benefited from having Dennis around.

"You've never been one to run from a fight. I still say you should go and give him a piece of your mind before you give up."

"It's different when I know I'm right, but this time I'm not. I told you, I've made up my mind. I'm moving on."

"To another Ed?"

"That's not fair."

There was no comparison between Ed and Dennis. They were one letter away from each other in the alphabet I guess, but they couldn't have been more different.

"Just saying, take a look at what you're walking away from." She turned and opened her door again. "Hey, Bill, time to get moving."

Her calling him Bill was another reminder of the impact Dennis had had.

Billy now did his homework before asking to turn on the television. And all it had taken was a comment from Dennis about it.

I found my purse. "I'll be back in a while."

THE M&M GIRLS WERE AT THEIR FAMILIAR TABLE.

"Got the day off?" Mona asked as I walked up.

"Something like that." I'd been so busy at work that I'd only been able to stop in to see them on Wednesdays since moving upstairs.

There were three cups on the table, and the extra one had my name on the side.

I sat at the chair with my cup. "This is nice of you. How'd you know I'd be by this morning?" I asked.

"It wasn't me," Martha said, nodding her head toward the corner. "It was him."

Dennis walked our way.

I froze in place. The fight-or-flight response got my heart racing, and the only alternative here was fight.

"Good morning, Angel."

The words slipped off his tongue almost as if he meant them.

I nodded. "Morning." I couldn't go so far as to say *good*.

Mona touched my shoulder. "Dennis told us how invaluable you've been at his company."

"And I told him he should have given you a bigger raise," Martha added.

Dennis nodded. "So I agreed."

That dropped my jaw to full fly-catcher mode. "But—"

"First," Dennis said, interrupting me. "I need you to be honest with these ladies about something."

The girls hung on his every word.

He sipped his mocha. "You see, ladies, Jennifer and I have been seeing each other for a while now, and hiding it from the people we work with."

I cringed. Where on Earth could he be going with this? Was he about to unleash some sort of twisted revenge?

He took my hand.

I pulled it back.

He held his hand out for me again.

Martha elbowed me, and I put my hand forward. The warmth of his touch welded me to him as it always had before.

He put his other hand over mine. "Jennifer, I don't want to hide our relationship anymore. I'm asking you to be my public girlfriend."

This was nowhere on any script I'd imagined. My eyes welled up.

Martha elbowed me again. "Well?"

"Please?" Dennis added. "I understand why you did what you did, and now I need your help at the company."

"Can you forgive me?" I managed.

"Of course. I love you, Angel."

Martha pushed on my shoulder and whispered, "This is where you kiss him, dear."

I leaned toward him, and our lips met in a simple but heartfelt kiss. The kiss I wanted to give him would have gotten us banned from the shop forever.

"If this place served liquor," Mona said. "I'd order us a round of champagne."

I liked the sentiment.

I broke the kiss to look into his eyes. "Just like that?"

"Just like that. You did what you did for an honorable reason, and someday I'll tell you about how I once did something even worse."

"I doubt it."

He pulled me up to stand. "We have to get to work, girl. We'll see you two next Friday."

"It's a date," Mona replied.

"I want to hear about the raise," Martha added.

Dennis pulled me toward the door. "Next time."

DENNIS

WE WALKED WITH INTERTWINED FINGERS TOWARD WORK.

She looked up at me. "Thank you."

"Don't thank me. Thank Cindy and Serena."

"Huh?

"I'll tell you later."

She squeezed my hand. "I love you too."

She hadn't said it in the coffee shop, but it was certainly good to hear it now.

I let go of her hand and circled my arm around her as we walked. "Are you ready for this?" I adjusted my stride to hers.

"Not really. Are you?"

"Definitely. It's been harder than you can imagine ignoring you at work."

"Hard, huh?" She giggled, looking down at my crotch.

"Keep it up and you're getting another introduction to my desk."

"Promises, promises."

I slowed our pace as my cock hardened. "Stop that. I won't be able to walk into work like this."

"Just put your hands in your pockets like you always do." She smiled.

I pulled my hand back and did just that. By the time we reached the building, I had things under control.

After Cindy had set up the Starbucks meeting, getting my Angel back had been easier than I'd expected, although there was certainly the possibility I'd need to do some groveling later for the way I'd treated her.

Soon the elevator doors parted upstairs, and we walked into our new reality.

Cindy was at her desk.

"Cin, let's get the large group together in the boardroom at nine."

She scribbled a note. "Sure."

I looked at Jennifer. "That means you too, Angel."

Cindy cocked an eyebrow, not missing what I'd said.

"And don't be late for dinner tonight," I added as I closed the door slowly.

Cindy was looking to Jennifer for an explanation. I listened at the door after it closed.

"You're staying, and it's not a secret anymore?" Cindy asked.

"Yes on both counts."

"Good, because frankly, he needs the help—and the attitude lift."

I walked to my desk. I didn't need to hear any more girl talk. *Go big or go home*, Dad always said. I'd made *us* public in a big way. The company grapevine would see to that.

Ten minutes later I walked out to Cindy's desk and handed her the envelope from the night at the museum.

She took it. "What's this?"

"A thank you for your help."

Her eyes lit up when she opened the envelope. "Hawaii?"

"You earned it." I turned for the door. If she hadn't been in contact with Serena, I'd probably still have my head up my ass.

~

Jennifer

AS I WALKED TO MY ONCE-AGAIN OFFICE, I WONDERED HOW MANY PEOPLE beyond Cindy had seen through our charade and guessed Dennis and I were seeing each other. It didn't matter, but it brought back the awkward feeling that I might be judged as having slept my way into this job, and I wouldn't even know it.

Yesterday every employee I'd passed had made me wonder if they knew what I'd done to hurt them. Today, I had to add the issue of whether they thought I'd slept my way to where I was. Agreeing to go public about us didn't feel as good as it'd sounded at Starbucks.

A little while later, I took a place at the far end of the long table as the group assembled in the boardroom.

Dennis had invited more department heads and managers than I'd seen him assemble before, and I didn't even know all their names.

Larry chose a seat next to me as the room filled, and the ambient noise of a dozen side conversations grew. Dennis was talking with Fisher.

"Let's get started," Dennis said.

The group instantly quieted, except for the young IT guy and his neighbor.

A few seconds later the two realized all eyes were on them and stopped.

Dennis surveyed the room. "Let me bring you up to date. An outside activist group called the Cartwright Group has taken a very substantial position in our stock, and they have visited us to say they're going to advocate for change in the company."

"Like what?" one person asked.

"They will say we're not running the company optimally for the shareholders, and they can do a better job. So expect that your employees are going to start seeing things either in the papers or in their mailboxes basically saying I'm a jerk."

That got a few giggles from the crowd.

"I'm a jerk, and they can do better," Dennis added.

"Why?" the same guy asked.

"This can likely play out one of two ways. Either they want to take over the company…"

The group grew restless at the statement.

"Or they'll end up blackmailing us into paying them to go away."

"Can they do that?" Paul, the guy from HR, asked.

"Yes and no. They'll be overt about it, but they'll imply that if we agree to purchase their stock back from them at a certain level, they'd sell and move on to their next target."

"Like hyenas," Larry added.

"What will this do to our stock options?" the IT guy asked.

Larry spoke up again. "In the previous companies they've gotten control of, they've ended up cutting stock options drastically. They view it as a way to save money."

"But the options are the main tool we have to attract people," Paul complained.

"I'm just telling you what they've done," Larry replied.

"They also have a history of advocating for significant staff reductions as a way of boosting profitability," I added. I'd researched this pattern in several of their recent attacks on other companies.

"That's a fancy way of saying layoffs," Dennis said.

The group grew sullen. Layoffs was the last thing they wanted to hear.

"What are we going to do to fight back?" the young IT guy asked.

Dennis smiled. This was obviously the question he'd waited for. "We're going to fight them aggressively on two fronts. First…" He looked around the room. "You and your employees own eighteen percent of the company and have a significant say in how this plays out. HR will distribute talking points to you laying out our position, as well as the facts of what happened to the employees at Cartwright's last two targets. This should help you convince your people that the Cartwright Group is not the benevolent force for good they claim to be. If the majority of our employees vote with us, that will be a significant help. The other thing we'll be doing is visiting a few of our major shareholders to shore up their support."

"But what if that's not enough?" a woman asked.

"Then I'll be out of a job," Dennis answered. "And you'll be on your own in dealing with them."

The looks of horror on the faces around the room were clear. They didn't want Dennis leaving. After answering a smattering of other questions, he called an end to the meeting.

After the managers filed out, I followed Paul, Syd, Larry, and Fisher into Dennis's office.

Syd was the first to speak. "We need to be careful what we say to employees, or we could get in serious trouble with the Securities and Exchange Commission."

Dennis leaned against his desk. "Larry, you and Paul work up the most persuasive literature you can, but run it by Syd before we put it out."

Paul nodded.

"It has to be factual," Syd said. "It can't be your normal marketing bullshit."

"I know that," Larry shot back. "And it's not marketing bullshit. It's persuasion material."

"I don't care what we call it," Dennis said firmly. "Larry, it needs to be persuasive. And, Syd, it needs to not get us in trouble with the SEC. But I don't want to shy away from anything. We need to snuggle up close to the line, just not go over it."

Syd sighed, likely not happy about being pushed out of his comfort zone. He looked over at our HR guy again. "Paul, I also don't want it just sent around. You need to see that all our managers and supervisors are trained on it. When we're done, no employee in his right mind should even consider voting with those Cartwright assholes."

Dennis shifted his focus to Fisher. "Jay, you need to make a list today of major shareholders we should meet with. You, me, and Jennifer are going on a road trip to shore up their support."

Fisher nodded.

I raised my hand. "I have a suggestion." I felt stupid for putting my hand up as if I were still in school.

Dennis looked at me expectantly.

"I think we might contact some others who have had dealings with Cartwright and ask them to go along and support our position."

"Who did you have in mind?" Fisher asked.

"Hugh Stoner. He had a nasty encounter with them a few years ago. I think he'd be on our side."

Dennis nodded. "He's been friends with Dad forever. We can probably get him to help."

"Talbot is also not fond of Cartwright," Fisher said.

I didn't think that would fly. "I'm not sure they'd be receptive."

Dennis smiled. "Jennifer, you and Jay go talk to them. Old man Talbot likes you."

I shrugged. An assignment was an assignment, even if I disagreed with his assessment.

"One more thing. Jenn, could you stay a minute?"

I took a seat again, while the others filed out.

Dennis closed the door after them. "I have something else to tell you." He retook the seat behind his desk. "The trip I took?"

"Yeah?"

He sucked in a breath. "My cousin, Debbie, is alive."

"That's great. Where is she?" I had a million questions, but he stopped me.

"We can't talk about it to anybody yet. We don't know where she is, but we have DNA evidence that she's alive?"

"What about your family? You have to tell them."

He shook his head. "Dad and Vincent know, but we can't tell the others yet."

"Why not?" I waited for more. There had to be more.

"She was involved in a bank robbery, and we know she's alive. But we don't know any more than that yet. We won't know the answers until we find her."

I couldn't make sense of it. Child kidnap victim, and now an adult bank robber.

"I needed to tell you, but we can't talk about this. We can't let it get out until we know more."

I nodded. I didn't agree, but it was his family and his decision.

As I walked back to my office, the import of the conversation struck me. He'd confided in me a secret he wouldn't tell his brother or sisters.

CHAPTER 40

Dennis

(Ten Days Later)

It was lunchtime Monday, the last day of the whirlwind of shareholder meetings Jay had lined up for us.

Royce Capital had been the final shareholder on our New York list after our meeting at Barron Funds earlier this morning. After eleven of these meetings last week, I'd had enough. I hoped we were where we needed to be.

I followed the group out of the mutual fund building onto the busy midtown Manhattan sidewalk.

"Jay, how do you think that one went?" I asked.

He scooted farther from the door before answering. "He might have been on the fence before, but that guy doesn't like Cartwright, is my read. He should go with us."

"Hugh, what about you?

Hugh Stoner checked toward the door before speaking. "Just like the others. Once Jim told them Fidelity and Price were behind you, they had no choice."

James Talbot agreed. "Bunch of sheep, the whole lot of them. Not a single one with the balls to cut away from the crowd and make his own decision. I think you've got it sewn up now. They won't give Cartwright the time of day."

Jennifer's smile told me she agreed.

Finally we had the support we needed for Monday's meeting with Cartwright.

Hugh checked his watch. "I'm due to meet Millie for lunch. Jim, you want to join us?"

"If you're buying," Talbot replied in his typical fashion.

Jay's phone rang, and he stepped away to answer it.

I thanked Stoner and Talbot profusely and shook both their hands as they broke off. They'd been invaluable.

"I'll tell him," Jay said into his phone. "It's Cartwright. They're all here in town, and they want to meet to make an offer."

"Now?" I asked.

Jay nodded. "Yeah."

Jennifer nodded as well. "Doesn't hurt to listen."

"Okay," I said.

Jay asked where and then hung up. "Restaurant two blocks north."

"Did you tell them we were going to New York?" I asked him.

"No."

"It doesn't take a genius to figure out we'd be making the rounds where the money is," Syd noted.

But what were the odds that they'd picked a place to meet that close?

~

Dennis

Walking to the meeting, Jay and Jennifer agreed that this would most likely be the "greenmail" offer Cartwright was known for—pay him enough, and he would go away.

After asking for the Cartwright party at the reservation desk, we were escorted to a private room upstairs.

Carson Cartwright greeted us. "Glad we could meet on such short notice."

When the obligatory hand shaking was done, I took the seat across from Cartwright, and Jay chose the seat across from his weasel lawyer, Beasley.

Jennifer took the next chair down the rectangular table, which was devoid of place settings.

A meal was apparently not part of the plan.

"You said you had something to discuss?" I asked.

Cartwright nodded to Beasley.

The lawyer opened a folder in front of him and slid a single sheet of paper across to me, and a copy to Jay. "Sorry. I only brought two copies."

Jennifer leaned over to read Jay's.

This was an agreement to give them a single board seat—down from their previous demand of three—and also to buy back their shares at a thirty-percent premium over today's stock price.

It was simple corporate blackmail, as expected.

"It expires as soon as we walk out of this room," Cartwright said. "Otherwise we'll be at your offices tomorrow morning with our official proxy proposal. From there, the offers only get worse."

I wasn't rushing into anything without a discussion with my team. "Then we can talk tomorrow. I'm not entering into anything today."

Beasley shook his head. "That's too bad. I heard a rumor that someone suspected you had an SEC problem."

Jay's face reddened. "Our accounting is flawless."

Cartwright stood. "We're on a tight schedule here. We just finished with Barron Funds, and we're scheduled at Royce Capital now."

Jay glanced at me.

Beasley laughed. "Yeah, looking forward to hearing what lies you told them."

I held my tongue as the two slimeballs departed.

Jay waited for the door to close. "Those terms weren't bad, as a Cartwright deal goes. It sounds like they've been following us around, and that's going to make it harder if they're getting the last word in."

"Your point?" I asked.

"You should have taken the deal."

"I'm not rushing into something without consulting the team."

Jay moved to the door. "The gall of that asshole to suggest the SEC has a problem with our accounting."

CHAPTER 41

DENNIS

IT WAS MONDAY MORNING BACK IN CALIFORNIA—MAKE OR BREAK TIME WITH Cartwright. Their group had arrived shortly before nine, and Cindy was getting them situated in the boardroom.

Jennifer had done her best to lift my mood all weekend. Another Saturday with her nephew had been a relaxing diversion, but seeing Cartwright in New York had been a complete surprise—a very unpleasant one. And how he could have managed to know our itinerary bugged me to no end.

Grabbing my lucky pen, I ventured out of my safe office and into the lion's den of the boardroom.

Cartwright pasted on a fake smile as we shook. "Good to see you again so soon, Dennis."

"Always a pleasure to talk with our shareholders," I offered.

"Yes, I'm sure it is. And so nice that in our corporate structures, the shareholders are the ultimate bosses, don't you think?"

Jay interceded before I could say something snarky. "We understood you had a proxy you wished to put forth?"

I took my seat, as did Cartwright.

His attack-dog lawyer, Beasley, passed us each a copy.

As I read, my blood started to boil.

Larry didn't hold back. "This is bull, and you know it."

Cartwright didn't flinch. "The company's charter allows us to submit this to a vote of the shareholders, and that's what we are requesting today."

"No way," Larry spat.

Syd put a hand on his shoulder. "Larry, they have the right."

"Not if it's full of lies like this," Larry said.

Beasley slid Larry a piece of paper. "I've circled the relevant section. The wording is at the shareholder's discretion." He looked proud of himself.

Jay reached over and slid it back to him. "We've met recently with most all of the major shareholders."

"We know," Cartwright said. "So have we."

Jay continued. "I'm confident they'll side with management on this."

The door opened, and Cindy came over to whisper in my ear. "Ed Baird has something he needs to talk to you about."

"Later," I told her.

"It can't wait."

I spun my pen on the tabletop and stood. "Excuse me for a moment."

Cartwright nodded with a smirk.

Once outside, I closed the door behind me and motioned for Ed to join me in my office.

He closed the door behind him.

"What is it that can't wait?" I demanded.

"The SEC is downstairs with a warrant, and *that* won't wait."

The words completely surprised me. "A warrant? For what?"

"Jennifer's office and computer." He hesitated. "And your computer."

JENNIFER

I HADN'T HEARD WHAT CINDY HAD WHISPERED, BUT THIS WAS NOT THE MEETING to pretend to be called out of.

The other side was quiet and, oddly, smiling at the delay.

Dennis rejoined us. "Syd and Jennifer, there's something that requires your attention."

I got up and followed Syd.

Cartwright's next line came before I reached the door. "After the SEC charges you two, I think the shareholders might rethink supporting the current management."

The SEC charges who with what? I wondered as I closed the door and faced Ed. It was our first face to face in a long time.

"What's going on?" Syd demanded.

Ed took a breath. "You need to go downstairs, sir. The SEC is here with a warrant."

"Is this a joke?"

"No, sir. And Miss Hanley, you need to stay here with me until they come up."

Syd took off for the elevator, muttering under his breath.

Ed whispered, "You should have talked to me before it got to this."

I led him away from Cindy's desk. "Got to what?"

"The SEC is here to seize your computer and the contents of your office."

My jaw dropped. *Why would the SEC be interested in me?*

The next few minutes were a jumble in my mind as agents of the government came upstairs with Syd and we watched them take Dennis's computer before moving on to my office. The goons boxed up everything in there. They only left me my purse and cell phone.

Syd didn't allow me to say anything or ask any questions.

I almost puked. The whole process was humiliating.

After Syd had a conversation with the head guy, he came over.

"Jennifer, you should go home and wait for me to call you. They're charging you and Dennis with insider trading," he said.

"That's ridiculous."

"They think they can prove you wrote those articles in the *Times* to push the stock down so Dennis could buy low. If you're contacted by the SEC, don't meet with them without me present."

His statement took a moment to sink in. I nodded, half in a trance.

"Do you understand?"

"No," I protested. "I don't understand a fucking thing about what is happening."

The only thing I knew was that what I'd done was somehow coming back to hurt Dennis even worse than before. I was at fault, because if I hadn't cooperated with Hydra, there wouldn't have been any articles, and these thugs wouldn't be here.

∼

DENNIS

THE CARTWRIGHT MEETING ENDED SHORTLY AFTER THE SEC'S SURPRISE VISIT.

Cartwright's words rattled around in my head. *"After the SEC charges you two, I think the shareholders might rethink supporting the current management."*

He'd known this was coming, and probably had a hand in it somehow.

Syd had handled the interaction with the feds, and had gotten on the phone with the SEC as well.

I called the group back into the boardroom as soon as Cartwright and his SEC accomplices were out of our hair.

"Cin, get Jennifer as well."

She shook her head. "Not here. Syd sent her home."

I turned to Syd. "Why?"

"Because their warrant focused on her. It's best if she stays out of the building until we understand the formal complaint, or we could have them back in here again tomorrow."

"I don't like it."

Syd stood his ground. "That's my legal advice, and the smart thing to do at this point."

I relented for the moment. "Let's get started." I ushered Syd back into the boardroom.

"Syd, what do we know from your guy at the SEC?"

He cleared his throat. "They got a tip—"

"What the fuck kind of tip?" I demanded.

"Let me finish. They got a tip that… They're investigating the likelihood that you've engaged in inside trading."

"That's stupid," I spat. "I file my form fours regularly." I'd filed with the SEC after every purchase, and I hadn't had any sales to report.

He took a slow breath. "They think you planted the stories in the *Times,* and then you took advantage of that to buy when the news tanked the stock."

"So, I'm guilty because I have confidence in the company, and I'm willing to invest when everybody else is running for the hills?"

Looking around the room, the entire group seemed to back away from engaging me in this debate.

"Well?" I asked Syd.

"It's worse than that. They think Jennifer wrote the stories under the Sigurd name at your direction."

Suddenly the situation looked a whole lot more complicated. Because Jennifer had confessed to me, I knew something the rest of the room didn't that made this SEC mess all the more dangerous. And I had no intention of sharing it with the group. In a long conversation, she'd come clean on her involvement with Sigurd—the person she knew as Hydra—and it was my call to forgive her for that. Nobody else needed to know, and I was keeping it that way.

Once again, only Syd was willing to speak up. "They expect to find evidence on Jennifer's computer or yours that will prove it."

"And when they don't?"

"Then it goes away," Syd answered.

Jay leaned forward. "It's not that simple, I'm afraid."

"Go ahead," I urged.

"This whole process will take way too long. It won't get settled before the proxy vote. Cartwright will use the news to his advantage, and he's right that a lot of our shareholders will move to his side with this stink hanging over you. This smells like a setup by Cartwright."

I prided myself in being able to keep a positive attitude, but this was too much. "So you think we're fucked?"

Jay's hesitation said it all. "Unless Larry has some rabbit to pull out of his hat, I don't see any way this plays, except to Cartwright's advantage."

Larry ignored the magic act comment. "He was probably hinting at a surprise coming during every meeting last week."

I nodded, agreeing with Larry. "It's what I would have done if I knew a bombshell was about to drop."

I let the group go and locked myself in my office.

Cartwright had been sneakier and smarter than I'd given him credit for, and now it was game, set, match.

He would win, and I would lose.

Everything had gone to shit, and I needed to talk to Jennifer, the one good thing in my life today. I tried to dial her, but my cell phone did its stupid reset thing again. I called out my open office door. "Cindy, I give up."

She appeared at the door. "What's the problem?"

I held up my phone. "You said we had a whiz kid in IT that could fix this thing?"

She walked in, hand out. "Yeah, I'll get it to Oleg."

"Is he the one who looks like he's fourteen?"

She took the phone from me. "That's the one. He's actually twenty-three, and he runs the group."

"Thanks."

I suddenly felt old having to get help from kids. The entire IT group looked like they belonged in high school. I dismissed the thought as wasted energy. I didn't need to be a phone genius to run the company. And maybe they weren't getting younger—maybe I was getting older.

"And, I need another fucking computer."

A scowl was my punishment for swearing at her.

"I'm sorry. Would you please ask IT to get me another computer so I can do my work?"

The scowl was replaced by her happy face. "Gladly."

I still needed to check on Jennifer. She'd been dragged into this mess as well. After closing my door, I dialed her number on my desk phone, but didn't get an answer. I didn't leave a message, face to face would be better.

The bottle of scotch in my credenza called to me, and I poured a glass.

The liquid burn did nothing to soothe me, so I put it down.

"I'm going for a walk," I told Cindy as I passed her desk.

With my phone in the shop, I was off my electronic leash and free to take as much time as I wanted.

Downstairs, I decided on a few quick laps of the block to get the blood flowing so I could think.

CHAPTER 42

JENNIFER

I SAT IN MY CAR. MY LEGS SHOOK SO BADLY I WAS AFRAID TO START IT. I couldn't drive like this.

Charged by the SEC? Insider trading? That was crazy. I hadn't written the articles, and Dennis hadn't known anything about my part in their creation at the time. But there was no way to prove a negative. The accusation alone would taint both of us. I'd never get another accounting job, and he could lose the company. Even being investigated by the SEC would be a black mark that would follow us both around forever. My actions had wounded him much worse than before.

As hard as I tried, I couldn't stop the tears. It wasn't like I could go back to being a bank teller either. Not only had I likely ruined my relationship with the one good man I'd managed to find, but now my career future officially sucked. Perhaps I could enter the wonderful world of hospitality services, or food preparation.

Pulling a tissue from my purse, I wiped my eyes and summoned the courage to drive home. I wasn't ever coming back to a job like this. An SEC investigation would preclude any kind of corporate finance work. It had been my passion, and this would end it.

The hardest part would be having to tell my sister and Billy I'd let them down.

I'd been naïve to think Dennis could easily forgive me for the damage the articles had caused. And even though somehow he had found a way to do so, it would be insane to expect his forgiveness for inadvertently bringing the SEC down on him, especially if he lost the company he'd created.

There was no coming back from this.

I drove slowly and reached home without getting in an accident.

Upstairs, I was pouring the first of my planned several dozen glasses of wine when my cell rang.

I'd already ignored a call from the company number, which was probably Syd with more bad news.

I pulled the last pin from my hair and shook it out before checking the phone.

Cindy's name was on the screen.

I couldn't bring myself to ignore her the way I wanted to. "Hello?"

"How are you holding up?" she asked.

"I'm already one glass into a bottle of wine, if that tells you anything."

"I know this isn't any of my business…but he needs you."

"Who?" I asked stupidly.

"The man who's been pretending forever to not be in love with you."

The words hit me hard. She thought he still loved me.

I plopped down on the couch. "You think so?"

"I think you're smart enough to know the answer to that."

I nodded silently. I knew how I felt, and even if he'd only recently said it, every day we spent together he'd shown me his feelings in his kidding, his little gestures, and in the way he looked at me. It added up to what every girl wanted from a man.

From the first morning he took me to his beach house, it had been all about me—about expanding my happiness horizons. From the silly listening to the ocean routine to the fun new things he got me to try every weekend, it had been about pulling me out of my shell. And it had worked, without me ever being focused on it.

It had all fallen apart when he learned what I'd done, but I'd been lucky enough to get him back after that. This, though? This was ten times worse. I couldn't dare hope to be forgiven again.

"Jennifer," Cindy said, bringing me back to the present. "The guys think this is all Cartwright's doing, and they're talking about Dennis losing the company."

I blinked back the tears that threatened. "I'm so sorry." I couldn't bring myself to admit to her the part I'd played.

"Come back in and help."

"Syd told me to stay away until he called."

"Syd can fuck off."

I almost dropped the phone. I'd never heard a swear word of any kind out of Cindy's mouth, or even one allowed in her presence.

"Dennis needs you," she repeated. "I'll get your badge reactivated."

"But—"

"But nothing. Don't leave him to fight this alone."

Her words stung. But maybe I owed it to Dennis to fight, not just slink away in the shame of what I'd done. What kind of woman did that?

Not any kind I wanted to be.

"I'm on my way."

I put the wine glass down. I was done with self-pity.

We hung up, and I didn't take the time to put my hair back up before grabbing my purse on my way out.

We hadn't lost yet, and my one regret from this morning was not going back into the boardroom to personally kick Cartwright in the balls.

DENNIS

THREE LAPS TURNED INTO MORE THAN A DOZEN BEFORE I ENTERED THE BUILDING again.

After my long walk that went nowhere, the heat in the elevator was more uncomfortable than usual.

I opened the door to our executive area, *my* executive area. This was still my fucking company.

Cindy nodded toward my door. "I got you a surprise."

"Not sure I can stand any more surprises today."

She merely smiled back.

I opened the door, and Jennifer was in my chair.

"I'm here to help," she said.

Her hair was down, the way I enjoyed it on the weekends.

I closed the door behind me and opened my arms.

We met mid-room for the kiss I owed her. My eyes closed, our lips met, and the scent of peaches filled my nostrils, bringing me back to the first kiss we'd shared in this room: the piss-off-Melissa kiss that had started it all.

Jennifer broke the kiss too soon for me.

I stroked her long locks. "I like the hair."

She smiled and twisted the ends around her finger. "Syd told me to stay home."

"Syd can go fuck himself."

She giggled. "Cindy said the same thing."

"I'll have to give her a raise for expanding her vocabulary."

Cindy's distinctive knock sounded.

I took a step away from Jennifer. "Yes?"

Cindy poked her head in. "IT has the computer you wanted."

"Let's have it."

An IT tech wheeled in a cart with a computer, monitor, and a fresh printer to replace what had been taken.

Oleg, the department head, followed him in.

"Did you fix my phone yet?" I asked.

Oleg stopped. "Still working on that."

The tech lifted the computer off the cart, placed it where the old one had been, and started connecting things.

I stepped forward to see what he was doing. "How long will it take to get software loaded so I can get back to work?"

Oleg answered. "Already done. We back up all the machines every night, so this is an exact copy of your machine the way it was when you came in this morning. All you've lost is anything you did today."

A few seconds later, the tech powered up my machine. "You're all set to go."

I thanked them as they left and asked Cindy to reassemble the brain trust, this time in my office.

Syd eyed Jennifer as he walked in. "I don't think this is wise, Dennis."

"She stays," I told him.

He shrugged. "Your call."

"Where do we start?" Jay asked.

Larry spoke up first. "Did you do it?" he asked me.

The question was beyond stupid.

If I'd had something to throw, I would have. "What the fuck do you think?"

"I think you didn't." He turned to Jennifer. "Did you write those articles in the *Times*?"

Her answer was swift—and truthful as far as it went. "I did not."

Larry looked back at me. "That means we need to figure out how Cartwright is framing you."

An almost-smile appeared on Syd's face. "I agree with Larry."

"That's a first," Larry said.

"What was on your computer that would be incriminating?" Jay asked Jennifer.

She shrugged. "Nothing that I know of."

"There has to be something," he countered.

Syd pointed out the obvious. "We don't have the machine, so we're not going to know until they tell us."

"Not necessarily true," I told him.

That drew a befuddled look from Syd.

I picked up the office phone and dialed down to IT. "Oleg, get your butt back up to my office."

Jennifer gave me a knowing look.

"We can make a clone," I told the group. I explained how I'd just gotten a copy of my machine from this morning delivered.

Oleg entered, breathless from what must have been a sprint back upstairs. "Is something wrong with the computer?"

"No. I want you to make a clone of Miss Hanley's computer, just like you did mine. Then I want you to work with Syd here to comb through until we find it."

He looked puzzled. "What are we looking for?"

"I have no fucking idea. That's Syd's job. Syd, you and Oleg and his guys are to keep at it all night, if that's what it takes."

Syd sighed and stood. "We better get started, then."

"Okay, guys," I said. "We get back together as soon as they find something."

Larry came over before leaving. "What do I tell the analysts when they call? Cartwright is probably already on the phone with them."

I didn't have a good answer to that.

"Tell them to look forward to the other shoe dropping soon," Jennifer offered.

"What's the other shoe?"

"Our counterattack, but don't tell them that."

Larry nodded. "I like it."

"We still need to carry on with our normal business," Jay said, pointing to me. "And you owe me some time reviewing the inventory analysis before I finalize it."

An hour later, we were going over the inventory analysis downstairs in Jay's office when his phone rang.

He answered and handed it over to me. "It's Cindy for you."

"Yeah?"

"Ed is here, and he says he needs to see you right away."

"I'll be up in a few."

I left Jay's office, wondering what Ed had this time.

Upstairs, I found Ed at my door with Oleg, the IT prodigy. "What's going on?"

Ed nodded toward my office door instead of answering.

Security guys were always overly paranoid about talking in public.

Oleg followed me in and Ed brought up the rear, closing the door after him. "Oleg's guys found something on your phone you should be aware of."

I took my seat behind the desk. "Okay. What?"

Oleg spoke. "It's a piece of tracking software."

He still didn't look or sound over eighteen to me. "How long?"

Oleg shifted in his seat. "We can't say how long it has been on the phone, or how it got there."

"Given the Cartwright situation, they could be behind this," Ed suggested. "Monitoring your calls and your physical location."

"Son of a bitch. And you know it's Cartwright?"

Oleg shook his head. "We can't say yet. That will take some time."

"We can clean the malware off the phone," Ed offered.

Oleg concurred with a nod.

I thought for a moment "Will they be able to tell?"

Ed looked to Oleg. "Yes. Definitely," he said.

That settled it for me. "I don't want them to suspect anything while you try to track it down. I'll get a new phone in the meantime. Thanks, guys."

Ed rose, and Oleg took the hint.

"One more thing," Ed said. "It'll have to be a new number. You have to leave the old number assigned to the old phone."

I rounded the desk and patted Oleg on the back. "Good work, and thanks guys. Keep working on Jennifer's computer."

∼

Two hours later, Cindy handed me a new iPhone box and a clear case.

"Who gets your new number?" she asked.

"The senior staff. And send it to Dad, along with the rest of the family. That should do it for now." I opened the box. "You didn't." The phone was a godawful rose gold.

"You'll be stylish for a change."

I knew she'd picked the color on purpose to annoy me.

I put the ugly thing down.

At least now I knew how Cartwright had followed us on our shareholder visits.

∼

Jennifer

Cindy called me back into Dennis's office around three.

The IT guy, Oleg, and Syd were already there.

Syd wore a sour face. "We found what they were after."

"What?" Dennis asked.

Syd handed Dennis several sheets of paper. "The private email you set up on the computer was hidden, but Oleg found it."

"What private email?" I asked.

Dennis was busy reading the sheets.

Oleg spoke up. "It wasn't that well hidden, and it contains—"

Syd interrupted him. "Jennifer, it's the emails you sent to the *Times* to publish."

My mouth went dry as I read the sheets with the articles I knew well, and each email said it had been sent by darkhorse666 to the *Times* shortly before the first two articles had been published, just like he said.

"This isn't me," I told them. "I didn't write these."

"They're on your computer, and they were sent to the paper. The dates match up with the stories."

I looked to Dennis, who hadn't said anything yet. "I swear I didn't write these."

Dennis read another page. "I don't see the latest one here."

"That's all we found," Oleg answered.

"How could you?" Syd said, looking squarely at me. He'd clearly already convicted me in his mind. "These are company trade secrets. You know sending these out to the paper is a federal offense."

"I told you I didn't write those."

"It's in black and white, perfectly clear to me," he shot back.

"It's not clear to me," Dennis said.

I blew out a relieved breath.

"Syd, you're not helping," Dennis added. He put the sheets down. "Oleg, could these have been placed on the computer by someone else?"

The computer guy cocked his head. "It's possible, but they would have had to access the machine directly. It's also possible that she clicked on some malware on the web that downloaded it."

"I don't go clicking around the web. I know better than that," I protested.

"I just said it's possible," Oleg explained.

Dennis steepled his hands. "And the SEC guys—would they be able to tell if that happened?"

"No. If I can't tell, they certainly can't. The most likely way for them to be there is that she wrote them."

"You keep your office locked, right?" Syd asked me.

I nodded. "Every night."

Dennis shook his head. "Hold on, Syd. Oleg, you told me you backup every day, right?"

"Three hundred sixty-five days a year."

"Then I want to know what day each of these documents appeared in our backups."

Oleg pulled out his phone and barked a few instructions to one of his guys. "Yes, day by day for each file in the darkhorse folder we found." He hung up. "It'll take a few minutes."

"Then we wait," Dennis said.

"Can I go?" Syd asked.

Dennis waved him away. "Sure."

I felt Syd's accusatory stare as he left the room.

The minutes ticked by slowly.

CHAPTER 43

DENNIS

FINALLY OLEG'S PHONE RANG. "YEAH?...ARE YOU SURE?... THANKS. YEAH that's it for now, I think." He hung up. "They all showed up four weeks ago on the fifteenth. There's no trace of them before that."

I drew in a relieved breath. At least now I knew what Cartwright's plan had been and how he'd executed it—at least, almost all of it. "Thanks, Oleg. That's it for now."

Oleg seemed happy to get out of my office, and he closed the door.

"You believe me, don't you?" Jennifer asked.

"Of course I do, Angel."

She settled into her seat, seeming relieved.

"You told me what you did and didn't do, and I have to get to the bottom of this without giving the guys that piece of the puzzle."

"I can quit if I have to," she mumbled.

I rounded the desk. "Not on your life." I pulled her up to stand and took her into my arms.

"Wouldn't that make it easier?" she mumbled into my shoulder.

"No. We're in this together, you and me. What kind of boyfriend would I be if I let you do that?"

"A smart one, maybe."

I let go of her. "Bullshit. Now get going. Go work with Oleg. Show him what you do on the web, answer any questions he has. We have to figure out how they set us both up, and I have a call to make."

She turned for the door.

"And leave your hair like that," I added.

She turned. "It's more professional up."

"I could make it an order."

She shook her head and left.

I lifted the phone and dialed downstairs.

Ed answered. "Yes, boss?"

"Ed, we think somebody got access to Jennifer's computer on the fourteenth or fifteenth, and I need to know who."

"Does this have to do with those *Times* articles?"

"It does. It looks like someone planted something on her computer, and I need to know who."

"You don't think she was involved?"

I sighed, ignoring his question. "I need to know who got into her office. And I need to know today."

"We'll start on it right away."

$\sim$

JENNIFER

I WALKED BACK FROM MY SECOND RUN TO THE COFFEE MACHINE. WAITING IN MY empty office with nothing to do was the pits.

A security guy stood outside my door.

I ignored him and went inside.

Ed got up from a chair. "Jennifer."

I put my cup down on the credenza. "Ed, you agreed to stay away."

"You should have talked to me earlier, when I might have been able to help you."

"Get out. We don't have anything to talk about."

"You have to come with me to the boss's office."

"What?"

The guy at the door made a move to enter, but Ed put his hand up to stop him. "Please don't make this any more difficult than it already is. We need to talk to Mr. Benson."

The other guy had a Taser on his belt.

I grabbed my coffee. "Whatever."

Ed followed me as I walked to Dennis's office. I'd had more Ed than I could stand, but whatever trouble he was making, I needed Dennis to straighten it out.

The door was open, so I marched in and took a seat.

Dennis looked up and put his pen down.

Ed closed the door after him, with his goon on the outside. "I need to give you some information about Miss Hanley."

Now he was going all cop-formal on us.

Dennis nodded. "Go ahead."

"She's been passing information to the Cartwright people."

"I have not," I spat. "This is just because—"

"Jenn, let him finish," Dennis said.

I grabbed the arm of the chair to control my anger.

Ed continued. "In addition to the meeting with Suzanne Murtog last month—"

"I explained that," I interrupted.

Dennis's eyes fixed me in place. "Jenn."

"In addition, I have this photo of her dropping off a folder in a park." Ed handed a picture to Dennis.

My stomach turned over, because Ed had discovered my interactions with Hydra. I could have asked why the hell he'd been following me like the stalker he was, but that wouldn't solve anything.

"And these." Ed slid over more small photos to Dennis. "The Cartwright person picking up the package."

Fuck. Things weren't looking up, if he'd caught Hydra.

I put my hand out toward Dennis. "I want to see those."

"Just a moment. Ed, email me this one." He held up a picture of someone getting into a car.

Ed fiddled with his cell. "Sure."

～

DENNIS

ED'S PICTURE OF THE CAR ARRIVED IN MY EMAIL. I OPENED IT, AND THAT clinched it. I recognized that car, and on my big monitor, I could make out the vanity license plate I knew all too well.

He'd caught Jennifer's Hydra, and it all made sense now.

Jennifer still had her hand out to see the pictures, but I ignored her.

"Thanks, Ed. I know who this is. I'll take it from here."

"But don't you think we should—"

I stopped him with a raised hand. "Like I said, I'll handle the next step. And good work. This is really good work."

Ed stood and puffed up like I'd awarded him a medal, which was fine, because he'd just given us a break. "Thank you."

He left, clearly not happy that I hadn't asked him to handcuff Jennifer or something equally active.

The door closed.

"Gimme," Jennifer complained.

I handed her the pictures of Hydra. Although none of them had a good shot of the face, I recognized the car. "Jenn, I know who it is."

"Who?"

I looked back at my screen to reread the license plate again.

TOTALWAR.

The plate did fit her. "Your swim coach."

JENNIFER

"YOUR EX-WIFE? MELISSA?"

He turned his monitor so I could see. "That's her license plate."

The plate read TOTALWAR. Should have been *total bitch*.

"Then we have her."

Dennis sighed. "Now that we know she was behind the articles and not Cartwright, this confuses things. How did the emails end up on your computer, and how did Cartwright know to send the SEC looking for them?"

"Do they know each other?" I asked.

"Probably, but that doesn't prove a connection. And that doesn't fix our SEC problem, or the proxy timing with Cartwright."

"You could confront her."

"That won't work. A picture of her picking up a package? That doesn't tie her to Cartwright, or prove the emails on your computer were planted."

I slumped in my chair. He was right. "I could email her and ask for a meeting."

"She won't fall for that. Tell me how she contacted you."

I sat up. "She would email me at home at nemesis666 using her HYDRA157 account. Her messages were file numbers, and nothing more. I'd email back when I put copies in the park, and then when I'd replaced the file where I'd gotten it."

He stroked his chin. "Do you have a list of the file numbers?"

"The most recent ones are on a Post-it in my purse."

"Were they all used in the articles, or are there still some left to publish?"

"A few were business plans that didn't fit with the articles, but everything else got published." I cringed, remembering the damage I'd caused the company with those articles, and all of it unwarranted.

Dennis closed his eyes and nodded, then opened them again. "Syd was more helpful than he realized." He pulled out his wallet and rummaged through it.

DENNIS

"I'VE GOT AN IDEA," I TOLD JENNIFER. AFTER PULLING THE CARD I WAS LOOKING for from my wallet, I dialed the number.

"Parsons," she answered.

"Agent Parsons. This is Dennis Benson."

"Dennis, I don't have anything further for you on Deborah."

"That's not why I was calling. I want to report that I've been the victim of a federal crime."

"Go ahead."

"Trade secrets have been stolen from my company."

"That's not my area, but I can put you in touch with the section head who handles that."

"I really want you on the case."

"Like I said, it's not my area."

I pulled out my trump card. "Do you remember Kirk Willey?"

She was quiet for a second. "This must be very important to you. How can I help?"

I let out a relieved sigh. "We performed a sting. A woman who works here was contacted by email to steal trade secrets."

Jennifer sent me a quizzical look.

"And?" Parsons asked.

"She dropped them off, and we have photographs of the thief picking them up."

"If you know who it is, we can bring him in for questioning," she offered.

"Her, actually. But I have a different question. Is that enough to get a warrant for the thief's email? And if you do get a warrant, will she know?"

"To your first question, if you and your employee sign affidavits that she was approached by this person, and that she turned over papers this person knew were trade secrets, the answer is yes. And no, she won't know about the warrant, most likely. We serve the warrant on the internet provider, not the person."

"Great. I'd like to get started this afternoon."

CHAPTER 44

DENNIS

(Two Days Later)

LATE WEDNESDAY MORNING, THE STOCK WAS TAKING ANOTHER NOSEDIVE. Larry's wait-for-the-other-shoe-to-drop line wasn't working anymore with the analysts, and Cartwright was trumpeting the SEC investigation every chance he got. Gumpert had called my direct number three times already this morning.

Cindy had handled him with more courtesy than he deserved.

Jennifer checked her watch. "She's late."

"That's normal."

Cindy popped her head in the open door. "She's downstairs. Should I have security bring her up?"

"Why don't *you* bring her up? That would be more hospitable. Set her up in conference room three."

"The boardroom is free, if you want to use that."

I shook my head. "No. Three is perfect. She won't be staying long. Oh, and have her seated facing the hallway."

Cindy left, muttering.

"You didn't tell her the plan?" Jennifer asked.

I tapped the folder. "Only you and Syd."

Syd had to know, so he could check that all the legal technicalities were correct. He'd enjoyed the irony of the plan and wanted to sit in, but I'd said no.

A few minutes later, Cindy was back. "The two of them are ready for you."

I stood and followed Jennifer to the conference room.

Melissa's face turned an angry red when Jennifer and I entered. "What is she doing here?"

I pulled out my chair after Jennifer took her seat. "She's my representative."

Melissa's lawyer slid a card across to Jennifer. "Karen Jenkins, Jenkins and Schwartz."

Jennifer took the card, but didn't offer one in return. "Oh, I'm not a lawyer."

Confusion filled the lawyer's face. "We thought this was going to be a resolution meeting."

"*Surrender* was the word you used," Melissa said.

It *was* the wording I'd used. She just didn't realize I meant *her* surrender.

Cindy knocked and opened the door. "The FBI is here to see you, Dennis."

"Tell them I'll be a few minutes." I turned far enough to see Parsons and Newsom waiting in the hall, wearing the FBI windbreakers I'd requested.

I'd chosen this room so that with the vertical blinds open, Melissa could see them clearly.

She smirked. "In trouble with the SEC, I hear."

I opened the folder and slid across the stapled copies of the emails I'd brought. "Yesterday the FBI served a warrant on your internet provider and found these emails."

She pushed them away with barely a glance. "I don't know anything about these."

It was Jennifer's turn to speak, and she aimed her words at the attorney. "I was approached by your client to steal trade secrets from the company. I passed them to her through a dead drop at a nearby park."

Melissa attempted a calm demeanor, but her facade cracked. "Lies."

Jennifer slid over the pictures of Melissa and her car. "The company surveilled the drop site after I left, and these are photographs of you picking up the material."

"I brought this to the attention of the FBI, and with the emails here…" I pointed to the paper stack. "…which are all tied to your home IP address, that gives us enough to have you charged with multiple counts of trade secret theft. That's up to ten years per count."

Jenkins's eyes bugged out. She put down the pictures and started to leaf through the emails.

"She's the one who stole them," Melissa complained, pointing at Jennifer.

"She did it at my direction, in order to find out who the real culprit was."

"That's a lie," Melissa spat. "It was all her idea."

"I don't think you should say any more," her lawyer cautioned.

"That's not the story the emails tell," I told her. "It's all in black and white, and it doesn't look very good for you. You recruited her, and you're the one who wrote the *Times* articles."

Melissa's face couldn't have been any redder.

I pulled out the documents Syd had prepared and slid them to Jenkins. "Either we come to an understanding, and you sign these, or I'm going to meet with those two agents, and we'll see you in court."

"But…" Melissa started to say.

I stood. "You have five minutes."

Jennifer followed me out of the room.

I winked at Parsons. "Can you two give me a few minutes?" I said loudly enough to be heard in the conference room. I herded Jennifer down the hall. "Do you think she'll go for it?"

"Of course. Did you see her eyes when you told her ten years per offense?"

CHAPTER 45

JENNIFER

A HALF HOUR LATER, CINDY HAD FINISHED NOTARIZING THE PAPERS, AND DENNIS and I were free of Melissa—hopefully forever. One of the papers she and her lawyer had signed ended the post-divorce dispute with Dennis.

I walked into the boardroom, where the next meeting was set to start soon.

Cartwright was due, and Dennis's fate hung in the balance. The Melissa legal dust-up was minor compared to Cartwright's attack.

Syd sat in his usual chair near the end, reading some of the papers Melissa had signed, and grinning.

I waited until he'd finished the last one. "Are those good enough to get us off the hook with the SEC?"

"Probably, but the timing isn't likely to be soon enough for the proxy vote. Even then, dropping the charges is not the same as the SEC declaring you innocent. Cartwright can still point to the original charges and claim that the SEC is just perfecting the case before they refile it. The whole thing casts a shadow over the company."

Larry wandered in. "Somebody said Cartwright was coming in. Should I join you?"

"Sure. You might find it entertaining," I said.

"You should ask Dennis," Syd told him.

Larry decided he liked my invitation better than Syd's warning and grabbed a seat. "What's the topic?"

"I'm just here to take notes," Syd grumbled.

"Why is he in such a good mood?" Larry said, leaning my way.

"My mood will improve when I stop being served court papers," Syd shot back.

A minute later, Cartwright and his slimeball lawyer arrived.

We went through the pleasantries without Dennis, and we all selected something to drink.

I stuck to Diet Coke—Dennis style, without a glass.

Dennis walked in and closed the door behind him. "Thanks for meeting us on such short notice."

Cartwright pasted on a smile. "You said you wanted to discuss restructuring the company, and that's a subject dear to my heart."

I doubted he had a heart. If he did, it was about to skip a beat.

Dennis took his seat, unscrewed the lid to his Coke, and downed a slug.

I did the same, and the glare we got from Cartwright was priceless. I unlocked my phone, selected the text message page, and put it in my lap in case I lost the bet.

Dennis spun his pen on the tabletop in front of him. "My ex-wife, Melissa, resigned from the board this morning."

"I take it you're offering us that seat?" Cartwright asked gleefully.

"Under the right circumstances. So you don't misunderstand, let me go through this slowly."

Cartwright sat back.

"Syd?" Dennis asked. "Do you have those papers Melissa signed?"

"Right here."

"Can I get a copy?" Larry asked.

"Pass them across, would you, please?" Dennis said, opening the folder in front of him and ignoring Larry.

Syd passed them to the two visitors. "I didn't bring extras," he told Larry.

Swartzman started the fireworks. "What is this bullshit?"

"Notarized statements that implicate your client in the stock manipulation you accused us of," Syd answered. "You orchestrated the negative press and bought on the down days."

313

"That's total crap," Cartwright spat. He pushed his chair back and stood. "We're not sticking around to be insulted."

I pressed send on the text I had ready. I'd lost the bet that they would stick around at least a minute to hear what we had.

ME: Now

Swartzman pushed his copy of the papers back at Syd and got up.

The text had gone to Cindy, and she opened the door as instructed. "Dennis, the two FBI agents you had an appointment with are here."

Swartzman and Cartwright froze at the word *FBI*.

"Have them wait a few minutes, please," Dennis told Cindy.

She closed the door.

Dennis spun his pen. "They're here to collect the evidence I have of your criminal conspiracy with my ex-wife."

The blood drained from Cartwright's face.

This was where it would get fun.

"Now, do you want me to pass it along, or would you rather listen to my proposed alternative?"

Cartwright answered by taking his seat again.

Swartzman followed.

Syd broke a smile.

"Very good," Dennis said. "Syd, show them the agreements."

Syd slid over a second set of papers.

Cartwright's eyes bulged. "A ten-percent discount? That's ridiculous."

The first page was an agreement for them to convert their stock to company debt at a ten-percent discount from their purchase price.

"And you expect us to help you finance a going-private transaction?" Swartzman asked. "Is this a joke?"

"No, and for that you get one board seat."

"That's worthless in a private company," Cartwright said.

"You're the one who wanted on the board. I want to take the company private, and this way we both get what we want."

Only, it wasn't anything like what Cartwright wanted. Because once the company went private, he lost all leverage.

"The agents are waiting," Dennis reminded them.

"A twenty-five percent premium, and I'll consider it."

Dennis took a long slug of his Coke. "Jennifer, you can handle it from here." He stood to leave.

"The case won't stand up," Swartzman argued.

"Syd, you can bring the affidavits along in a few minutes."

Syd nodded, and the door closed behind Dennis.

Swartzman pointed at me. "Nice try, but the SEC found the emails on your computer already, and that implicates you, not us."

Cartwright nodded, and his smile reappeared.

Larry's smile faded.

It was time, so I opened the folder I'd brought. "You directly attacked me, and if it were up to me, we'd be talking to the FBI right now. But Dennis is a nice guy and insisted on giving you a chance to find a mutually beneficial resolution."

Cartwright huffed. "You have a losing hand, young lady."

I held up the first paper. "You haven't seen all our cards yet. I have here an affidavit from Melissa Benson stating that she sent you, Carson…" I pointed a finger at him. "An email containing the files that were to be planted on my computer."

The happiness melted from his face.

I held up the USB Suzanne had given me with the resume on it she'd asked me to print and distribute. "You then had those files transferred to this thumb drive."

Swartzman objected. "We did no such thing."

"You instructed your employee Suzanne Murtog to give it to me." I lifted the last paper. "I also have an outside analysis confirming that this USB contains malware that would transfer the files to any computer it's plugged in to. I attached it to mine on the day I met her."

Cartwright glanced at his lawyer and back to me.

"The analysis also shows that the files on my computer are identical to the ones on this USB drive, and also identical to the ones emailed to you by Melissa Benson. They appeared on my computer that same day I met with your employee. And yes, the FBI retrieved those emails of Ms. Benson's yesterday with a warrant, so there is no question of their authenticity."

Happy Larry spoke up. "I'd say that is game, set, match."

Syd nodded, now back in confident mode. He'd not known what I had up my sleeve.

Cartwright shifted in his seat. "We'll need some time to read these over and consider it."

Swartzman nodded his agreement.

I checked my watch. "You have sixty seconds before I send Syd to join Dennis with the FBI agents. Decide quickly."

Cartwright looked at his attorney, who shrugged and put pen to paper.

A minute later they were gone, and Larry and Syd were high-fiving it.

EPILOGUE

"LIFE IS A FLOWER OF WHICH LOVE IS THE HONEY." — VICTOR HUGO

JENNIFER

It was Saturday morning, and as usual, the bedroom window was cracked open at the beach house. The wind made the curtains billow slightly, letting in the morning light. This early, the only noises outside came from the surf in the distance.

I rolled toward Dennis.

He was fast asleep after our late-night bottles of celebratory champagne. The go-private transaction had closed yesterday, and the company was now out of Cartwright's or anyone else's reach. The king's throne was secure.

Lifting up to see the red numerals on the clock, I realized we didn't have much time this morning. We were due over at the big house early, to get it ready for all the employees he'd invited to celebrate with us this afternoon.

The magazines said a man's testosterone levels were highest in the morning, and I had no intention of letting that go to waste. I got wet just thinking about the prospect. Slipping beneath the comforter, I lay my head on his abdomen, grabbed for my prize, and started to stroke.

He was already erect, and growing harder.

"Morning, Angel," he said groggily.

That name still sent a tingle down my spine every time—especially now that I knew I wasn't destined to disappoint him by being the avenging angel.

"Morning. Does Little Denny want to play?"

"Always, but you know that name sucks."

"How 'bout Big Willy?"

He pulled me up from my cave under the covers. "That still needs work."

I kept stroking him. "You have two choices this morning."

"Who's being bossy today?"

"You said I could have a turn." I made that part up, but it was worth a try.

"When?"

I kissed him lightly. "Last night after your third or fourth glass."

"I don't remember it that way."

I pulled my hand away. "Are you going to renege on a promise?" I scooted to the side of the bed to get up.

He pulled me back to him. "Never, my love. What are my choices?"

I took his nipple in my teeth.

He tensed.

I released. "We could go out and do it under the lifeguard tower."

"In the daylight? No way."

"It's dangerous."

"It's that, and a good way to get arrested. That'll have to wait until really late at night."

The danger of it obviously excited him.

"Or I'm in charge. My rules." *Take that, Mr. Control Freak.*

"Today is your day, Angel. You can have anything you want."

I pushed him over onto his back and threw the covers off. Moving down south, I gave his cock a long, slow lick from root to tip before taking him in my mouth for a few quick strokes in and out. It was sexy the way his cock jerked slightly as I blew cold air on the wet underside, or tickled just below the tip.

I stroked his hard length with a light grip and moved down to cup his balls.

He pulled at my shoulders to get access to my breasts, but I resisted. "My rules."

I climbed up over him and positioned myself over his super-hard cock.

He reached for my breasts, kneaded them, and thumbed my nipples with the circular motion that always got to me.

I lowered myself onto him, a bit down and then back up, and a little more down, teasing him with my slow approach.

His eyes showed the lust I'd induced in him. Holding back and not taking charge was killing him.

His gentle moans as I lowered myself, and his gasps as I pulled up were my guide. I took more of him with each stroke until I reached his root. I rocked into him, and he guided me up and down with his hands on my hips.

He moved to thumb my clit, but I jerked his hand away. He tried again, and I pulled him away again.

I shoved down fully, and his steely cock stretched me. "My rules today. You come first."

He always made me come first, and often more than once, before he did. It was his superpower, but this morning I wanted things to be different.

He relented and resorted to guiding my hips with his hands. He thrust up into me with my every downstroke. Each thrust seemed deeper and more filling than the one before.

I neared my limit as every cell of my body tensed with the thrusts down. Every lift up had all my nerves on fire, but I held off. I had to. I had to make him come first today. With concentration, I could win. I knew I could.

He tensed, and his breathing became shallow and rapid as he neared his limit.

I rocked down hard on him. I reached behind to grab his balls and used my other hand to pinch his nipple. He came with a loud groan and a final deep push. He gushed into me as he held me down on him.

His legs shook, and his cock continued to throb inside me as I ground down on him. He moved his thumb to my clit, and this time I allowed it.

I'd won for once.

His circling pressure on my sensitive nub quickly took me over the top. I couldn't hold off any longer and came undone on a shudder.

I leaned forward on him. I couldn't catch my breath as the spasms shook me and my body dissolved in a heap.

He hugged me tightly. "Angel, I love you," he groaned into my ear.

"I love you, too."

A perfect smile filled his face as I lifted up off his chest to kiss him.

I relaxed down against him again. The pulses of his cock inside me slowly diminished. This was always the best part, the ultimate closeness between us, physically and emotionally linked to each other.

I rolled off of him and headed to the shower. I turned at the door. "How about Dickzilla?"

He huffed. "Keep trying, Angel."

~

JENNIFER

DENNIS HAD HIRED LUSSO'S CATERING FOR THE EVENT AT THE BIG HOUSE, AND I felt like a bit of a fifth wheel instead of the hostess. The backyard was overflowing with people from the company.

Tony Lusso had taken over the huge kitchen, and he barked orders at his staff.

I quickly grabbed a can of the Bud from the fridge, which I'd stocked for Ramona's new squeeze, Ian.

He was fireman with the LAFD. Ramona had met him at her new job at Mercy Hospital, now that she'd graduated. He seemed nice, and because he was divorced with a six-year-old son, the two had a lot in common as single parents.

I located them out back by the pool, and handed the chilled beer to Ian. "You know we have other choices as well."

"It's Bud or nothing, and I have to stop drinking by three. I've got a shift tomorrow."

Ramona deserved a responsible guy after what she'd been through with Billy's father, and Ian definitely checked that box.

It also didn't hurt that when we'd gotten together a few times on the weekends, Ian had impressed Dennis as well.

Ian had been spending quite a bit of time at our new place, which had allowed me to spend more time at Dennis's.

Billy crouched down to feel the pool's temperature. "Can we go swimming later?"

"Bill, you have to ask Uncle Dennis," his mother replied.

Every time I heard Ramona use that nickname, I wished it were true. But after the disaster of his quick marriage to Melissa, I understood that *slow* was Dennis's watchword for relationships.

Ian's son tugged on his father's leg. "Can I be Ron? I don't like Ronnie anymore."

"You're not old enough yet," Billy told him proudly.

I left them to find my Denny.

As I searched for him, I was relieved that one face was missing in the crowd.

Ed had moved to another company. Dennis had written him a nice letter of recommendation, which he honestly deserved. We wouldn't be where we were today without his help nailing Melissa.

Fortunately, months ago he'd come to grips with the situation and picked up with a new girl. The texts had stopped permanently, and I'd come to realize that the later ones had been his way of trying to help me. After he'd realized what I'd been doing, he hadn't turned me in, but instead reached out to talk.

Eventually I located Dennis talking to his father.

Serena joined us.

"So you were behind that?" Dennis asked Lloyd.

"I knew you weren't going to ask *me* if you needed help, so I had Hugh approach you."

Dennis had finally told Hugh Stoner last month that we weren't interested in his livestock feed business.

Stoner had admitted it had been Lloyd's idea all along.

"That's underhanded," Dennis complained.

"It worked, didn't it?"

It had worked. We'd been in contact with Stoner for a long time, and he'd been there when Dennis needed help talking to shareholders.

Serena elbowed me and whispered, "He didn't suspect?"

I whispered back. "Not a clue."

"I told you Cartwright was a snake. He always has been," Lloyd said. "I still wish he'd gotten jail time. It's what he deserves." The animosity was palpable.

Dennis finished his sip of wine. "He's gone for good now."

"I wouldn't count on that. The Cartwrights are like a bad rash, always appearing at the worst times."

"But you were wrong about the attack on Josh being Cartwright's doing," Dennis noted.

We'd been informed that the police had made an arrest in another road rage incident where shots were fired, and the gun they found on the guy matched the bullets in Josh's car. Since they didn't have any other evidence, they couldn't prosecute him in Josh's incident, but they would get him on the current charge.

"There's a first for everything," Lloyd said. "I've been right about them all the rest of the times. Bad apples, the whole lot of them."

While they went back and forth on the Cartwright family, I asked Serena, "Is there a history I don't know about?"

She nodded. "Dad won't tell us the details. All we know is it's bad."

I filed that comment away for later.

Although Dennis's solution to getting rid of Cartwright didn't sit well with his father, it was a win-win, which was pure Dennis. We were done with both him and Melissa. And by taking the company private with Cartwright's forced help, Dennis no longer had to deal with the Wall Street types he despised.

To add irony to the situation, Dennis told me he'd given Gumpert's number to Melissa.

I hadn't understood why, until Dennis had said they had similar moral compasses, and he deserved her.

Having experienced Melissa, I wasn't sure anybody deserved her.

"Hey, Larry, get control of your dog," Dennis called out.

Serena and I cracked up.

Larry's little mutt Binky was dry-humping Dennis's leg.

The attractive brunette on Larry's arm raced over to fetch the little monster. "Binky, behave yourself." She picked him up and whisked him away.

Larry had decided to keep Binky after women started approaching him at the park to meet the hairless wonder.

Dennis and I'd had Larry and several of his ladies over for dinner, and so far this latest one, Sylvia, had lasted the longest.

After a fair amount of food and alcohol had been served, Dennis dragged me with him up to the deck. "Gather round," he yelled a few times.

Ramona and Ian joined us on the deck.

Larry whistled loudly to get everybody's attention, and Syd went inside to pull anyone else out.

Dennis had worked on a speech for this crowd of mostly Vipersoft employees, intended to tell them how he felt about the future of the company now that it had gone private. The speech emphasized the company's new ability to plan for the long term instead of the short. He'd been totally focused on how it would provide a more stable workplace for the employees.

I was proud of the job he'd done with it and expected it to go well.

Dennis pulled the folded sheets of his speech from his pocket. "Thank you all for coming. We officially completed the go-private transaction yesterday."

There were a few claps.

He still hadn't opened his notes yet. "I know the last half year or so has been a rough time for all of us, and I appreciate all your support in this process. I prepared a few words for you." He unfolded and held up the pages. "But I feel they are inadequate for the occasion."

He refolded the papers. "The reorganization we accomplished isn't yet complete."

He'd lost me, and judging by the faces in the crowd, most of them as well.

"Jennifer, Larry, and Syd have been a great help in this. But one thing remains incomplete that I need Jennifer's help with."

He was seriously off script.

I surveyed the crowd, and with everybody looking at me, my blush went to three alarms. I looked back at Dennis, and he was on one knee.

"Jennifer Susan Hanley," he began.

I couldn't believe my eyes.

Ramona had handed him a box—a fucking Harry Winston jewelry box.

He opened the case.

A gorgeous diamond solitaire sat in the blue velvet.

Tears of joy welled in my eyes. This was really happening.

"And this is not an opportunity for negotiation," he said.

The crowd laughed.

"Will you marry me?"

The crowd hushed.

"Yes," I squeaked. "Yes."

The applause started, and Dennis rose to kiss me. It was another one of those breathless kisses that made the noise of the gathering drop into the background, behind the thundering of my heart.

He released me, too soon, and slipped the ring onto my finger. We were official.

"You make me so happy," he said loudly.

We descended the deck into the throng of well-wishers, and Lusso's people were miraculously everywhere, passing out champagne.

After the congratulations died down, Dennis and I wandered the thinning crowd.

"I have one problem," I told Dennis as I waved my sister over.

Dennis held my hand. "The deal is done. No re-negotiation allowed, and no arguments."

"I still have to help out with Bill. She can't handle him alone."

"I heard that, and no you don't," Ramona said as she and Ian walked up.

Her boyfriend put his arm around her. "We're moving you out, and Ronnie and I are moving in."

Dennis squeezed my hand. "I asked your sister's permission first."

Ramona giggled. "It was sorta sweet. He was worried about Bill."

I snuggled up to my man. "How did I get so lucky?"

"I'm the lucky one," Dennis replied.

I knew I was truly the lucky one, but decided to live with his request for no arguments.

At least for today.

THE END

∾

THE FOLLOWING PAGES CONTAIN AN EXCERPT OF THE NEXT BOOK IN THE SERIES: **Undercover Billionaire**.

Available on AMAZON HERE.

SNEAK PEEK: UNDERCOVER BILLIONAIRE

CHAPTER 1

KELLY

I LOCKED THE DEADBOLT TO MY HOUSE. THE SCUFF ON MY SHOES REMINDED ME OF my umpteenth useless date last night. I'd walked away so fast from Harold —if that was even his real name—that I'd tripped on the curb.

As I turned, the man in the dark suit looked away. How did he almost always end up walking down my street when I came out of the house?

Probably because I was predictable as hell. That was my life alright: predictable and boring.

He looked married, but maybe that was just the attire. Hell, lots of people in Washington DC worked for the government and wore suits.

I forced myself to ignore the hopelessness of my dating life and searched the bottom of my purse for my car keys as I walked. After climbing in, I started up.

Fucking shit.

The low fuel light was on. Like an idiot, I'd forgotten to fill up yesterday, and now there wasn't enough time before I was due at work.

I started after Mr. Dark Suit down the street toward the Dupont Circle station, and cursed my awful luck. The DC Metro was swift, comfortable, and clean by American subway standards, but it was slower than driving, and Monday was not a good day to be late to work at the Smithsonian.

Helmut Krause scheduled his weekly status meetings bright and early every Monday, and attendance was mandatory.

I'd been late to the first one of these he'd scheduled after his arrival, and just my luck, he'd made a public example of me.

Being called up in front of everyone to explain why I was late had made me the instant poster child for bad employee of the month.

He'd even made me repeat my name to the group.

I didn't know everybody in the building, but they certainly knew me after that. The under-the-breath murmurs and sideways glances had taken months to die down.

Shame, thy name be Kelly Benson.

Reaching the tracks, I chose a different Metro car than Mr. Dark Suit, and changed to the blue line at Metro Center. The LED screen inside the car showing the next stop couldn't change fast enough. Finally we reached L'Enfant Plaza, and I made a dash for the escalator.

Arriving at our building, I made it through security and up to my desk to drop off my umbrella with a few minutes to spare.

Upstairs, the light tan inter-departmental envelope with my name on it sat on my work surface. OPS was written in the *From* column. The guys in the Office of Protective Services all thought using OPS made them sound more important that just writing Security.

It wasn't heavy enough to be a copy of the access logs I'd requested.

I unwound the red string holding it shut and pulled out the single sheet of paper.

The printed words make my knees go weak.

On Tuesday night reset the key code of the southeast door by the loading dock to 1-1-1-1
    Or end up like Brooks
    Do not contact anyone or end up like Brooks
    We see everything

I collapsed into my chair. I could hardly breathe. My throat constricted, preventing the scream of terror lodged in my throat from escaping.

I closed my eyes in an effort to restart my breathing.

When they reopened, the deadly threat on the page only looked worse.

"Ready?" Kirby Stackhouse asked from behind me. Somehow I hadn't heard her approach.

I quickly folded the note closed and turned.

She tapped the cubicle wall.

"Come on, Kell. We don't want to be late."

I opened a drawer and hid the ghastly paper inside.

"You can tell me about Harold on the way."

I rose on unsteady legs. "Nothing to tell."

"That bad, huh?"

I looked down at the scuff on my new shoes. "Worse."

Kirby went quiet while we descended the stairs, and my mind returned to the note. Six months ago Melinda Brooks, who'd worked two cubicles down from me, had left work on a normal Monday night. She was kidnapped and found dead four days later in the Maryland woods. The details hadn't been pretty.

Life here in the Smithsonian had slowly returned to normal as the incident was forgotten. *She* had been forgotten, but not by me.

Following the crowd to the cafeteria, we made it in time for the start of the meeting.

Kirby and I took up residence on some chairs near the back. That way Krause wouldn't notice if we snickered at something ridiculous he said, which was pretty much every week. The meeting was supposed to get us all off to a very efficient German start to the day. Bullshit. It had most of us needing a second cup of caffeinated beverage to stay awake while he prattled on.

Mark Porter smiled at me as he took the seat on the other side of Kirby. "Morning, ladies."

Having him find a seat nearby had become a weekly occurrence, but at least he'd stopped asking me out. I'd learned to nod back to him, rather than encourage him with words, and the only words that came to mind anyway were *why me?* What had I done to be targeted by the memo writer? Who could I or should I bring the note to?

Looking over the sea of people, I realized the note could have come from any of them. I couldn't trust anybody in the building.

Helmut Krause started his talk, getting me off the hook with Porter.

Krause had brought this meeting system over from his last job at the

Deutsches Museum in Munich, Germany. The Munich museum was, after all, the world's largest museum of science and technology, he liked to remind us. Never mind that *we* had the Apollo 11 command module that had ferried Americans to the moon and back. That was my definition of technology.

Wendy had been the first on our floor to make the mistake of mispronouncing where Krause was from. *Munich,* he told us, was an English bastardization of the real spelling, München, and was to be pronounced *Moon-chen.*

I could never get the U sound quite right and avoided the word entirely.

Krause's speech this morning went right by me. Every time I blinked, I saw Melinda's face staring back at me. She'd been the second tragedy I'd experienced in the past year. The first had been the kidnapping and murder of Patel, another Smithsonian employee.

The only thing I heard while Krause talked was the sound of the newscaster in my head from the night they found Melinda. *"Tonight we have the tragic story of a young woman found strangled in the woods."*

Her face had been the first thing on the evening news. For a week or so, the story had continued to dominate, but then it didn't. No more details became available, so the news people shifted to something about North Korea, then a budget impasse the following week, and life went on.

But Melinda was always with me. She'd provided the recommendation that got me my job here. I would never forget her, or what had happened.

She'd left a letter for me in her apartment, sealed and addressed but unstamped. Her family had located it while clearing out her things and given it to me.

It shocked me when I opened it. It contained a note almost identical to the one in my drawer. "Look what I got for Halloween" had been handwritten on it. Instead of Brooks, hers had said she would "end up like Patel."

I'd walked Melinda's note to the local FBI office, and told them how I came to get it. I'd never heard another thing from them.

Daya Patel had stopped coming to work roughly six months before Melinda disappeared. It had taken a week for her to be declared missing. Her boyfriend and she had fought, and the first theory had been that she'd left town to get away from him. That ended when her car was located abandoned in a desolate area. No sign of her had ever been found.

I'd transferred upstairs to replace Patel, even been assigned her old cubicle, a detail I hadn't known until after I started on this floor.

"Kell, let's get moving." Kirby pushed my shoulder and jostled me back to reality. The meeting was over.

I stood and shuffled down the line of chairs.

"The biggest waste of time ever," she said. "Can you believe he wants to start another inventory this week?"

"Huh?" I'd been so preoccupied by the ugly note that nothing had registered.

"The inventory again already?"

"Yeah, a waste of time." The Smithsonian had over a hundred fifty thousand items, most of them packed away in storage, and inventory was a monumental task.

I stumbled on the way out, but caught the frame of the doorway before ending up on my ass.

Mark grabbed my elbow to steady me. "Careful there, Kelly. You okay?"

I forced a half laugh. "Damned heels."

He released his hold and left with a smile. "They do look hot on you."

The compliment pulled a half-smile from me. He wasn't a bad guy, easygoing it seemed, but I'd learned my lesson about dating a guy from work. That was a mistake I wasn't about to repeat. Instead I'd found lots of new mistakes to make.

Back at my desk, I turned on my computer and signed in. I blinked, but the icons on the screen swam back and forth, refusing to stay in focus. My thoughts went back to the two dead girls, and the note in my drawer.

Kirby reappeared. "Coffee? You looked like death warmed over after that meeting."

"Sure." I followed her to the coffee room.

"Wanna try the Columbian blend? It's better than the regular stuff," she said.

She was a superstitious sort and had decided I needed to break old habits if I was ever going to get laid.

I chose an English Breakfast teabag and added hot water. "No thanks. I don't need anything to clean the rust off my bicycle chain."

She laughed. "It's not that bad."

"It's not that good either."

Back in my cube, Melinda's face reappeared, and I was back to today's reality.

Act normal, I kept telling myself. If he was watching, I shouldn't do anything out of the ordinary. Today was not the day to take Kirby's advice.

I needed to talk to someone in the family, someone I could trust implicitly. To be safe, I couldn't call until lunchtime when I could be out of the building.

The minutes ticked by slowly.

If this didn't go well, would people remember me six months from now?

∾

ADAM

MY PHONE VIBRATED WITH A TEXT MESSAGE.

HARPER: Be about ten late

Sal Harper was always late. The motto of the FBI didn't include punctuality, he'd once joked. If it had, he'd no longer be with the Bureau.

I'd gotten stuck with the midnight watch on this stakeout, and not once in the last week had he managed to relieve me on time.

The word *relieve* was not a good one to have go through my head. I'd already filled the bottle I was peeing into in the car, and my bladder was about to burst. Leaving my post for a break at the coffee shop two blocks away was not an option. The last DC agent who'd been caught doing that was now in Anchorage. Our field office was only a few blocks from HQ, so more was always expected of us.

I started to type a text back to Harper.

ME: get here on time for a change

I deleted it without sending. He was not only senior to me, but he played weekly poker with our boss, which is why I gotten the overnight duty in the first place, and he got the day shift. Pissing Harper off would likely lead to even worse assignments. Shit ran downhill in the Bureau, and I wasn't far from the bottom.

Harper finally pulled up behind me in his minivan and waved through the windshield. He'd even been assigned a minivan with enough room to stand up when he had to piss. I had to contort myself to get it in the bottle without dribbling on my pants.

I started up the piece-of-shit undercover car, and it rattled its way down the street, past the location we were watching. I was careful not to look left at the rundown house containing the dirt-bag human traffickers. Our intel had said they were expecting another "delivery" soon, and we had to catch them in the act when the girls arrived, before they all got sent off to other cities.

The DC police had handed the case over to us when they realized the operation crossed state lines.

I made it to my place, and the bathroom, without bursting. In the kitchen, I ground a scoop of my special St. Helena beans and loaded the grounds into a French press. A few minutes later, the savory smell of the coffee I decanted into my mug filled the kitchen.

I was going to need several cups to make it through another day. We were short staffed for the case load, thanks to more budget wrangling in Congress. While they debated priorities, we didn't have the manpower to properly handle the crimes that came our way. But, that's what we had the top brass for: to deal with the elected jerkoffs.

Upstairs, I shed my undercover outfit of intentionally dirty clothes. My coffee cup came with me into the shower. The hot water eased the soreness of sitting in the car seat all night.

My family was among the uber-rich, and I had a ton of zeros in my bank balance. I hadn't joined the Bureau to make a living. I did this to make a difference, and that meant making sacrifices. Sacrifices that mattered.

From a very young age, I'd known that pushing papers around the way my old man did was never going to be my future.

Today's assignment was the kind of admission I had to pay to get a chance at the counterterrorism division with my family name, a name that needed rehabilitation in the Bureau.

There was evil in this world. It had to be confronted, and I meant to make a difference doing just that.

CHAPTER 2

KELLY

I STOOD AND WALKED TO THE RESTROOM, THEN TO THE COFFEE ROOM FOR another cup of tea, and back to my desk. All the while I looked around the office. Nothing seemed out of place that I could tell. I didn't detect anyone watching me, following me, or paying any attention at all. Only when I noticed the little black spheres at opposite corners of the room did my blood turn cold.

Any of us could be watched by the cameras behind the black plastic. It was impossible to tell which way the camera within pointed, or who was at the monitor on the other end.

As I sat, my skin started to itch. What could I do to keep from being the next victim? Or was it too late?

I pulled the note from my drawer and opened it on my lap, away from prying eyes. Whoever he was wanted me to change the entrance code on the southwest doorway.

Could it just be a prank? Or could this be a test by Protective Services to see if I was trustworthy? If I was being watched and Melinda's killer was in Protective Services, I couldn't go to them.

Closing my eyes, I shook my head at the impossibility of my position.

Going to my boss, Mr. Heiden, made the most sense, but Melinda had also worked for him. What if she'd taken the note to him instead of doing what it demanded, and that had sealed her fate? My face could be the next one on the evening news if I made the wrong choice.

I needed to talk to somebody about this. The only people I could trust without any reservations were my family, and none of them lived anywhere nearby. All but me and Vincent were still in California. If I called my father, or any of my protective brothers, I'd be grabbed and shoved into Daddy's jet and on the way back home in a matter of hours. My sister, Serena, was the clear choice. She'd listen and help me puzzle through who to talk to and what precautions to take.

I'd come to DC to get away from LA, and away from Daddy's control, although I hadn't put it that way in talking to him. The last thing I wanted to do was give him a reason to pull me back there.

The note went back into the drawer after I'd taken a picture of it with my phone. I would call Serena when I went out to lunch, someplace I wouldn't be overheard.

~

THE LITTLE INDIAN RESTAURANT WAS ONE OF MY REGULAR HAUNTS. IT HAD ONLY two tables on the sidewalk separated by the walkway to the door. The far one was already occupied by an older couple.

Normally I sat inside, but today I chose the nearer sidewalk table and took the seat with its back to the restaurant. There wasn't much pedestrian traffic on this street, and I could see well in both directions.

The waiter brought water, and I ordered my usual—Diet Coke, naan, and chicken tikka masala—without bothering with the menu.

After checking in both directions, I dialed my sister.

Serena picked up. "Hi, Kelly. Miss me?"

"Always." That was certainly true. "Do you have a few minutes? I need some advice."

"I always have time for you. What's his name?"

I laughed. "It's not a man." It lifted my spirits to talk to her.

"That's too bad." She went silent, waiting for me.

"I have a problem at work."

"Yeah?"

335

"I got a threatening note, and I'm not sure what to do?"

"You could take it to HR, I guess."

"This is worse than that.

"How much worse?"

"Here's what it says." I'd memorized the words and repeated them verbatim.

"Who's Brooks?"

The waiter arrived with my drink.

"Just a sec…" I thanked him and continued after he left. "She used to work here. She was murdered six months ago."

An audible gasp came across the line. "You have to get out of there, like, right now."

"And what happens when he picks another girl and sends her a note?" I countered.

She sighed. "What about security?"

I explained the problem with going to them or my boss, hoping she'd have a better idea.

For about five seconds all I got from Serena was silence. "Then I'd call Ashley."

I hadn't considered Vincent's wife. She was in the FBI, and Serena's suggestion was a good one.

"Not Vincent?" I asked.

"Not unless you want a one way ticket back home." It was good to know she understood my brothers' likely response. "I'll send you her direct number. Let me know what she says."

We hung up, and I only had to wait a minute for my food to come.

After more checking of my surroundings and a bite of my food, I dialed Ashley.

"Benson here." There was a lot of background noise, but her voice was familiar even though I'd only met her at the wedding.

"Ashley, it's Kelly Benson. Serena gave me your number."

"Hi, Kelly. I'm about to go into a meeting. What can I do for you?"

"If I talk to you about something FBI related, can we keep it from Vincent?"

"I don't discuss delicate Bureau business with him."

"Let's call it delicate FBI business then. I've gotten a threatening note, and I need help."

"Give me a sec to get to a quieter room…"

I heard a door close, and the background noise died away.

"Okay, can you send me the note?"

"Sure." I texted her the picture I'd taken.

A moment later she'd received it. "Is this Brooks, Melinda Brooks?"

"Yes. How'd you know that?"

"The abduction and murder of a federal employee is a high-priority case at the Bureau."

That made perfect sense.

The older couple at the other table left.

She sighed. "I have to be honest. In a case like this that looks like the perp wants to get leverage, and it's not personal, you have two choices. I won't judge you regardless."

I took another bite of my food as the waiter appeared to bus the other table.

She continued. "You could run away and let the Bureau and the museum look into it, or we could get you security and try to catch this guy."

I'd already made up my mind. "I couldn't live with myself if I left and someone else paid the price. I just don't know who to go to with this at work."

"This has to be handled by the Bureau, no question about it. How did you get the note?"

"It was in an interoffice envelope on my desk after the weekend."

"Okay, here's what we do. I'm going to call the DC Field Office, and they'll figure out a plan to get you protection. I'll call you back with the plan on your cell. If you can talk, call me Ash. If you can't talk, call me Ashley. Got it?"

"Okay."

"It'll be all right. The Bureau will take care of you. I'll make sure of it."

I thanked her profusely, and we hung up.

Adam

THE MORNING AT THE DC FIELD OFFICE HAD BEEN MONOTONOUS—NO CALL outs to break up the video watching. My partner, Neil Boxer, and I had just finished lunch.

I relaunched the video player on my machine. "I'm at T minus eleven days."

"I'm still on minus eight," he replied.

He was reviewing the even days, and I was doing the odd ones of the bank surveillance video. We were combing through for a glimpse of our masked bank robber with the limp.

It was the second bank job in a month by the same pair who'd shot up the bank in Gaithersburg. This one had gone down in Falls Church, Virginia. The woman drove and stayed in the car, and the man went inside, fired two shots into the ceiling, and was out in less than a minute. No one had gotten hurt, but with an itchy trigger finger, anything could happen on their next job. A robbery where the guy was recklessly firing off rounds was a dangerous situation.

The man wore a mask, but he had a limp. We hoped to use that and his general body type to ID him.

Television shows made it look simple, but that was far from the truth. We were doing the grunt work—going through weeks of prior surveillance footage from the two banks, looking for a shot of the robbers casing the location. Even your average bank robber wasn't stupid enough to rob a bank they'd never been inside before.

An hour in, I caught my eyelids closing for more than a blink, and stood to stretch. My knee cracked again.

Fucking ACL.

It was a constant reminder of what could have been—what should have been.

I started for the coffee machine. "I need another cup."

He hit pause and leaned back in his chair to stretch. "Knock yourself out."

Two other guys from the floor below were ahead of me when I arrived at the machine. I'd bought the expensive machine on my own dime, and now a lot of the agents in the office made the trip to our floor for the good stuff. Each of the other floors had the government-issue coffee maker that dispensed a brown liquid that could hardly be called coffee.

The double shot I'd programmed in was dispensing when our ASAC,

Assistant Special Agent in Charge, Dempsey yelled for me and Boxer to join him.

At last, something to break up the video scrolling.

"Close the door," he barked. Something had riled him today.

I closed it, and took the second seat across from the ASAC.

"I hate getting these calls," he complained. He passed us each copies of a typewritten note.

I looked at Neil, who didn't seem to have a clue either.

"The AD just called, and we have to drop everything for some hotshot in Boston." Dempsey didn't often get anything straight from the Assistant Director, but when he did, it didn't pay to take it lightly.

He punched the hold on his speakerphone. "I've got Boxer and Cartwright here with me now."

A woman's voice came over the box. "Did you get the note I sent?"

"Yes," Neil said.

"This was received this morning by an employee at the Smithsonian. The Brooks mentioned on the note is Melinda Brooks, the second of two Smithsonian employees who've been abducted and murdered in the last year."

"We know," Dempsey said. "They're our cases."

I recalled the Brooks murder. Neil and I hadn't been on it, but a lot of agents in the office had. The trail had quickly gone cold, and was unsolved so far.

"We believe the note writer is the same UNSUB as the two previous cases."

Neil hit the mute button. "Why is she telling us our business?"

Dempsey ignored him and took it off mute. "You want us to interview this employee?" Dempsey asked.

"No. She needs undercover protection in place to let this play out until we can get a handle on the UNSUB."

Neil shook his head. "What does museum security have on this?"

"The UNSUB could be in their security, so we don't think we can loop in anyone in the building."

"Who is we?" Dempsey asked.

There was a hesitation on the other end. "The Director and me."

She'd just pulled out the biggest trump card in the deck, and Dempsey's face showed it. A case involving the death of a federal employee was a big deal, two murders was a bigger deal, but one with the Director's attention was the biggest. Dempsey wasn't fool enough to argue with her if she'd brought it up with the Director. Being assigned a case by the AD was serious; mentioning the Director took it up another several notches.

"The previous abductions were both offsite." Again, she was telling us things we knew.

"She should be secure in her building. We need you guys to go under, to cover her off premises."

Neil huffed. He didn't like being told what to do, and she'd already decided how we were going to run our operation.

Dempsey ignored Neil. "We'll get right on it."

"Thanks, guys. I'll send over the meeting detail," she said.

Dempsey punched the speakerphone off. "Needless to say, this is your top case starting today."

"She's got some brass ones, telling us what we're going to do. Who the hell was that?" Neil asked.

"Ashley Newton. Now she's Ashley Benson."

Neil nodded. He and I had heard the same rumors about her. He wisely decided to shut up. You didn't argue with someone who had the Director's ear.

I hated the name. But she was good. Singlehandedly taking down a corrupt Assistant US Attorney and keeping it out of the papers was a major coup, even if she had the poor taste to marry a Benson later.

Dempsey pointed at me. "Cartwright, you're up. Neil will provide back-up." This would obviously entail a lot more than day-shift hours for me, and Dempsey always favored Neil when these decisions came up. My family name was always in play it seemed.

Once again, I had no choice in the matter. "Great. Who's the protectee?"

Dempsey passed over the thin file. "Rich girl, just your type."

I dreaded opening the cover. He was probably kidding, and it would turn out to be a middle-aged cat lady.

The name surprised me—Kelly Benson, the sister of the man who'd ruined my knee, and my life. No wonder Ashley Benson had gotten involved.

It took us a few minutes of discussion to come up with a workable plan, given the information we had on her.

The Bensons were fucking everywhere recently, and now they were screwing with my life again.

CHAPTER 3

KELLY

AT THE END OF THE DAY I RUMMAGED THROUGH THE EXTRA LARGE HANDBAG I carried every day. It took a minute, but I found the eyeshadow I brought along for just such an emergency. A girl had to be prepared, and I could almost always find what I needed at the bottom of this bag somewhere.

Kirby walked into the bathroom as I was finishing the first eye. "What are we getting all pretty for?"

"Another SuperSingles date. Sooner or later I have to find the prince among the frogs." A harmless lie.

She turned on the water to rinse her mug. "I have a nice cousin in Alexandria I could set you up with."

"Yeah? What does he do for a living?"

She rinsed her mug again before answering. "Assistant mortician."

"I'll pass." The idea of even shaking hands with a guy who'd been touching dead bodies made me cringe.

"He's not a frog."

I switched to my other eye. "Still pass."

She left, and I was alone again with my apprehensions.

Ashley had promised me FBI protection outside of work, and I hoped that was enough. If I got too scared, I'd have to consider going back to LA, which was not my favorite alternative. But it was better than ending up like Melinda.

Just the thought of what she'd endured before death had freed her from the agony made my stomach turn. I owed it to her to give this my best shot. This maniac had to be stopped.

I'd picked the restaurant, and my instructions from Ashley were to get a table and wait to meet my "detail," whatever that meant.

~

I ARRIVED EARLY, AND THE HOSTESS SEATED ME AT A TABLE NEAR THE WINDOW while I waited for my detail to arrive. Without any names, I was looking for men to show up in off-the-rack dark suits, white shirts, thin plain ties, probably sticks up their asses, and definitely super-short hair. Or maybe they were sending a woman as well. What did female FBI agents wear? Pants for sure…after that I drew a blank.

One guy too attractive to be an FBI prospect arrived. Blond, tall, and well muscled, he was underdressed for an FBI dude. Blondie briefly looked in my direction, but then took up residence at the bar. Definitely lick-worthy, he ranked several points above any of the recent dates I'd been on. How come there weren't more of him on SuperSingles?

A minute later an attractive blonde with the world's deepest cleavage joined him. Lucky girl.

Maybe that was my problem—not enough cleavage in my SuperSingles profile picture. While I waited, I thought through the tops in my closet.

I glanced down. Definitely insufficient cleavage to be fishing in this pond. I undid a button.

An even taller, more muscled guy walked in. Mr. Muscles stopped to take in the room. The leather flight jacket over his button-down shirt didn't fit the FBI dress code. His eyes landed on me and a hint of a smile tugged at the corners of his mouth before his scan moved on to the other tables.

At least showing a little more cleavage had gotten me noticed, a real improvement.

He continued past the bar to the bathrooms.

I went back to watching the front door for my detail.

"Kelly?"

I turned. It was Mr. Muscles, and this close, he looked oddly familiar.

He moved around to take the other seat. "Your profile picture doesn't do you justice."

He knew my name, and I realized why. He was Adam Cartwright from years ago in LA.

I blushed and cringed at the same time, if that was possible. Daddy would kill me if he knew I was even talking with a Cartwright. Daddy had been at war with his father, and my brother Dennis and Adam had serious bad blood between them. The Hatfields and the McCoys had probably been friendlier.

He pulled out his chair. "It's been a long time. How have you been?"

I fumbled for the right words. "Okay. But... But I'm expecting to meet some people, actually."

He sat down. "I know. I'm your date. Adam Carter." He said the last name slowly.

My mouth fell open.

"What's good here?" He acted as if this were a real date, and our families didn't hate each other. Or maybe he was pretending to not remember.

"You?"

He skipped my query. "What do you recommend here?"

I'd picked this place because it was close to work. "I've only been here once before, so I don't really know." I paused. "Are you?" I didn't want to say *FBI* out loud.

"Ashley asked me to dine with you, if that answers your question."

That did answer one of my questions. If Ashley sent him, he was in the right place.

"You and?"

"I think a dinner for two is much more intimate, don't you?" That answered my other question. My detail was apparently a single protector.

As he scanned the menu, I took in the person across from me. No longer the high school senior I'd last seen, this was a man—light blue eyes, an angular chin that could probably cut glass, and shoulders Apollo would be envious of. The too-short dusty blond hair was the only part I'd gotten right about him.

His eyes came up to meet mine, and a smile formed on his lips. "I meant it."

"What?" I squeaked, self-conscious at having been caught checking him out.

"Your picture doesn't do you justice."

The heat in my cheeks went up a notch. I looked down and took a sip of water. "Thank you."

A waitress arrived to break the embarrassing silence. "Can I get you something to drink? A cocktail? Wine? A beer?"

I ordered a chardonnay, but he stuck to lemonade.

"How is this going to work?" I asked.

"Usually you order first and eat second."

I let out an exasperated sigh. "Really?"

He looked around before leaning forward. "We should talk later."

The hint was clear. I hadn't spotted anybody from the office here, but I didn't know everybody in the building either, and being overheard wouldn't be good.

"What is it you do, Adam?" That was the most innocuous, date-like question I could come up with.

He put down the menu. "Did you bring the item with you?"

I nodded. I'd brought the note in a plastic bag.

"Hold on to it 'till we get outside."

"Okay." I couldn't control my curiosity. "Are you—"

He stopped me with a raised finger. "I'm a guidance counselor."

"That sounds interesting"

"Frustrating is more like it. Sometimes I get the most spoiled children assigned to me." His eyes bored into me with the words *spoiled children.* "And I have to keep them out of trouble." Charming had been replaced by insulting.

Our waitress returned with our drinks, breaking up the mini insult-fest that had erupted. She departed after taking our dinner orders.

"Do you end up whipping them into submission?" I shot back.

A smirk appeared. "Only the ones that like it."

"And if they don't appreciate your approach?" I asked.

He sipped his lemonade. "They don't get a choice. They do as they're told, or very bad things happen. That would get me in trouble, so I don't allow it. But we should talk later."

Protection was starting to sound like confinement.

I nervously played with my fork. "Do they get field trips?"

"Supervised, yes. Solo, no." His hand came across to cover mine. "I take very good care of my clients."

The electricity that shot from his skin to mine was unmistakable. I willed my hand to move, but it froze in place, welded to his by the warmth of his touch and the look in his eyes. Antagonism was now nowhere to be found in those light blues, only softness. Once again, heat accumulated in my cheeks.

He took his hand back, and I missed the touch more than I should have, particularly given his family name. I really did need a date.

Our food arrived, and the conversation transitioned to a familiar, date-like pattern. He answered my questions about his life since we'd last seen each other, using euphemisms for this current job, but being truthful about college. In turn, I relayed my path from Los Angeles to the Smithsonian.

I didn't need to make up terms or job titles as he did. I had no reason to hide being a museum rat.

Every time I looked up, I saw a bit more of the person, with a bit less of the filter of my brother's or father's animosity tainting the image.

"What's that smirk I see every once in a while?" he asked, catching me in one of those moments.

"Nothing."

He pointed his fork at me, and his grin turned into a grimace. "There are a few rules. One of them is that you have to be completely honest with me. Hiding even the smallest thing can be dangerous." He leaned forward and whispered the next words. "It's the only way I can protect you." Even whispered, his words conveyed conviction. He really did want to protect me, almost as if he were family.

I looked down. "I was just thinking you're not so bad."

"Thank you," he said before moving the fork to his plate and spearing a piece of meat. "Not that '*not so bad*' is such a great compliment, but for being honest." He pointed the meat-filled fork at me. "You're not so bad yourself."

Momentarily I felt like throwing something from my plate, but I controlled myself. "Thank you."

I recovered my composure, and we finished the dinner without any more blowups.

After I declined dessert, he put down his menu and didn't mention the key lime pie he'd asked the waitress about.

Personally, I was anxious to go somewhere we could talk frankly about what to expect, and if I should do what the note had asked.

We split the check and walked outside.

"Can we talk out here?"

Instead of answering, he asked, "Did you drive in today?"

"No, my car had a stupid flat this morning, so I took the Metro."

He pointed toward the garage down the street. "My car is this way. I'll drive you home, and we can talk on the way."

I followed him. "You know where I live?"

"Of course."

What had I been thinking? They probably had a three-inch file on me. "What's my favorite color?"

"I don't know yet."

Maybe it wasn't three inches thick after all.

He slowed and took my hand, interlacing his fingers with mine.

The shock of his touch made me pull away.

"To anybody watching, we're on a date," he said, offering his hand again.

I used the hand I'd pulled away to move my purse to the opposite shoulder and took his hand again.

This time, his grip on me was stronger.

In a move that surprised me, he shortened his stride to match mine.

I looked up at him. The streetlights gave his chin an even more chiseled look than earlier, and I liked it.

~

ADAM

KELLY BENSON HAD BEEN INSTANTLY RECOGNIZABLE WHEN I ENTERED THE restaurant. Not as obviously seductive as the blonde at the bar with her tits hanging half out of her top, but a sophisticated, beautiful girl somewhat insecure about her looks, by the way she dressed. Although, that could have been dictated by her work environment.

She'd been watching the door, but hadn't recognized me.

I scanned the room while passing through toward the restrooms. A sweep on the way back, and I didn't see anyone overtly watching her.

Her surprise when I took the chair across from her had been real. The girl had filled out in all the right places since I'd last seen her when I left for USC

—full tits and a smile that could kill, when she let it loose. Her emerald eyes were striking against the light brown of her hair, and they carried a twinkle that hinted at an intelligence that wasn't to be underestimated.

Neil had entered and taken a seat at the bar a few minutes after we ordered, to provide another set of eyes and so he'd recognize her more easily if needed later.

I'd had to keep reminding her we couldn't talk freely with people around, and because I hadn't prepared her, she'd reacted poorly to my taking her hand outside.

The sidewalk was empty, and we weren't likely being watched.

She adjusted her purse and took my hand again.

"That's the idea," I told her.

She looked up at me with a smile

"Does your job keep you very busy?" she asked.

"The client I just started with is getting my attention twenty-four seven."

This fox could run the entire spectrum from seductive to playful to cunning. If she weren't a Benson—and this were a real date—I'd be having her for breakfast, lunch, and dinner by the weekend.

I escorted her into the garage and to my car. For this assignment I'd switched from last night's junker to my Lexus.

She swung her legs in as I held the door for her—legs that had been out of view during dinner, killer legs.

I rounded the car and climbed in. "I'll take that note now."

She fished a plastic bag with a paper inside it from her purse.

"And the envelope?"

"I didn't keep it. It was just a brown interoffice envelope."

"And who was it from?"

"It said our security department, but I don't believe that."

Neither did I. The evidence went in the backseat, but before I could hit the start button, the interrogation began.

"Is it just you?"

I pulled my finger back from the starter. "No, I have a partner. He was at the restaurant as well, but you won't see Neil unless he's needed, and I can call in more people as required. This doesn't work if the UNSUB sees you surrounded by agents."

"Oh."

"I'm really tired. Can we go now and talk on the way?"

She nodded, but my phone vibrated immediately, and I took it out to check.

NEIL: No tails from here

After showing her the message, I put it away and started the car. "Neil doesn't think we were followed."

"You expected to be followed?"

"Didn't expect it. That was just a precaution. The note you got implied you're being watched, and to be safe, we have to assume that can include away from work."

"You're scaring me."

I turned right out of the garage and moved a hand briefly to her shoulder. "Be strong. I'll keep you safe. I promise." When I looked over, she was smiling.

"Thank you."

I returned my hand to the wheel and navigated toward her house. "Tell me what you know about the Brooks case."

"She got a note just like the one I got, telling her to change the door code, except it referenced Daya Patel, and then she ended up dead. That's all I know."

The note had been turned in a month after the murder, and hadn't provided us any forensic evidence. "Did she really get it on Halloween?"

"Like I told them when I brought it in, she never said anything to me."

"When did you get your note?"

"Like I told Ashley, it was on my desk this morning. What do you think this is about—I mean, the door code part?"

I didn't want to scare her, but I had to be honest. "I would think it's a test."

"And Melinda refused?"

I turned left and sucked in a breath. "I don't know if she thought it was a joke or refused. Either way, she disappeared two days after Halloween."

She wrapped her arms around herself. "I'm not sure I can do this."

KELLY

. . .

ADAM PULLED THE CAR OVER AND PUT HIS HAND ON MY SHOULDER AGAIN. "It's okay to be scared. It's your choice, but it's one you have to make by tomorrow."

I turned to him. "What can I do? He has to know where I live."

He took my hand in his. The strength and warmth were comforting. "You can leave town. If you do, you'll be safe. Patel didn't help him, so he picked Brooks. When she didn't help him…"

I finished the sentence he left off. "He picked me. Why me?"

"We've got no idea. But he still wants something, and he needs your help."

"If I leave, you think I'll be safe?"

"Yes. If you leave, you won't be of any use to him, or a threat either. So he'll probably…"

I sniffed. "He'll pick someone else in my building, won't he?"

"That's likely."

The word likely was meant to soften the blow, but it didn't. If I left, I'd be sentencing the next person to my predicament, and what if they didn't go to the FBI? They could end up dead, and it would be on my head.

I shivered. "I don't have a choice, then, do I?"

He squeezed my hand. "Yes, you do. You can choose to do this or not, and nobody's going to judge you."

Even in the limited light from the street lamps it was clear he meant it.

The problem was, I would still judge myself if I left. I wouldn't be able to live with the consequences if the name of another coworker appeared in the news some number of months from now.

I took a breath. "How do we do this?"

"You have till tomorrow afternoon to make up your mind. That's when he expects you to reset the door. If we do this, you have to commit to following my instructions completely."

I nodded. "I think I want to do it."

He let go of my hand and pulled away from the curb. "Think it over tonight. If you decide to move forward, you will follow the instructions on the note tomorrow, and we'll see where this leads. Once you pass that test, I expect you'll get more instructions."

It sounded simple enough to start with. "Okay."

This was a decision I'd have to make on my own. One word to my family, and Daddy would make the decision for me.

"You need to explain how this protection is going to work," I said. "Are you driving me to work and stuff?"

He looked over briefly. "It's simple, and it's complicated. Your building is well secured, so while you're at work during the day, you'll be safe. Outside of work, it's my job to keep you safe."

"What are you going to do? Shadow me everywhere?"

"Pretty much. Yolanda's out of town for the month, right?" My house-mate had left on Saturday.

"How do you know about her?"

"We do our research, and her itinerary is on her Facebook page."

"Oh." That made sense. Yolanda was always oversharing.

"And you don't have a boyfriend right now, do you?"

"That's pretty personal."

"Do you?"

Since he'd checked out my SuperSingles profile, I was pretty sure he knew the answer. "No. Not right now."

"Good. Then I won't have to shoot him to win your affections. I'm your new boyfriend."

I pulled back. "Nobody's going to believe that." *Boyfriend* and *Cartwright* were two things that didn't go together in my world.

"I need to be around you all the time, so we need to make them believe it. Everybody needs to believe it."

This just got a whole lot more complicated.

My new fake boyfriend reached over and took my hand. After a few blocks, we hit a red light. He looked over. "I had a very nice time with you tonight. I think you're an incredible lady."

I couldn't tell if this was him getting into character or being serious. I decided he was acting, and responded accordingly. "You're not so bad yourself."

He smiled. "Think hard about whether you're prepared for this. You have until tomorrow night. After that, changing your mind is a problem."

The blocks went by quickly, and he pulled up in front of my house.

He pulled a business card out of his pocket after setting the parking brake.

The card read *Adam Carter* and looked official. "State Department?"

"My cover." He shocked me by snaking a hand behind my neck and pulling me to him. "The other part of my cover." He leaned over and kissed me quickly on the lips before letting me go. "Call me tomorrow."

The tingle on my lips disoriented me for a moment. I grasped the card tightly as I opened the door and climbed out. "I will."

I had a long night of thinking ahead of me.

UNDERCOVER BILLIONAIRE IS AVAILABLE ON AMAZON.

Printed in Great Britain
by Amazon